Coping with Trade Reforms

Note

The views expressed in this book are those of the authors and do not necessarily reflect the views of the United Nations.

The designations employed and the presentation of the material do not imply the expression of any opinion whatsoever on the part of the United Nations Secretariat concerning the legal status of any country, territory, city or area, or of its authorities, or concerning the delimitation of its frontiers or boundaries.

Coping with Trade Reforms

A Developing Country Perspective on the WTO Industrial Tariff Negotiations

Edited by

Sam Laird

and

Santiago Fernández de Córdoba

Forewords by

Supachai Panitchpakdi

and

Tony Venables

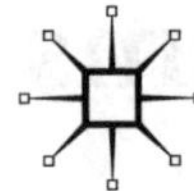

First published 2006 by
PALGRAVE MACMILLAN
Houndmills, Basingstoke, Hampshire RG21 6XS and
175 Fifth Avenue, New York, N.Y. 10010
Companies and representatives throughout the world

PALGRAVE MACMILLAN is the global academic imprint of the Palgrave Macmillan division of St. Martin's Press, LLC and of Palgrave Macmillan Ltd. Macmillan® is a registered trademark in the United States, United Kingdom and other countries. Palgrave is a registered trademark in the European Union and other countries.

ISBN–13: 978–0–230–00472–6 hardback
ISBN–10: 0–230–00472–5 hardback

This book is printed on paper suitable for recycling and made from fully managed and sustained forest sources.

A catalogue record for this book is available from the British Library.

Library of Congress Cataloging-in-Publication Data

Coping with trade reforms : a developing country perspective on the WTO industrial tariff negotiations / edited by Sam Laird and Santiago Fernández de Córdoba.
p. cm.
Includes bibliographical references and index.
ISBN 0–230–00472–5 (cloth)
1. World Trade Organization—Developing countries. 2. Developing countries—Commercial policy. I. Laird, Sam. II. Fernández de Córdoba, Santiago.

HF1385.C68 2006
382′.7091724—dc22 2006043558

10 9 8 7 6 5 4 3 2 1
15 14 13 12 11 10 09 08 07 06

Printed and bound in Great Britain by
Antony Rowe Ltd, Chippenham and Eastbourne

Contents

List of Figures

List of Tables

List of Abbreviations

AGOA	African Growth and Opportunity Act (United States)
ATC	Agreement on Textiles and Clothing
CARICOM	Caribbean Community
CEE	Central and Eastern Europe
CEFTA	Central European Free Trade Area
CET	common external tariff
CGE	computable general equilibrium (model)
CMEA	Council for Mutual Economic Assistance
CMT	cut, make and trim
COMESA	Common Market for Eastern and Southern Africa
CSO	Central Statistical Office
EBA	Everything but Arms (an EU Initiative)
EBZ	Export Board of Zambia
EFTA	European Free Trade Area
EPR	effective protection rate
EPZ	export promotion zone
EU	European Union
FDI	foreign direct investment
FTA	free trade agreement
FTAA	Free Trade Area of the Americas
GATT	General Agreement on Tariffs and Trade
GDP	gross domestic product
GSP	Generalized System of Preferences
GTAP	Global Trade Analysis Project (model)
IBRD	International Bank for Reconstruction and Development
IDB	Inter-American Development Bank
IFS	International Financial Statistics
IMF	International Monetary Fund
ISIC	International Standard Industrial Classification
LDC	least developed country
MFN	most favoured nation
NAFTA	North American Free Trade Agreement (or Area)
NAMA	non-agricultural market access
NTB	non-tariff barrier
OECD	Organization for Economic Co-operation and Development

OPEC	Organization of the Petroleum Exporting Countries
OTEC	ocean thermal energy conversion
PPI	producer price index
QR	quantitative restriction
RBI	Reserve Bank of India
REER	real effective exchange rate
RTA	regional trade agreement/arrangement
SACU	Southern African Customs Union
SADC	Southern African Development Community
SAP	structural adjustment policy
SDT	special and differential treatment
SEZ	special economic zone
SME	small and medium-sized enterprise
TRAINS	Trade Analysis and Information System (UNCTAD tariff protection database)
TRIMs	Trade-related investment measures
TRIPS	Trade-related Aspects of International Property Rights
UNCTAD	United Nations Conference on Trade and Development
USAID	United States Agency for International Development
WITS	World Integrated Trade Solution (Joint World Bank and UNCTAD software)
WTO	World Trade Organization

Acknowledgements

UNCTAD wishes to acknowledge the support of the Department for International Development (DFID) of the Government of the United Kingdom for funding this project on 'Supporting Developing Countries' Assessment of the Non-Agricultural Market Access Negotiations and Trade Preferences', particularly the direct support of Diana Melrose and Jean-Christophe Maur.

The book project, under the overall direction of Sam Laird and Santiago Fernández de Córdoba, could not have been completed without the support of a number of UNCTAD staff members, consultants and interns who worked tirelessly to produce this book under considerable pressure: Mirko Abbritti, Veronica Chau, Fabien Dumesnil, Nathaniel Mamangun, Lauren Murphy, Jenifer Tacardon-Mercado, Jose Maria Serena and Andrea Zazzarelli.

Particular thanks to the UNCTAD consultant editor, Praveen Bhalla, and the Palgrave Macmillan editor, Christine Ranft.

Foreword

Supachai Panitchpakdi, Secretary-General of UNCTAD

International trade has been the driving force behind some of the more successful achievements in development, and the current WTO trade negotiations hold out hopes of further gains by the developing countries. However, the realization that trade reforms also pose adjustment challenges has made developing countries sceptical about taking on new commitments that could also limit their options for industrialization. Resolving this dilemma is one of the more serious problems confronting the negotiators.

It is remarkable that after some 20 years of reforms, there is still no clear-cut policy formula that guarantees development success. Yet this is one of the lessons that comes out of the country studies in *Coping with Trade Reforms: a Developing Country Perspective on the WTO Industrial Tariff Negotiations*. While countries like India and Bangladesh have done well, Zambia and Malawi have stagnated and even undergone some de-industrialization. Growth rates in Brazil and the Philippines have fallen below the pre-reform levels. Jamaica has only avoided increased unemployment by large-scale emigration of its skilled workers. Bulgaria has massive support from the European Union that helped it to pick up strongly after its initial decline. Flawed design in the reforms, inadequate attention to institutions, the need to prioritize physical infrastructure, the provision of social safety nets, maintaining price stability and a competitive real exchange rate are some of the problems identified in the book.

The analysis in this book, however, shows that there are indeed important gains yet to be made from the multilateral trade negotiations, and the challenge is how to take advantage of these opportunities while overcoming the downside risks. The international community needs to support the WTO negotiations with real efforts on social safety nets, infrastructure, institution- and capacity-building. As is pointed out in the book, aid for trade – proposed by the UN Millennium Project's Task Force on Trade in its report on *Trade For Development 2005* – can help the poor to trade more effectively and ease the social costs of adjustment. But if it is to be effective, it will require real new resources and coordinated activity by the donor community. In this respect, the Declaration adopted at the WTO's Ministerial Conference in Hong Kong in December 2005 suggests that the international community is ready to tackle the issue of developing efficient adjustment mechanisms and ensuring their funding so that ultimately the Doha negotiations can fulfil their development promise.

Foreword

Tony Venables,
Yu Kuo-Hwa Professor of International Economics, London School of Economics and Chief Economist Department for International Development

This volume makes two major contributions to knowledge about the impact of trade reforms on developing countries. The first is to provide careful and detailed evaluations of the possible effects of alternative liberalizations of non-agricultural market access. The potential gains from such liberalizations are substantial, but outcomes depend on the scheme that is implemented, as well as countries' capacities to respond to changing economic circumstances. This volume goes beyond existing work in its detailed quantitative analysis of alternative trade liberalization scenarios, and its message is that modalities matter less than the overall level of ambition for liberalization that is pursued in negotiations.

The second contribution is to provide eight case studies of the effects of developing country trade liberalizations that have been undertaken in recent years. These address head-on the fundamental issue of the possible asymmetry between export and import responses. Experiences vary across countries, with some examples of booming export response, for example India, the Philippines and Bangladesh. In other cases, especially Malawi and Zambia, the two African studies in the volume, export response was disappointing and reform was accompanied by falling manufacturing output. What are the lessons? Often liberalization has been partial, and barriers remain on both the developed and developing country side. Trade liberalization is not a panacea, and effective export supply response requires a good business environment and infrastructure upgrading. This is expensive in both political and economic resources, and actions need to be targeted to address the needs of export sectors and to remove bottlenecks. Transitional adjustment should not be underestimated, and policies need to be put in place to handle the adjustment costs that will be encountered. At a broad level these messages are familiar, but the case studies in this volume provide clear illustrations of their importance at the country level. They also remind the donor community of the need for policies, such as aid for trade, to support the economic adjustments that must accompany a successful liberalization.

List of Contributors

Carlos E. Aggio is a development economist working as a freelance consultant based in Buenos Aires with research experience in Latin America and South Asia. He has written on trade policy impacts, both in the north and the south, on economic growth, employment and productive upgrading in developing countries.

Ramon L. Clarete is Professor of Economics at the University of the Philippines School of Economics in Diliman, Quezon City. He has worked on trade policy reforms in the Philippines since the 1980s, advising policy makers and private sector trade and industry organizations.

Santiago Fernández de Córdoba is an UNCTAD economist and Special Professor of Economics at the Universidad de Navarra, Spain. He has been a consultant for the World Bank, Ecuadorian government and Andean Community. He has published a number of studies on economic policy, modelling trade negotiations, and regional trading arrangements, as well as advised governments on trade policy.

Joe Francois is Professor of Economics, Erasmus Universiteit Rotterdam, and Fellow of the Tinbergen Institute and the Centre for Economic Policy Research, Director of the European Trade Study Group, and Board Member of the Global Trade Analysis Project. He has written a number of books on modelling and is author of numerous articles on trade policy.

Veena Jha is the coordinator of the UNCTAD/DFID/GOI initiative on 'Strategies and preparedness for trade and globalization in India'. She has published over a hundred articles on trade and has edited and authored several books. She was a member of the Multilateral Trade and International Financial Systems Task Force of the Millennium Development Goals Project. She has served in an advisory capacity to several trade initiatives both governmental and non-governmental in several countries.

Sam Laird is Inter-regional Advisor, UNCTAD, Special Professor of International Economics, University of Nottingham, UK, Research Associate, Trinity College, Dublin and Visiting Professor, World Trade Institute, Bern. He was formerly Senior Economist, the World Bank, and Counsellor,

World Trade Organization. He is the author of numerous articles on trade and trade policy.

Jean-Christophe Maur is an Economic Adviser, Trade Policy at DFID, London, and Research Fellow, Groupe d'Economie Mondiale de Sciences-Po (GEM). His recent published work focuses on regional trade integration, and antidumping policy.

Kennedy Mbekeani is Senior Research Fellow (International Economics), Botswana Institute for Development Policy Analysis. He has published on trade policy issues, financial markets and investment in Malawi and Southern Africa.

Patrick A. Messerlin is Professor of Economics at the Institut d'Etudes Politiques de Paris (Sciences Po) and Director of the Groupe d'Economie Mondiale de Sciences-Po (GEM). From 2002–2005, he was co-chairman with Dr Ernesto Zedillo, Former President of Mexico, Director of the Yale Center for the Study on Globalization, of the Task Force on Trade in the UN Millennium Development Goals Project which produced a Report on Trade for Development released in May 2005. He has published a dozen books and a hundred papers on trade theory and policy. His most recent book is *Measuring the Costs of Protection in Europe: European Commercial Policy in the 2000s* (2001).

Dale Mudenda is a lecturer in the Department of Economics at the University of Zambia. He teaches international and development economics. His research interests are in international trade, development and health economics. He is currently a member of the national committee drafting the National Export Strategy for Zambia.

Manenga Ndulo is a lecturer in the Department of Economics at the University of Zambia. He teaches international and industrial economics. He has done research on services trade in Zambia and Southern Africa. He has been a consultant to the Ministry of Trade and Industry in Zambia.

Victor Ognivtsev is currently Senior Economic Affairs Officer, UNCTAD, with responsibilities for global, regional and country trade and economic analyses. Prior to this he served (in 1995–2004) as the Coordinator of UNCTAD technical assistance activities in favour of the WTO acceding countries. He is the author of many articles on trade policy issues and has also edited several UNCTAD publications devoted to the Uruguay Round results and WTO accessions.

Lia Valls Pereira is Senior Economist, Instituto Brasileiro de Economia, Fundação Getulio Vargas, Rio de Janeiro, and Professor in International Economics, Universidade do Estado do Rio de Janeiro. She has written a number of books and articles, mainly on Brazilian trade policy.

José María Serena is an Economist at the Bank of Spain in Madrid, Spain. He has carried out research in labour economics and international trade. Work in progress includes: 'Do Wage Contracts Differ in Booms and Recessions? Theory and Evidence'.

Narun N. Rahman is a freelance consultant. She previously consulted for UNCTAD and UN/DESA (New York) on international trade and sustainable development issues.

Diana Tussie directs the Research Programme on International Economic Institutions, FLACSO, Buenos Aires, as well as the Latin American Trade Network. She is a senior research fellow at CONICET, National Council for Technical and Scientific Research, Argentina. She has written numerous books and articles on development policy and regional trade agreements.

David Vanzetti is Visiting Fellow at the Asia-Pacific School of Economics and Government, Australian National University, Canberra. He has been a consultant for FAO, UNCTAD and the World Bank. His publications cover farm investment analysis, applications of game theory to the international wheat market, modelling trade negotiations, trade sanctions, regional trading arrangements, desert locust control, climate change, trade and environment policies, and food security.

Michael Witter is a senior lecturer and the Head of the Department of Economics at the University of the West Indies, Mona, where he has been based for the past 31 years. During this time, he has conducted many studies of the Jamaican economy. Some of the insights have been brought to this paper on the liberalization of the economy from prior studies on the impact of structural adjustment and globalization on the Jamaican economy. He is also currently completing a programme of research on the economic vulnerability of small island states.

Overview

Sam Laird and Santiago Fernández de Córdoba

Introduction

The trade negotiations launched at the World Trade Organization (WTO) ministerial meeting in Doha in November 2001, which aim at further liberalization of trade in goods and services, hold out hopes for potentially important gains for developing countries in terms of improved access to overseas markets. Many of these countries are expected to undertake further liberalization commitments and this could bring them even further gains, at least in the longer term.[1] However, while there might well be long-term gains from liberalization, liberalizing economies are, nevertheless, likely to face short- to medium-term adjustment costs. This is because, as economies open up, imports use existing channels while new exports often come from different sectors that have to gear up production and find new markets. The structural unemployment that occurs as this transition takes place is, perhaps, the major social cost of adjusting to trade reforms. Unfortunately, most developing countries do not have well-developed social safety nets, such as unemployment benefits, retraining programmes and portable pensions, to address these problems. Other areas of adjustment to be addressed include: the need to replace tariff revenues as a major source of government funding as protection is reduced; tackling the likely loss of preferences in overseas markets as MFN rates are lowered under multilateral liberalization; and intrasectoral and intersectoral reallocation of resources in response to changes in the levels of protection.

To gauge the possible developmental implications of the current WTO trade negotiations, it is important to examine the various proposals and attempt to assess their likely economic impact. Part I of this book provides a quantitative analysis of the various proposals being considered in the WTO negotiations launched at Doha in November 2001, as well as a review of other studies of adjustment to trade reform. Part II examines the experiences of a number of countries at different levels of development and across various regions to try to ascertain the impact of their trade reforms and the factors that contributed to the outcomes.[2]

Part I: Quantitative assessment and literature review

What are the numbers?

Chapter 1, Now What?, by Santiago Fernández de Córdoba (UNCTAD) and David Vanzetti (UNCTAD and the Australian National University) reviews key features of the main proposals that have been tabled in the WTO Negotiating Group on Non-Agricultural Market Access, and attempts a quantitative assessment of the likely economic impacts of those proposals.

The analysis by Fernández de Córdoba and Vanzetti, which covers all the sectors but is more detailed in its treatment of industrial tariffs, estimates global annual welfare gains from liberalization to be in the order of $90 billion to $200 billion, similar in order of magnitude to a number of other, more conservative studies, including those of the World Bank. While these results seem impressive, the percentage changes in aggregate welfare and trade are relatively minor – in many cases, less than 1 per cent. However, crucially, these modest results in the aggregate conceal potentially important sectoral variations; while the exports and production of some sectors are likely to expand considerably, other sectors are likely to suffer large contractions of output and employment as imports increase. Among the more significant increases would be the output of services. If the tariff cuts are large enough to significantly reduce applied rates in developing countries, as in the so-called free-trade scenario, there will be a big shift to services. The most significant increases in absolute terms are estimated to occur in China.

Perhaps of greater interest are the substantial negative changes in sectoral employment. In percentage terms, the largest falls in employment over the partial liberalization scenarios fall under an ambitious application of a Swiss-type formula in sectors such as motor vehicles for the Rest of South Asia (i.e. other than India) (−36 per cent) and non-ferrous metals for India (−25 per cent). Under a more moderate scenario, in the leather sector, there is a loss of skilled and unskilled employment of over 30 per cent in Japan and nearly 21 per cent in Canada, while in developing countries, the losses tend to be less than 10 per cent. These results provide an indication of the structural adjustment that would be needed.

The potentially high adjustment costs associated with these estimated changes are one of the reasons for the hesitation of some developing countries to take on board some of the more ambitious liberalization proposals. Temporary unemployment of labour and capital can have a significant negative effect on output and welfare. On the other hand, if the reforms lead to a greater use of previously unemployed labour, the welfare gains would be significant, perhaps as much as the gains from using resources more efficiently. However, as discussed in the next section, there is relatively little documented evidence concerning the scale and nature of these costs or of the adjustment process of local economies in the aftermath of trade liberalization, despite some 15 years of unilateral reforms in developing and transitional economies. For informed policy-making, governments need a better understanding of the costs to their economies following changes in their tariffs.

Comment by Joe Francois

Professor Joe Francois of the Tinbergen Institute, in commenting on the chapter by Fernández de Córdoba and Vanzetti, draws attention to the fact that all the formulas yield larger cuts in percentage terms for developed countries, and larger cuts in absolute terms for developing countries (at least under the ambitious scenarios). He says that the modelling results, in common with all recent CGE studies of the Doha negotiations, produce the strongest percentage increase in exports from a reduction in average tariffs across developing countries.[3] He also argues: 'A message between the lines . . . is that tariff preferences may be a second order economic issue, despite its high profile as a political one.' The overall effect of tariff reductions by OECD countries would be a net expansion of exports by LDCs (many of whom are in the sub-Saharan Africa aggregate in the model). Discussing problems with the administration of preferences, he concludes that, 'because of limitations placed on trade preferences, NAMA negotiations matter even more for developing countries than if preferences worked better'.

Experiences of adjustment to trade reform: a review of the literature

There have been a number of studies of adjustment costs and even some prior reviews of other studies, as discussed in Chapter 3 by Fernández de Córdoba, Laird, Maur and Serena. While the various studies take different views of the nature of adjustment costs, and use different methodologies, many have concluded that the gains from trade liberalization are often less than the adjustment costs, particularly in the presence of rigid labour markets. The difference in treatment of social and private adjustment costs helps to explain some of the variations in the findings of some empirical studies, and highlights the importance of being prepared to face the adjustment process.

An important issue raised in the literature is that adjustment occurs not just due to changes in trade policy at home (or abroad), but also from a wide range of factors, such as technological change, changes in demand/tastes, changes in national law, weather/natural phenomena and political (in)stability, or as a result of international agreements, including trade agreements. There is no agreement in the literature as to whether it is feasible or desirable to try to separate the causes of adjustment costs: the key is to put in place policies and institutions that facilitate structural adjustment, whatever the source. The emphasis in various studies on labour market issues (structural unemployment), rather than other factors of production, highlights the major social concern of trade reforms, and clearly needs to be addressed with social safety nets and programmes for re-insertion into the labour force if workers are to be persuaded of the long-term benefits from the reforms. One implication of the main body of studies is that the phasing-in of liberalization is strongly recommended.

Part II: Country case studies: experiences of trade reforms and adjustment

The case studies

Developing countries have undergone major trade reforms in the last 10 to 15 years, often under World Bank/IMF lending programmes, regional trade agreements (RTAs) – mainly in the 1990s, commitments undertaken in various Uruguay Round agreements, and as part of preparations for accession to the WTO.2. With some important exceptions for sensitive products, tariffs are now low to moderate in most countries, and the main question being asked in Part II of this book is how these countries fared under the reform process. We are also interested in the explanations for their performance. If they fared well, what were the factors that contributed to a successful outcome? If they faced problems, why and what could they or others have done to obtain a successful outcome?

The Bangladesh study, by Narun Rahman, a private consultant, notes that 'over the last three decades, Bangladesh has come a long way in the evolution of its economic and policy orientation, from a highly interventionist regime with widespread control on trade, the exchange rate and investment, to a substantially liberalized economic framework.' The study gives details of the changes in policy in Bangladesh, which seem to have gathered momentum since 1991, and then goes on to discuss their economic impact. The results appear to be mixed: 'an improved, but not strong enough growth performance; expansion of trade, but without meaningful diversification; reduction in poverty, but an increase in inequality'. The share of manufacturing in exports increased from 77 per cent in 1990 to 92 per cent in 2003. The textiles and clothing sector, particularly low-end ready-made garments, accounts for over 80 per cent of total merchandise exports, while the shares of agricultural raw materials and food have fallen drastically. The number of workers employed in the ready-made garments sector has increased almost tenfold over the past 15 years, but the overall employment rate has fallen both in relative and absolute terms. As an LDC, Bangladesh benefits from preferential treatment in Europe, but there are significant limitations on its preferential access to the United States. Overall revenue receipts of the government have risen in recent years, due to increased imports and improved revenue collection. During the 1990s Bangladesh succeeded in reducing the aggregate level of poverty, but the evidence in the study suggests that income inequality has increased. In the WTO context, the elimination of textiles and clothing quotas at the end of 2004 is expected to pose some challenges for Bangladesh, as competition, particularly from China, intensifies, while preference erosion will increase pressure on domestic firms to become more competitive. WTO rules may also have implications for the ability of the country to enter new dynamic sectors of world trade (e.g. pharmaceuticals, leather goods, information and communications technology (ICT) products and ICT-enabled services, agro and marine products, and niche items of interest to expatriate Bangladeshi and other South Asian nationals).

The Brazil study, by Professor Lia Valls Pereira of the Fundaçao Getulio Vargas in Rio de Janeiro, notes that, after more than two decades of restrictive trade policies, in the early 1990s Brazil started to implement a comprehensive plan of economic reforms including a stabilization programme and other initiatives to modernize and increase the efficiency of the public sector. Under the first broad trade reform in 1990, most quantitative controls were eliminated and tariffs were significantly reduced. Brazil was also a founder member of the Southern Common Market (MERCOSUR), established in 1991. The financial crisis of 1998 featured an overvalued exchange rate and increasing deficits in the trade balance, leading to growing protectionist sentiments and a partial reversal of trade liberalization. The devaluation of the Brazilian currency in 1999, however, alleviated the protectionist pressures.

The post-liberalization period in Brazil has been characterized by relatively low rates of growth (2.4 per cent in the 1990s, compared with the world rate of 3.8 per cent). An overvalued exchange rate explains the trade deficit and the persistent growth of imports until 1999, while the freeing of the exchange rate in 1999 led to the growth of exports and the decline of imports, resulting in a trade surplus. There is evidence that total factor productivity increased across most sectors, but there seems to be no agreement about the specific impact of trade liberalization on this increase. Unemployment rose from 5.7 per cent in 1992 to 7.9 per cent in 1999. Job losses in the manufacturing sector, although this was partly due to competition and to 'increases in productivity through the adoption of new technologies and/or greater management efficiency (a non-reversible trend)'. There is some evidence that part of the newly unemployed were absorbed by the informal market, where low earnings predominate. Uneven income distribution and the lack of opportunities, especially in education, are still the main factors that explain the poverty in Brazil, and there is no clear-cut evidence of the impact of trade liberalization on them.

The Bulgarian study, by Victor Ognivtsev of UNCTAD, notes that Bulgaria has undergone 15 years of profound reforms in the process of its transition to a market economy, and in pursuing its main current strategic goal: to accede to the EU by 1 January 2007. Before 1989, Bulgaria's trade was mainly directed to countries of the Council for Mutual Economic Assistance (CMEA), and was in some sense 'centrally planned'. After the collapse of the Soviet bloc, trade became 'market-driven'. Liberalization of Bulgaria's trade regime, in particular through RTAs, has been much faster for industrial products, while trade in agricultural products has been only partially liberalized. Export growth has been one of the main contributors to the growth of GDP in the last few years, with the EU now accounting for 52.4 per cent of Bulgaria's total trade, compared with 38.5 per cent in 1995. The recovery of the economy after 1997 has been accompanied by persistent current-account and trade deficits, financed mainly by foreign direct investment (FDI). The EU accession process is helping to improve the competitiveness of the economy by increasing regional trade, encouraging FDI and providing additional funding for social safety measures. However, Bulgaria still faces a high and persistent level of unemployment, and poverty indicators have deteriorated.

In the India study, Veena Jha of the DFID-UNCTAD India project in New Delhi explains that India has been engaged in a wide-ranging economic reform programme since the early 1990s. It began with progressive liberalization in areas such as the exchange rate regime, foreign investment and industrial policy. This was followed by autonomous trade liberalization measures that included the reduction of trade restrictions, the abolition of import licensing, and the rationalization and reduction of import tariffs, which were reduced from almost 50 per cent in 1990 to 26 per cent in 2003 (and reportedly have been further reduced to 17–18 per cent). India has further liberalized under a number of regional trade agreements.

Economic growth surged after liberalization was introduced, averaging 6 per cent in the 1990s. Poverty indicators have also improved, but interstate and regional disparities have widened. Both exports and imports have grown significantly – by almost 50 per cent between 1998 and 2003 – and they have become increasingly diversified. The current account has moved into surplus. There has been a rise in the overall level of unemployment (from 6 per cent in 1993/94 to an average of 7.3 per cent in the period 1999–2003), mainly in agriculture and in the informal sector. Dr Jha concludes that India's gradual approach to liberalization has helped to spread adjustment costs and to ensure better preparedness among industries. In particular, the sequencing of reforms, whereby fiscal, monetary and investment reforms preceded trade liberalization, may explain India's positive experience with adjustment.

The Jamaica study, by Michael Witter of the University of the West Indies in Kingston, mentions that under several waves of reforms that began as early as 1982, the average tariff was reduced from 25 per cent in 1989 to 8.9 per cent in 2002, while the tariff structure has been rationalized and almost all import licensing and quota requirements have been abolished. In the 1990s, trade liberalization was given a further boost with 'the reform of the common external tariff of the CARICOM, the pressure to comply with the WTO's international trade regime, the restructuring of trade relations with Europe that is embodied in the Cotonou Agreement and commitments taken in the context of the process to establish a Free Trade Area of the Americas (FTAA)'. Other important reforms implemented in the period include fiscal reforms, financial liberalization and the elimination of exchange rate controls, and divestment of public enterprises.

Despite the reforms, GDP growth in last two decades has been very slow: per capita GDP has grown on average by 0.5 per cent a year, partly as a result of the financial crisis of the mid-1990s and the consequent monetary tightening, and partly due to the negative international economic conditions for bauxite/alumina and the tourism sector. Overall, Professor Witter concludes: 'the evidence indicates that trade liberalization led to the decline of manufacturing for the domestic market, and to an increase in apparel exports from the free zones, but there was an overall decline in the contribution of the manufacturing sector to GDP.' Unemployment rate fell from 27.4 per cent in 1980 to 15 per cent in 2001, but this was mainly due to the slowing of the rate of growth of the labour force, while outward migration rose to over 20,000 per year, mostly skilled workers.

In the Malawi study, Kennedy Mbekeani of the Botswana Institute of Development Policy observes that prior to the trade liberalization programme that began in 1988, Malawi had maintained a restrictive and complex trade and exchange rate regime based on discretionary allocation of foreign exchange, non-tariff barriers (NTBs), high tariffs, restrictive licensing requirements and surrender requirements on imports and exports. Malawi's trade reform process consisted of: the elimination of NTBs, the consolidation of its tariff structure, a reduction of tariff protection, and the liberalization of its export regime. Malawi substantially rationalized its tariff structure by lowering and harmonizing duty rates. As Dr Mbekeani notes: 'By mid-1999, Malawi's liberalization programme had produced one of the most liberal and transparent regimes in Africa.' Externally, Malawi enjoys preferential market access to the EU market through the Cotonou Agreement and the 'Everything-but-Arms' (EBA) Initiative, and to the United States market through the African Growth and Opportunity Act (AGOA). Malawi is also a member of two regional agreements: the Common Market for Eastern and Southern Africa (COMESA) and the Southern Africa Development Community (SADC).

Malawi's post-liberalization economic performance has been disappointing. Growth had reached as high as 15 per cent in 1994, but thereafter it began to fall steadily. By 2001, growth was below 2 per cent, and in 2002 the economy shrunk even further. The manufacturing sector shrank by 30 per cent between 1989 and 1998, and by 11.4 per cent in 2002 alone. Other contributory factors included macroeconomic instability, weak infrastructure and poor institutions. The main obstacles are transport costs (due to Malawi being a landlocked economy with a poor road infrastructure) and supply-side constraints. The author notes that Malawi's main exports, including tobacco, face high tariffs in key export markets (products and markets not covered by the EBA or AGOA). In the WTO negotiations on further liberalization of trade in goods and services, the 'biggest challenge for Malawi is how firms will adjust to global competition'. Preference erosion may also be a problem. Limited technical capacity implies that Malawi cannot participate effectively in the WTO processes.

The Philippines study by Ramon Clarete, a private consultant from Manila, notes that the Philippines has implemented various unilateral trade reform programmes since 1981. The reforms gradually lowered nominal and weighted average tariff rates, and simplified the tariff structure. Throughout the reforms, there were temporary periods of reversals: for instance, the government raised the tariff rates in 1998 and 1999 in response to difficulties caused by the Asian financial crisis. More recently, in 2003, there has been another increase in tariff protection for selected industries (steel, sugar, polymers).

Since 1990 aggregate exports have expanded dramatically, overtaking aggregate imports. However, growth has occurred in only a few sectors (manufacturing, machinery and transportation equipment), while in others (raw materials, animal and vegetable oils) it has remained stagnant or even declined. Per capita income has not changed, and there is mixed evidence as to whether the reforms have improved income distribution or alleviated poverty. This unsatisfactory economic performance can be attributed mainly to macroeconomic instability (economic contraction in 1985, the Asian financial crisis in 1997–1998), natural disasters (El Niño-induced drought in 1997) and poor economic institutions (high transaction costs, lack of property rights, high logistical costs). Even if market access is facilitated through unilateral or negotiated trade liberalization, the Philippines may not be able to avail fully of the new access opportunities because of high transaction costs that dampen the country's competitiveness. Dr Clarete argues that investment has been slow to react to new export opportunities because of a poor investment climate and the relative difficulty of enforcing property rights.

The Zambia study by Manenga Ndulo and Dale Mudenda of the University of Zambia in Lusaka, highlights the fact that the Zambian economy is heavily dependent on the production of a single commodity: copper. In 1974 the price of copper plunged by 40 per cent, and thereafter continued to remain weak and unstable. Zambia has experienced two major episodes of reforms, first in 1985–1987 and the second since 1991. Key reforms, besides trade liberalization, included privatization of the State-owned firms, liberalization of agricultural input markets and marketing, public sector reform, financial sector liberalization and the removal of exchange rate controls.

In general, trade liberalization has failed to contribute to substantial economic growth, and GDP per capita continues to decline. On the one hand, the reforms have stabilized the macroeconomic situation and boosted competition and efficiency. On the other hand, reforms have entailed significant adjustment costs and have failed to help the development process. The import-competing industrial sectors suffered heavy losses after liberalization, and their contribution to GDP fell by 50 per cent. Formal employment as a share of the total labour force fell from 23 per cent in 1981–1990 to 8.3 per cent in 2003. Thus, recent trade liberalization and the associated adjustment measures have resulted in a fall in employment levels in Zambia by over 50 per cent. Moreover, most of the development indicators have worsened. Due to the HIV/AIDS pandemic, life expectancy has declined; and due to the deterioration of the economy and rising levels of poverty, education indicators have also worsened. The analysis by Professor Ndulo and Mr Mudenda is that the implementation of the reforms was too rapid, unsequenced and often without the support of the stakeholders, and that there were serious limitations in administrative capacity.

Comments by Messerlin and Tussie

In addition to the country studies, at the request of DFID, Professor Patrick Messerlin of the Institut d'Etudes Politiques de Paris (Sciences-Po) and Professor Diana Tussie and Carlos Aggio of the Facultad Latinoamericana de Ciencias Sociales (FLACSO) of Buenos Aires were asked to comment on the country studies. They provided valuable advice to the project and also to the authors of the individual country studies. Their observations are also included in this book.

Professor Messerlin, while acknowledging that average tariffs have fallen, says that trade liberalization in most developing countries has substantially consisted of reducing protection imposed on goods that are not produced (or produced in small quantities) at home. A consequence is that resources are likely to move only slowly out of the traditional sectors and towards new activities. He suggests there may even be an increase in resource misallocation from uneven liberalization. In Professor Messerlin's view, it is therefore difficult to expect a boost to economic growth and a noticeable move to diversification, which is why the disappointing economic performance from such liberalization is not surprising.

In considering the policy implications, Professor Messerlin believes that special and differential treatment (SDT) has not worked well because key sectors for developing countries – shoes, clothing and agriculture – were excluded from SDT. However, he accepts that the poorest countries still need preferential access to rich countries, which could do much more, including opening their farm and clothing markets and simplifying their rules of origin. The poorest countries could also gain from other developing-country markets. He proposes that cuts of high tariffs by developing countries be compensated by finance from the rich countries for transport infrastructure and to make up for revenue losses.

Professor Messerlin suggests that the full benefits from trade liberalization are likely to require complementary domestic reforms, and that there are many instruments for development purposes at their disposal (production and consumption subsidies, or taxes on goods, services and factors of production) that can better achieve the desired objectives at a much lower cost than trade barriers. He argues that, in services, introducing economically sound and politically acceptable special and differential treatment will be no easy task. Attention should be on regulatory creativity focusing on a well-defined cluster of services, such as those related to trade facilitation, which might afford the largest net benefits.

Professor Diana Tussie and Carlos Aggio note that, after decades of highly interventionist trade regimes, all eight countries covered by this project initiated major trade reforms, leading to increased trade openness; they also signed various forms of trade agreements with country neighbours and/or other trade partners. Since the trade reforms were usually part of much broader policy reforms, it is difficult to disentangle the effects of the different policy changes.

With some exceptions, the results of the reforms have been disappointing with respect to growth rates and social indicators, especially employment. Preferential access to major markets was important for Bangladesh and Bulgaria, especially in textiles and clothing (assisted by FDI), and contributed significantly to their overall economic and export growth. However, Malawi and Zambia were unable to take advantage of similar preferential access because of their extremely limited supply response capacity. Further liberalization under the WTO will pose additional challenges as it will erode preferential access for the African countries and Jamaica. In Brazil, growth rates fell below those of the 1960s and 1970s, but the main problems seem to lie in domestic policies – exchange rates, public debt, high interest rates, and difficulties in implementing all the economic reforms. Professor Tussie and Mr Aggio observe that, by contrast, Indian economic growth in the past decade has been impressive, although there is disagreement about how much of this can be attributed to the trade reforms. They conclude that the incidence of poverty is so dramatic in India and Brazil that trade alone cannot provide a way out; improvements in income distribution will be necessary to achieve poverty reduction.

Overall assessment from the country studies

From the case studies, it is clear that one size does not fit all. However, most of the reforms followed a standard pattern of eliminating non-tariff barriers, followed by a rationalization and progressive reduction of tariffs to moderate or low levels. (In the last 10 years, these autonomous reforms, often carried out under World Bank/IMF programmes, were also supplemented by the formation of regional trade agreement, leading to deeper cuts in applied tariffs with partners in such agreements). The studies suggest that in the design of the national programmes it is necessary to take greater account of the level of development, the quality of institutions, resource endowments and the availability of resources to support reforms. Despite years of experience with reform programmes, there is no recipe for monotonically increasing levels of welfare; reforms are tools/instruments, and serious mistakes are still being made with regard to timing, sequencing, implementation and inclusion of all relevant essential elements.

Little account seems to have been taken of adjustment costs in the design of liberalization programmes, other than to provide balance-of-payments support as countries undertake reforms, while waiting for a supply response that does not always arrive. Yet proactive support seem to run afoul of ideological stances (e.g. 'if there is a problem, not enough has been done' – and not that the programme has design flaws). Moreover, the possibility of using policy tools, such as subsidies, to overcome market failures is increasingly running up against limitations imposed by expanding WTO rules. Curiously, apart from some emphasis given to establish export processing zones, there seems to have been little use in the countries under study of positive industrial policies such as the promotion of cluster groups, etc., that were a key part of polices in successful economies like Ireland, the Republic of Korea and Singapore.

A number of the country studies certainly challenge the view that trade liberalization alone is the key to development, while almost all of the studies emphasize the importance of supportive policies and institutions, and hence agree with Rodrik (1999). As expected, most studies confirm the importance of a stable macro-economic environment and maintaining a competitive real effective exchange rate. Complementary policies that need to be factored in more carefully are labour market policies designed to reduce rigidities, as well as education policies to produce a skilled work force. Another area for complementary action lies with income distribution, as there is no evidence from the studies that reforms improve income distribution (consistent with Dollar and Kraay, 2004).

Among the studies, India stands out as having achieved the greatest gains from its reforms, which began with openness to foreign direct investment and only subsequently proceeded with trade reforms which have brought average tariffs down to what is still a moderately high level. The studies also highlight important negative effects on unemployment after reforms – often continuing for a number of years – and this contrasts with the findings of the studies by Papageorgiou, Choksi and Michaely (1992), but is consistent with relatively recent work by Rama (2003). These findings suggest a need for caution in asking countries to embark on ambitious reform programmes, since reform-minded governments could risk being replaced by others that take a more protectionist stance, which would result in reforms being stalled, if not reversed.

Concerning the capacity of countries to carry out reform programmes, an observation from these studies that is not stressed by others, is the greater capacity of the larger economies to absorb reforms – perhaps because there are other sectors that can more easily expand to take advantage of economic restructuring, while small economies have few such alternatives.

The studies also place considerable emphasis on the importance of expenditure on transport-related physical infrastructure in generating a supply-side response, and this is perhaps the greatest weakness in the land-locked African countries in the study, but is mentioned in most cases. Most likely a related issue is the significance of substantial targeted funding to facilitate reforms, which also points to the importance of aid for trade, as indicated below. The studies also note the need to address the high cost of capital that seems to be endemic in many developing countries.

A number of countries in the study are highly dependent on unilateral preferences in developed markets, for example under the Cotonou Agreement, the African Growth and Opportunities Act, etc. These countries are expected to face new pressures as most favoured nation (MFN) tariffs are reduced in the current WTO negotiations.

What is also clear from the studies is the almost total lack of attention given to the need for social safety nets to offset the negative effect of reform as labour markets shake out during structural changes. This may be the single most important social issue that has been given scant attention in reform programmes, but one which can make or break governments as public support for reforms are implemented. Martin Rama (op. cit.) at the World Bank has been one of the few economists who has focused extensively on the design of adjustment programmes to address the labour market issue and it is clear that much more work is needed along these lines.

How can the WTO processes help?

The study suggests that the trade negotiations launched at the WTO ministerial meeting in Doha in November 2001 present both challenges and opportunities with respect to adjustment by both the developed and developing countries. There are challenges in that the more ambitious scenarios seem to offer greater export possibilities and welfare gains, but they also imply increased imports, greater intersectoral shifts in production and employment, and further losses of tariff revenue. On the other hand, the negotiations also offer opportunities to correct imbalances that have resulted from the uneven evolution of rules and the removal of measures in previous negotiations; these have left both a systemic bias in the multilateral trading system as well as higher barriers against developing countries' key exports.

In the past the GATT moved faster on areas that were relatively easy to tackle. It liberalized areas of export interest to the developed countries and tightened rules or the application of rules on subsidies, balance-of-payments (BOP) measures, infant-industry support, trade-related aspects of intellectual property rights (TRIPS) and trade-related investment measures (TRIMs), while providing lacunae or exemptions of one form or another on agriculture, and textiles and clothing. It also made the provision of differential and more favourable treatment for developing countries into 'best endeavour' clauses.

By creating new opportunities for developing countries ahead of any new commitments that they may have to undertake, the economies of these countries should start to attract new investment and generate a supply-side response that should help them cope with the expected negative effects of the challenges posed by WTO negotiations, whether through their own liberalization or the loss of preferences.

The developing countries need to be provided with flexible timetables for the implementation of new commitments. Pushing too hard, too fast could generate the kind of negative effects that have been identified in a number of countries from prior episodes of liberalization. Any backlash from such effects could have negative consequences for longer term liberalization.

Among the issues to be addressed are the provision of:

- Improved access for developing countries' key exports of agricultural goods, manufactures and services.
- Policy space for developing countries, consistent with received economic views on the importance of externalities, and taking account of market imperfections as well as WTO rules.
- Realistic time frames, and financial and technical support for implementation of any new commitments, and support for structural adjustment. Ideally, such assistance should be provided by the donor community, especially to the highly indebted countries, perhaps with technical support from the international financial institutions in their respective areas of expertise under the coherence arrangements, and without further conditionalities.

- Compensation for losses due to preference erosion, similar to that available within the EU's Common Agricultural Policy (CAP) compensatory payments scheme.
- Assistance and adequate time for developing countries to restructure their fiscal systems to offset revenue losses where tariffs are reduced as a result of new commitments.
- Special and differential treatment, including less than full reciprocity, in all areas of the negotiations, as identified in the Doha Ministerial Declaration.

These issues need to be resolved prior to the conclusion of multilateral negotiations (or indeed any reform programme), in keeping with normal business practice that proposals should be costed, and implementations realistically programmed, with provision made for financing. The failure to take account of similar issues, and the consequent unexpected and often high costs, may well have led to the disillusion with the outcome of the Uruguay Round and to the failed WTO meeting in Seattle. Although it may take longer to strike a deal that takes account of such issues, such a deal would be more likely to retain the confidence in the multilateral system of all the WTO Members.

Conclusions

After the extensive reforms of the last 10 to 15 years, developing countries face additional adjustments following WTO negotiations. These adjustments, positive and negative, will result from their own liberalization affecting sectoral production and employment as well as aggregate revenues, and from changes in access to overseas markets. The adjustments will be positive as barriers are brought down and negative as preference margins are eroded. All this has implications for their human development.

Preliminary analysis from case studies and reviews of other experiences suggest that it would be desirable to anticipate such adjustment in a number of ways: by encouraging domestic and foreign investment, including through legislation and institutions that are business-friendly; by developing capital markets to provide access to finance, especially by SMEs, by providing social safety nets, introducing labour retraining, and extending other skills-oriented education programmes; providing or improving physical infrastructure, especially in the transport sector; trade facilitation; debureaucratization; helping developing countries meet SPS/TBT standards, which at present constitute barriers in major markets; and encouraging cluster group formation.

The international financial institutions, with their considerable technical expertise in a wide range of projects, can play an important role in helping developing countries to implement or extend programmes in many of the ways outlined; they have already indicated their willingness to help (e.g. the IMF's Trade Integration Mechanism). However, the donor community can also play an important role, particularly where the affected countries are already heavily indebted.

The WTO process can also help by providing for anticipated liberalization in areas where the developing countries have comparative advantage. This would help create jobs ahead of job losses in sectors that are likely to suffer from increased competition as their own barriers are lowered. The WTO could also usefully address systemic and rules-related issues with the aim of allowing policy space for development purposes. This was partly envisaged in the original GATT, but it seems that such options, including the use of support policies in the presence of externalities, are being closed off to developing countries.

One last comment. It is clear that newly open economies invariably face adjustment problems (WTO, 2004). Although largely overlooked in the past, it is now more widely recognized that short- to medium-term adjustment assistance to trade shocks is indispensable to facilitate acceptance of freer trade. In the absence of any adjustment assistance or social safety nets, trade liberalization may be resisted or even reversed.

The multilateral trade agreements of the GATT/WTO were traditionally silent on the issue of adjustment, leaving this entirely up to national policies to address, with or without the support of the Bretton Woods institutions in the case of the developing countries. An international consensus appears to be emerging on this issue, and on building supply-side capacity, under the rubric of 'aid for trade'. However, if this approach is to influence attitudes towards multilateral trade negotiations, there may be a need for a more formal organic link within the WTO itself, creating rights and obligations in relation to adjustment that go beyond the 'coherence mandate' covering cooperation between the WTO and the Bretton Woods institutions.

This is especially important for developing countries, most of which lack adjustment assistance instruments to be able to withstand increased import competition; they would require substantial international support in this regard. Some recent initiatives address this issue: a temporary 'aid for trade fund' was proposed by the UN Millennium Project's Task Force on Trade in its Report on Trade For Development, 2005, while Mandelson, the EU Trade Commissioner, proposed on 4 February 2005 the establishment of a special Trade Adjustment Fund to 'help the poor to trade more effectively and ease the social costs of adjustment'. The new challenge for the multilateral trading system would be to design efficient adjustment mechanisms, ensure their funding and find ways to effectively integrate them into the negotiating outcomes.

Notes

1 The main debate on the relative merits of openness and growth is encapsulated in Sachs and Warner (1995) and Rodrik (1999).
2 Most of these country studies were commissioned under a project funded by the United Kingdom's Department for International Development (DFID), and supplemented by studies under UNCTAD's own work programme. The studies published here are shortened but updated versions of the original studies presented at a conference in Geneva in 2005.
3 This is also an argument for South–South trade. Note that the largest increases in the value of exports are still in developed markets.

References

Dollar, D. and Kraay, A. (2004) Trade growth and poverty, *Economic Journal*, 114(493): F22–F49, February.

Papageorgiou, Demetrios, Choksi, Armeane and Michaely, Michael (1992) *Liberalization Foreign Trade: The Lessons of Experience in the Developing World*, Washington DC: World Bank.

Rama, M. (2003) Globalisation and workers in developing countries, World Bank Working Paper 2958, Washington DC: World Bank.

Rodrik, D. (1999) *The New Global Economy and Developing Countries: Making Openness Work*, Washington, DC: Overseas Development Council.

Sachs, Jeffrey and Warner, Andrew, S. (1995) Economic reform and the process of global integration. *Brookings Papers on Economic Activity*, Vol. 1, pp. 1–96, Washington, DC: The Brookings Institution.

WTO (2004) The future of the WTO: addressing institutional challenges in the new millennium, Report by the Consultative Board to the Director-General Geneva, World Trade Organization.

Part I
What to Expect from the WTO Negotiations

1

Now What? Searching for a Solution to the WTO Industrial Tariff Negotiations

Santiago Fernández de Córdoba and David Vanzetti

1.1 Introduction

The WTO negotiations on non-agricultural market access (NAMA) could lead to significant gains for developing countries in exports, employment and economic efficiency. An analysis of various scenarios shows potential global annual welfare gains ranging from $70 billion to $110 billion. However, the generally modest overall results conceal important changes in trade and output in individual sectors. Some countries will achieve important gains in key sectors, but in other countries some sectors will face important adjustments, including significant loss of employment and output. Estimated losses in tariff revenue could have a strong negative impact on government revenues for a number of countries.

1.2 Existing protection

Several rounds of multilateral trade negotiations have achieved significant reductions in tariffs. They have led to a process of liberalization resulting in: (i) a substantial reduction in overall tariff barriers; (ii) a commitment to keep tariffs below a given level (binding tariff lines); (iii) greater transparency of trade impediments through the conversion of quantitative restrictions to tariff barriers;[1] (iv) a legal framework to minimize the use of policies and measures that unfairly distort trade; and (v) a set of measures and safeguards to provide flexibility to developing countries and least-developed countries (LDCs). However, despite the shift in emphasis towards the use of tariffs, this does not always facilitate measurement or estimation of the effects of proposals to modify rates as there are a number of difficulties in measuring even tariff protection, as noted in Box 1.1.[2]

1.2.1 Tariff barriers

Binding coverage

Bound tariff lines are products on which there is a commitment not to increase tariffs above a specified level. The binding of tariff lines makes trade more predictable by reducing the discretionary ability of governments to increase tariffs. The binding coverage (i.e. the percentage of tariff lines that are bound) among developed countries is almost 100 per cent, while among developing countries it is much lower, and as low as 10 per cent for some countries (on average 77.5 per cent for developing countries). Proposals within multilateral trade negotiations have called for increased binding coverage, especially by developing and least-developed country members. However, increasing the binding coverage can reduce flexibility and raise the level of obligations in future rounds of tariff reductions. Once a tariff line is bound, countries are obliged to subject it to any across-the-board tariff reductions that are agreed within multilateral negotiations.

Average tariffs

Average tariffs are higher in developing countries and LDCs than in developed countries (Table 1.1). However, among developed countries there are still significant tariff barriers in some sectors, resulting in tariff peaks and tariff escalation. Table 1.1 also shows that developed countries impose tariffs on imports from developing countries that are twice as high as those from other developed countries (2.1 to 1.3 per cent), and their tariff rates on imports from LDCs are three times as high. These tariffs are insignificant on average, but fairly high on a few items.

Tariff peaks

Tariff peaks are high tariffs, usually defined as tariffs that are three times the national weighted average. Because of trade reforms under World Bank and IMF programmes, developing countries have relatively few tariff peaks, compared with developed countries (Table 1.2). Developed countries' tariff peaks tend to have a higher incidence on products of export interest to developing countries such as textiles, apparel and footwear. Therefore, it is important for developing and least-developed countries to ensure that a tariff reduction approach addresses not only average tariff rates, but also tariff peaks in key sectors of export interest to them.

Box 1.1: Difficulties in measuring protection

There are several difficulties in measuring protection, arising from:

(i) **The distinction between bound and applied tariff rates**
Bound rates are the maximum levels, while applied rates are the rates that are actually imposed. Since developing countries have very high bound rates, there can be a considerable difference between bound and applied rates.

(ii) **Conversion of specific tariffs to ad valorem equivalents**
Ad valorem tariffs are based on the value of the product, while specific tariffs are a set amount, usually for a given quantity of product, irrespective of price. Specific tariffs can be converted to ad valorem equivalents. However, care must be taken when selecting the appropriate base prices to use.

(iii) **Trade-weighted averages**
Averages that are weighted on the basis of trade volumes are often used to indicate levels of tariff protection. However, a problem with interpreting these measures is due to the endogeneity of trade flows; that is, the higher the tariff rates, the lower the trade flows will be. In the extreme, a prohibitive tariff is given a weight of zero. As a result, simple average tariff rates tend to be higher than weighted averages.

(iv) **The influence of preferential tariffs**
Due to the proliferation of regional trade agreements and preferential arrangements for developing countries, a significant share of the world's trade takes place at below most-favoured-nation (MFN) rates; therefore special attention is needed to ensure that the appropriate tariff rates are being measured.

(v) **Shortcomings in using average tariff rates**
Averages do not tell the whole story: they do not capture tariff peaks and tariff escalation that are additional forms of protection. Tariff peaks are tariffs that are greater than three times the national average, while tariff escalation involves an increase in tariff levels with the transformation of a product, resulting in higher tariffs for high value-added products.

(vi) **Non-tariff barriers**
Assessing the degree of protection afforded by non-tariff measures, such as quantitative restrictions and technical barriers, can often be quite complex due to the lack of reliable data.

Table 1.1: Average applied tariff industrial rates by country grouping (%)

	Exporter		
	Developed country	**Developing country**	**LDC**
Importer			
Developed country	1.31	2.12	3.05
Developing country	9.00	6.26	6.33
LDC	10.88	14.79	9.95

Table 1.2: Definition and number of tariff peaks on industrial products

Group of countries	**Applied tariff rates**		**Bound tariff rates**	
	Minimum tariff that qualifies as a tariff peak(%)	**Number of peaks**	**Minimum tariff that qualifies as a tariff peak(%)**	**Number of peaks**
Developed	9	338	10.2	185
Developing	24	149	37.5	18
LDCs	40.5	37	37.2	15

Notes: Minimum tariff that qualifies as a tariff peak is equal to three times the average applied rate; number of tariff peaks are at the six digit level of the Harmonized System (HS).
Sources: WITS, UNCTAD TRAINS database; WTO CTS database; UNCTAD analysis.

Tariff escalation

Tariff escalation occurs when tariff levels increase with the degree of processing. To assess tariff escalation, it is useful to classify products into three groups: low, intermediate and high value added. Governments have traditionally sought to impose tariffs on highly processed products and zero or very low taxes on raw materials. This affords value-added sectors a higher rate of effective protection than is apparent from the tariff schedule because taxes on input are less than taxes on output. Tariff escalation in developed countries may inhibit the development of value-added industries in developing countries where they might more suitably be located.

As shown in Figure 1.1, tariff escalation, with tariffs higher for intermediate and final products, is clearly observed in all groups of countries. Among developing and least-developed countries, there is considerable tariff escalation between raw materials/low-technology products and intermediate technology goods, but the extent diminishes between intermediate goods and final products.

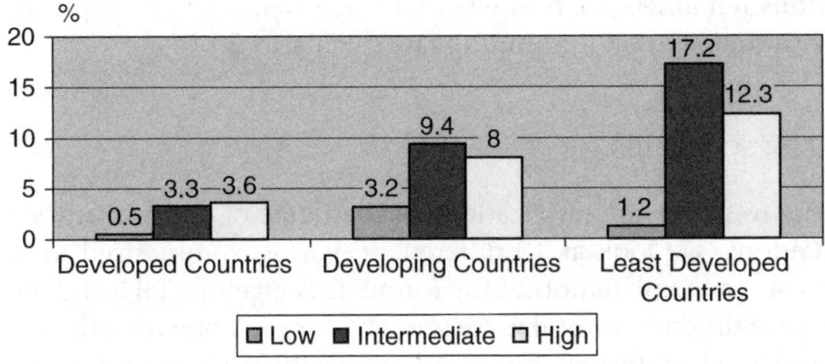

Figure 1.1: Tariff escalation of weighted applied tariffs on industrial products
Sources: WITS; UNCTAD TRAINS.

1.3 WTO negotiations: from Doha to Hong Kong

In 2001 the WTO Doha Ministerial Conference launched an ambitious programme, intended to achieve substantial liberalization in both agricultural and non-agricultural sectors. The Doha Declaration mandated that tariffs and other barriers should be reduced. In particular, special efforts were to be made to take into account the interests of developing countries and LDCs, through measures such as the provision of less than full reciprocity, longer implementation periods and exemptions.

The Hong Kong, China, Ministerial Conference in December 2006 confirmed an approach based on the so-called 'July Package' adopted by the General Council of WTO in August 2004 (referred to as the 'NAMA Framework' in the Hong Kong, China, Ministerial Declaration). In practice the 'July Package' of 2004 set the stage for the end-game in the NAMA negotiations. From that point, discussion became more focused on variations in the 'Swiss' formula of the earlier Tokyo Round, by which a preselected coefficient would establish a maximum rate, while reducing higher rates by a greater proportion than lower rates. An alternative proposal[3] sets the coefficient at the national average (or a multiple thereof). Other proposals are based on the idea of a 'Simple Swiss' formula, with one coefficient for developed countries and another, higher coefficient for developing countries. Some variation would depend on the use of other flexibilities, e.g. on binding. Consensus on participation in sectoral elimination was still lacking, awaiting a decision in the formula. The provisions for special and differential treatment for developing countries also needed further refinement. No transition period had been agreed for implementation of the Agreement. On a more detailed level, several key questions remained, such as whether trade-weighted or simple average tariffs should be used for binding rate calculations.

1.4 The scenarios

In order to gauge the implications of the range of options in the WTO negotiations, we look at 10 different scenarios, summarized in Annex Table 1.A1 (an explanation of the formulae is given in Table 1.3, below). First, three different formulae are selected, for each of which three 'cases' are considered: ambitious, moderate and flexible.[4] These cases are created by varying the tariff cuts, sectoral elimination, binding coverage, exemptions for developing countries and low/nuisance tariff reductions. The tenth scenario is a free trade scenario, used as a benchmark. We start with a discussion on the formulae and other elements under negotiation.

1.4.1 The formula

As noted, the main formulae currently under consideration are variations on a 'Swiss' harmonizing formula, but there has also been interest in a 'Capped formula' in which tariffs are subject to across-the-board uniform cuts, with a capping mechanism based on a multiple of the average applied rates (as originally proposed by India in 2003).

The selection of values for the coefficients within a formula approach can have a significant impact on the resulting tariff reduction obligations. Some proposals call for a common set of coefficients to be used for all countries. Other proposals call for different values for the coefficients for groups of countries as a way to build more flexibility into the formula. Some of the options for dividing countries into groups include the following:

- *Most weak and vulnerable.* This separates out the LDCs plus other weak and vulnerable economies (e.g. the G90) for even more generous treatment.
- *Initial average bound tariff rate.* This calls for varying the coefficients in the WTO formula based on the initial average bound tariff rate, so that countries with higher initial tariffs would face less stringent reductions.
- *Capability to adjust.* This WTO formula calls for grouping countries into three categories according to their 'capability to adjust and commitments they are willing and able to accept'. The categories are 'leaders' (smallest coefficient), 'adjusters' (moderate coefficient), and 'new entrants' (highest coefficient). For a given tariff, countries with the

Table 1.3: Descriptions of formulae to be used in the negotiations

Formula	Explanation
Swiss formula	A harmonizing formula that is effective at reducing tariff peaks and tariff escalations: $T_1 = \frac{(a \times T_0)}{(a + T_0)}$ Where a is the maximum coefficient and no final tariff can be higher than this coefficient.
WTO formula (also known as the 'Girard Formula'):	A harmonizing formula with a coefficient, B, that can be varied to reflect different initial tariff levels. $T_1 = \frac{(B \times t_a \times T_0)}{(B \times t_a + T_0)}$ Where t_a is the national average of the base rates, T_0 is the initial tariff rate and T_1 the final rate.
Capped formula	$T_1 = (a \times T_0)$ An across-the-board, uniform reduction in average bound tariff levels with a capped mechanism three times the average national applied rate. Where $(1 - a)$ is the per cent of tariff reduction.

smaller coefficient are obliged to reduce tariff levels more than those with the higher coefficient.

Three representative formulae are modelled: the WTO formula, the 'simple' Swiss formula and the Capped formula. The Capped formula applies uniform reductions to tariffs with a cap at three times the average national applied rate. This cap has a harmonizing effect and helps address tariff peaks and escalation. The 'simple' Swiss formula envisages the use of different coefficients for developed and developing countries; scenarios using coefficients based on both simple and trade-weighted averages would be used. These are laid out in Table 1.3.

Agriculture and services

All scenarios include a fixed reduction in tariffs on resources (oil, gas, unprocessed minerals, petroleum and coal), services and agriculture. These sectors are responsible for an estimated 30 per cent of the total distortions impeding goods and services trade. As part of the single undertaking in the negotiations some of these distortions are likely to be removed along with reductions in tariffs on non-agricultural goods. If these are not removed resources may flow out of a protected sector, such as textiles, into an even more distorted sector, such as agriculture, worsening the overall efficiency with which resources are used in an economy. For this reason the scenarios include reductions in tariffs on services and agriculture, but these are the same in each of the scenarios to facilitate comparison of the impacts on the non-agricultural sectors. Bound agricultural tariffs are reduced by 36 per cent for developed countries and 24 per cent for developing countries. Protection in the services sector[5] is reduced by 30 per cent. The appropriate reductions in protection are simulated by imposing a productivity shock.

1.4.2 Other elements under negotiation

Binding coverage

Proposals for binding rate coverage vary, with some offering flexibility, while others call for up to 100 per cent coverage. In the modelling exercise, the rate for newly bound tariffs is varied by scenario. The 'ambitious' scenario binds the tariffs at twice the applied tariff rate. The 'flexible' scenario allows developing countries the added flexibility of selecting either twice the applied rate for developing countries (11.6% × 2 = 23.2%), or twice the simple average bound rate (29.4% × 2 = 58.8%).

In the ambitious scenario, countries that fall under paragraph 6 of the 'July Package', with less than 35 per cent of binding coverage ('paragraph 6 countries'), bind their tariffs at the simple average bound rate for developing countries (29.4 per cent). The flexible scenario allows them to bind at twice this amount (29.4% × 2 = 58.8%).

Within the negotiations, there are ongoing discussions on the extent to which binding unbound tariffs is in itself a concession, and whether or not reductions should then be applied to the newly bound tariffs. For the purpose of modelling the scenarios, the key question is how to treat the newly bound tariff rates, and whether or not they should be included in the formula tariff reduction approach. In the 'ambitious' scenario both developed and developing countries first bind those tariff rates that are currently unbound and then the formula is applied on the newly bound tariffs. On both 'moderate' and 'flexible' scenarios developing countries only bind their tariffs and developed countries bind and cut their newly bound tariffs.

Sectoral tariff elimination

Sectoral tariff elimination, or a 'zero-for-zero' approach, involves selecting certain sectors for tariff elimination. Some view this approach as achieving the objective in Paragraph 16 of the Doha Ministerial Declaration, that tariffs be eliminated, 'in particular, on products of export interest to developing countries'. At Hong Kong, China, it was agreed that participation in these sectoral agreements would not be mandatory. Some proposals call for participation by Members that constitute a 'critical mass' of trade in a given area. As yet, however, product coverage, participation and exemptions for developing countries are still to be negotiated. Least-developed countries would not be required to participate in any sectoral approaches, but instead would be expected to make binding commitments.

The scenarios covered by the modelling effort use the seven sectors listed in the original Girard text as possible sectors for elimination of tariffs under sectoral initiatives.[6] These sectors are electronics and electrical goods; fish and fish products; textiles, clothing, footwear; leather goods; motor vehicle parts and components; and stones, gems and precious metals; and textiles and clothing.[7] One scenario includes all countries in sectoral initiatives; another includes developed countries only, while a third assumes no sectoral elimination.

Other tariff reduction modalities

While WTO Members decided to pursue a primarily formula-driven approach; they also agreed that opportunities for supplementary approaches, such as zero-for-zero sectoral elimination, and request-and-offer, would remain open. The proposal also calls upon developed countries to consider eliminating low tariffs, but no firm decision appears to have been reached on this. Several countries have proposed using a mix of the above approaches in order to better take into account the different needs of Members and sensitivities with regard to certain sectors. This is the so-called mixed or cocktail approach.

No account is taken of any possible request-and-offer outcomes in the modelling scenarios.

Exemptions from the formula

The July Package, accepted in Hong Kong, China, contains provisions for developing countries to be exempted from formula and binding coverage commitments; paragraph 8 of the July Package proposes two options for flexibility with respect to product coverage:

(i) Reduce formula cuts by up to 50 per cent for 10 per cent of the tariff lines as long as the tariff lines do not exceed 10 per cent of the total value of a Member's imports.
or

(ii) Exempt up to 5 per cent of tariff lines from formula cuts or binding commitments, as long as they do not exceed [5] per cent of the total value of a Member's imports.

The square brackets in the text imply the number within is subject to negotiation. As per paragraph 6 of the July Package, countries with less than 35 per cent of binding coverage on non-agricultural tariff lines would be exempt from formula-based tariff reductions.

The scenarios to be modelled take account of paragraph 8 of the July Package by which the top 5 per cent of tariff lines in terms of tariff rates are selected for exemptions. In cases where there are several tariff lines with the same rates, those with the highest tariff revenue are used. The binding coverage obligations for countries with less than 35 per cent binding coverage (covered by the paragraph 6 of the July Package) are varied within the scenarios (e.g. 90–100 per cent). The scenarios also vary the binding rates for the unbound tariff lines.

Under paragraph 9 of the July Package, LDCs would be fully exempted from formula tariff reductions (but would be expected to substantially increase their binding coverage), and this has been taken into account in the modelling reported below.

Credits for autonomous liberalization

A number of proposals have suggested that countries that have undertaken autonomous liberalization (e.g., under World Bank and IMF programmes) should be rewarded with credits that can be used to offset obligations in other elements of the market access agreement. Since these credits are not expected to be of significant value for most developing countries, this element is not included in the modelling.

Simple versus trade-weighted averages

Paragraph 6 of the July Package calls for the tariffs to be bound at the overall average rate of bound tariffs for developing countries. Historically under the GATT, trade-weighted averages have been used for non-agricultural market access negotiations, although in the Uruguay Round simple averages were used in the agricultural negotiations. Within the current round of WTO negotiations, it is not clear whether trade-weighted or simple averages will be used for the non-agricultural market access negotiations. This can have a significant effect on the outcome of the binding level commitments, as the current simple average of bound tariff rates for developing countries is double that of the trade-weighted average.

Since this issue can have significant effects on the outcome of the negotiations, the scenarios alternatively use both trade-weighted and simple averages to determine the binding rates.

1.5 Tariff changes

Table 1.4 shows the estimated changes in bound and applied rates for developed countries of applying the various postulated scenarios, Table 1.5 for developing countries and Table 1.6 for LDCs. These tables show the tariff changes after applying the different scenarios described above. It is important to mention that the average tariff depends on the number of tariff lines that are bound, and varies from one scenario to another, as each implies different binding coverage.

Table 1.4A and B shows that the binding coverage in developed countries does not significantly affect the simple average tariffs after applying the various scenarios. This is to be expected, as developed countries have almost 100 per cent of their tariffs bound. Average tariffs in developed countries do not vary too much after applying the various scenarios. All 10 scenarios reduce the initial bound weighted average from 3.4 per cent to less than 1 per cent, except for Swiss flexible and capped flexible, which reduce it to only 1.4 per cent and 1.6 per cent respectively. As may be observed, it is not the choice of formula, but rather the level of ambition that most affects the final average tariffs.

Increasing the binding coverage has implications for the final average tariffs for developing countries where the initial binding coverage and final binding coverage are not the same. This is shown in Table 1.5A and B. In some scenarios, such as the WTO moderate and flexible, the bound weighted average tariff for developing countries actually increases from 12.5 per cent to 15.3 per cent and 17.1 per cent respectively. This is due to an increasing share of tariff lines becoming bound.

It is noteworthy that for developing countries' applied tariffs, the scenarios for the Capped and WTO formulae give similar values. The Capped formula offers the additional benefits of being transparent and simple, two of the key criteria for assessing a tariff reduction approach. Since LDCs are exempt from tariff reduction formulae no change is evident in their average tariffs (Table 1.6).

Disaggregating the changes by country grouping reveals that all three formulae offer developed and developing countries roughly equivalent improvements in market access to developed countries (Table 1.7). However, the data on tariff averages do not reflect the remaining tariff peaks on sensitive products, especially those of export interest to developing

Table 1.4: Developed countries
A. Changes in simple average industrial tariffs (%)

Developed countries	Bound simple averages			Applied simple averages	
	Before	After			
		Initial coverage	Final coverage	Before	After
Swiss					
Ambitious		1.1	1.1		0.8
Moderate		1.1	1.1		0.8
Flexible		2.9	2.9		2.3
WTO					
Ambitious		3.0	2.9		1.6
Moderate	12.3	2.0	1.9	5.5	1.3
Flexible		3.2	3.1		2.2
Capped					
Ambitious		2.6	2.6		1.7
Moderate		2.6	2.6		1.7
Flexible		4.6	4.6		3.4
Free trade		0	0		0

Source: Derived from UNCTAD TRAINS database.

B. Changes in weighted average industrial tariffs (%)

Developed countries	Bound weighted averages			Applied weighted averages	
	Before	After			
		Initial coverage	Final coverage	Before	After
Swiss					
Ambitious		0.5	0.5		0.5
Moderate		0.5	0.5		0.5
Flexible		1.4	1.4		1.3
WTO					
Ambitious		0.7	0.7		0.6
Moderate	3.4	0.5	0.5	3	0.4
Flexible		0.8	0.9		0.8
Capped					
Ambitious		0.8	0.8		0.8
Moderate		0.8	0.8		0.8
Flexible		1.6	1.6		1.5
Free Trade		0	0		0

Source: Derived from UNCTAD TRAINS database.

Table 1.5: Developing countries
A. Changes in simple average industrial tariffs (%)

	Bound simple averages			Applied simple averages	
	Before	After		Before	After
		Initial coverage	Final coverage		
Swiss					
Ambitious		8.7	9.1		5.3
Moderate		11.1	16.8		7.6
Flexible		14.6	20.4		9.1
WTO					
Ambitious		12.4	12.7		6.3
Moderate	29.4	23.1	29.7	11.6	10.4
Flexible		25.2	31.8		10.6
Capped					
Ambitious		11.6	12.1		6.8
Moderate		16.5	22.3		10.3
Flexible		18.3	23.9		10.6
Free Trade		0	0		0

Source: Derived from UNCTAD TRAINS database.

B. Changes in weighted average industrial tariffs (%)

	Bound weighted averages			Applied weighted averages	
	Before	After		Before	After
		Initial coverage	Final coverage		
Swiss					
Ambitious		2.6	3.4		2.5
Moderate		4.0	6.4		4.0
Flexible		5.9	9.2		5.2
WTO					
Ambitious		3.9	5.0		3.3
Moderate	12.5	9.4	15.3	8.0	6.1
Flexible		10.4	17.1		6.3
Capped					
Ambitious		4.4	5.7		3.8
Moderate		7.0	9.2		5.9
Flexible		8.2	10.5		6.2
Free Trade		0	0		0

Source: Derived from UNCTAD TRAINS database.

Table 1.6: Average industrial tariffs in least-developed countries

	%
Initial bound simple average	45.2
Initial applied simple average	12.6
Initial bound weighted average	12.4
Initial applied weighted average	13.5

Source: Derived from UNCTAD TRAINS database.

Table 1.7: Initial and final weighted average applied tariffs by country grouping

Exporter	**Importer**					
	Developed country			**Developing country**		
	Developed	**Developing**	**LDC**	**Developed**	**Developing**	**LDC**
Before	1.31	2.12	3.05	9.0	6.26	6.33
Swiss						
Ambitious	0.32	0.20	0.01	2.75	2.09	2.20
Moderate	0.32	0.20	0.01	4.58	3.13	2.84
Flexible	0.69	0.90	1.04	6.00	3.91	3.28
WTO						
Ambitious	0.40	0.24	0.01	3.64	2.65	2.64
Moderate	0.27	0.16	0.00	7.09	4.46	3.82
Flexible	0.44	0.45	0.39	7.29	4.61	3.95
Capped						
Ambitious	0.45	0.29	0.01	4.20	2.97	2.92
Moderate	0.45	0.29	0.01	6.85	4.28	3.69
Flexible	0.70	1.14	1.47	7.21	4.55	3.90

Notes: LDCs are exempted from the table because their tariff regimes do not change.
Source: GTAP simulations.

countries. Therefore an important issue for developing countries is not necessarily the choice of formula, but rather the extent to which the agreement will address the high tariff peaks on products of strategic importance to their economies. Modelling bilateral trade flows can help identify what is important.

1.6 Modelling trade policy

1.6.1 Models as a tool for understanding trade policy changes

Looking at average tariffs provides a good indication of the level of ambition of a proposal. However, it is also possible to use trade models to make estimates of the potential effects of changes in trade policy on exports, imports, tariff revenues, production, prices and welfare. Models allow an understanding of the interplay of different economic forces and the relative impact of different policies. They can often help to highlight unexpected or counter-intuitive outcomes, which can assist policy-makers in their choice of policy options and/or development of support measures.

The standard GTAP model used in this analysis is a static, multiregion, multisector, computable general equilibrium (CGE) model that assumes perfect competition and constant returns to scale. Bilateral trade is handled via the Armington assumption that differentiates imports by source. Input-output tables reflect the links between sectors. GTAP is ideally suited for analysis of trade policies, such as the liberalization of industrial tariffs, which are likely to have international and intersectoral effects. The input-output tables capture the indirect intersectoral effects, while the bilateral trade flows capture the linkages between countries. A shock or policy change in any sector has effects throughout the whole economy. Tariff support for one sector, such as textiles, tends to have negative effects on downstream sectors (apparel) by raising prices and costs. Changes in policies in sectors such as steel and petroleum tend to have relatively important economy-wide effects because many sectors use these inputs. Support in one market often has a negative effect on others because each sector competes with the others for factor inputs, capital, labour and land. CGE models attempt to capture these effects. The methodology involves specifying a data set which represents a specific year, postulating a change in tariffs or other policy variable, and comparing the simulated outcome with the base data. Impacts of the removal of trade barriers on trade flows, government revenues, welfare and resource allocation within countries can then be ascertained.

1.6.2 Limitations of various models[8]

Trade models are useful analytical tools, but they have certain limitations; this is important to keep in mind when drawing inferences from the results. For example, static models do not provide estimates of the adjustment process; they say nothing of the transition between one state and another. Yet the adjustment process is becoming a major concern vis-à-vis international trade, and is often cited as the main reason for the absence of reform. Dynamic models throw more light on the adjustment process, but the results tend to be driven by the underlying assumptions. A more significant limitation is the inability to capture dynamic gains, the effects on productivity from investment, competition, the transfer of technology and other factors that are associated with trade liberalization. These factors may be as important as the static impacts, but are difficult to estimate.

Another limitation is that market entry is not always assured, because of other barriers, such as sanitary and phytosanitary measures and technical barriers to trade barriers, which appear to be gaining in importance, especially in the agricultural sector. Exports may also be limited by supply constraints (ports and roads) or the preferences and practices of large marketing companies.

1.6.3 Data

The GTAP 6.5 database is used in the present study. The value (of output and trade flows) data relate to 2001 and the behavioural parameters, such as elasticities, are taken from the literature rather than econometrically estimated specifically for use within the model. Input-output data are taken from national accounts and vary from year to year, depending on their availability in particular countries. For this application the bilateral tariff data are taken from the World Integrated Trade Solution (WITS); the UNCTAD Trade Analysis and Information System (TRAINS) database is the source of the applied tariff data; and the WTO Integrated Database provides the bound tariffs. The standard GTAP model also uses data collated by UNCTAD, but it is aggregated in a different way, particularly when converting specific tariffs to ad valorem tariffs. This is more relevant for agricultural than industrial tariffs. Preferences are included in the tariff database, and data for the EU are aggregated to 25 members, with internal tariffs removed. China's tariff data reflect its accession terms, with its average industrial tariffs at 9 per cent. China's textile and apparel exports face tariffs of around 10 per cent in each of its major markets: the EU, the United States and Japan. Quotas on exports to these markets were removed at the end of 2004. The database includes substantial export taxes on Chinese textile and apparel exports to the EU and the United States, reflecting quota rents. However, these quotas are not removed in the simulations, as their removal was agreed to in the Uruguay Round.

1.6.4 Aggregation

GTAP is a spatial model in that it contains bilateral trade flows and tariffs. This enables us to say something about regional trade agreements and the erosion of preferences. However, it is not feasible to include all 87 regions and 65 sectors when simulating GTAP. For the analysis in this paper, we use 23 regions and 23 sectors. The choice of aggregation reflects the questions to be addressed.

Regional Aggregation. Single region models permit additional detail, and may be useful when assessing the impact of exogenous shocks on a single country. For multilateral trade negotiations, a multi-region aggregation is obviously more desirable. The selection of the 23 regions reflects geo-political groupings. It is desirable to aggregate together countries at a similar stage of development and those with similar rates of protection. The aggregation used here separates the major developed and developing countries, and the available case study countries (Bangladesh, Bulgaria, Malawi, the Philippines and Zambia). The remaining groups are aggregates of developing countries.

Sectoral aggregation. The aggregation chosen here reflects an attempt to separate sectors with high rates of protection, such as textiles, leather, apparel, motor vehicles and electronics. For this application to industrial products, the agricultural and services sectors are highly aggregated into only two and four sectors respectively. However, these sectors need to be modelled because resources flow into and out of all sectors, leading to possible second-best effects. This can occur if resources released from the industrial sector are re-employed in a more highly protected agricultural sector, resulting in loss of allocative efficiency.

1.6.5 Closure

Closure refers to the specification of exogenous and endogenous variables in the model. Exogenous variables are fixed, whereas the endogenous ones vary according to changes in the policy variables. The specification depends on how economies are run, the time horizon envisaged and the particular scenarios to be modelled. Of interest here are the labour, capital and foreign exchange markets.

Labour market. The standard labour market closure specifies that the amount of skilled and unskilled labour is fixed and cannot move between regions, although it can move readily between sectors. Wage rates are assumed to be flexible. This closure is somewhat at odds with reality, given that unemployment varies with the business cycle. In addition, in developing countries in particular, there appears to be a pool of unemployed or members of the labour force that work with low intensity. Previous work by UNCTAD (Fernández de Córdoba, Laird and Vanzetti, 2004a) and others has shown that changes in the amount of labour employed has a far greater effect on output and welfare than merely reallocating resources in response to changes in relative prices. An alternative to the standard closure used in this application is to assume fixed wages and allow unskilled labour use to vary in developed countries. Skilled labour remains fixed. This is based on the intuition that the informal sector in developing countries is characterized by significant unemployment and underemployment. Because the demand for labour is indirectly derived from the demand for labour-intensive goods, liberalization tends to increase employment in developing countries and reduce it in developed countries. Thus, with this closure, developing countries appear to gain more from liberalization at the expense of developed countries.

It could be argued that some developed-country economies which are characterized by rigid wages, such as those of Japan and some EU members, should also be treated in a similar way. However, these economies also have regulations governing the shedding of labour, which restrict downward changes in labour use. In these simulations, the standard closure is applied to these economies.

Capital. Macroeconomic closure refers to the specification of endogenous and exogenous variables to satisfy the balancing of the capital and current accounts (i.e. the difference between national savings and investment must equal exports plus international transfers less imports). The standard GTAP closure assumes that investment adjusts endogenously to changes in savings. The trade balance can vary, so that at a national level the change in exports need not equal the change in imports. An alternative macroeconomic closure used here is to fix the trade balance in all countries except one – the United States. This implies that changes in regional investment must equate with savings to maintain the current-account and the capital-account balance. With the trade balance fixed, there is little change in investment. This assumption can affect the distribution of gains from liberalization.

Exchange rates. Real exchange rates (i.e. adjusted for inflation) are implicit in the model and are assumed to be fully flexible. However, several countries, such as China, have or have had managed nominal exchange rate regimes. A fixed nominal rate implies that adjustment must occur elsewhere, for example in prices, interest rates or employment. If this is ignored in the simulations, the trade flow estimates may be biased.

In summary, we use the standard model closure with two modifications. (1) Real wages of unskilled labour in developing countries are fixed and the quantity flexible. Although not entirely satisfactory in several respects, this closure is relatively transparent and permits replication of results by others. (2) The trade balance is fixed for all countries but one.

1.7 Simulation results

This section provides the estimated effects of the various trade policy scenarios described above on exports revenues, imports, government revenues, welfare, sectoral output changes and changes in labour use. In general, the degree of ambition in the various scenarios can be evaluated by the global change in export revenues, with the more ambitious scenarios creating a greater impact. However, this rule does not necessarily apply to all countries or all sectors in an economy.

1.7.1 Export revenues

The implications for export revenues from the ten scenarios described above are shown in Table 1.8. There are increases in export revenues for almost all regions under all the scenarios. Overall, the more ambitious tariff reduction formulae lead to greater changes in export revenues. Of the ambitious, moderate and flexible variations in each of the Swiss, WTO and linear Capped approaches, the ambitious scenarios generate greater export revenue gains in almost all cases. Moreover, there is relatively little difference between the Swiss, WTO and Capped approaches. For example, in each 'ambitious' scenario the magnitudes of the export revenue effects are somewhat similar. Global export revenue effects are 4.6 per cent, 4.3 per cent and 4.1 per cent respectively under the three 'ambitious' scenarios. This observation also holds for most individual countries.

A second observation is that the increase in exports is not evenly distributed. The major beneficiaries, in percentage terms at least, are China, India, Brazil and Rest of South Asia.[9] In absolute terms, the gains in export revenue are shared roughly equally between developed and developing countries. For example, under the Swiss 'ambitious' scenario – the most liberalizing of the partial scenarios – global export revenue gains are estimated at $317 billion, of which $163 billion accrues to developing countries, particularly China ($73 billion), South- East Asia ($17 billion), India ($15 billion) and the Middle East and North Africa region ($15 billion). Export gains for the EU, the United States and Japan are estimated to be $51 billion, $44 billion and $27 billion respectively (figures not shown in table).

The results for China and India are noteworthy: China's exports increase by 15 per cent under the Swiss 'ambitious' scenario. The major increases are to the developed markets: the EU ($16 billion), the United States ($18 billion) and Japan ($11 billion). There are also significant increases, in percentage terms, to developing-country/regional markets: India (50 per cent), Brazil (39 per cent), Bulgaria (71 per cent), Rest of South Asia (30 per cent), South-East Asia (28 per cent), the Andean Pact[10] (31 per cent) and the Southern Cone region (Argentina, Chile and Uruguay) (36 per cent). But these exports, which amount to a total of $18 billion, account for only 24 per cent of China's export growth. By sector, the major increases in exports in value terms are in apparel ($16 billion to the EU, Japan and the United States), electronics ($13 billion to the EU and the United States), textiles ($10 billion) and machinery and equipment ($8 billion).

Table 1.8: Changes in export revenue relative to base under alternative scenarios

	Free trade (%)	Swiss			WTO			Capped		
		Ambitious (%)	Moderate (%)	Flexible (%)	Ambitious (%)	Moderate (%)	Flexible (%)	Ambitious (%)	Moderate (%)	Flexible (%)
EU[11]	2.6	1.9	1.7	1.2	1.8	1.3	1.2	1.7	1.3	1.1
United States	6.9	4.9	4.8	3.5	4.9	5.1	4.5	4.8	4.8	3.5
Japan	8.9	5.9	5.3	3.7	5.8	5	4.5	5.4	4.7	3.4
Canada	2.0	1.3	1.3	1.1	1.3	1.3	1.2	1.2	1.2	0.9
Rest of OECD	6.0	3.1	2.9	2.1	2.6	2.7	2.3	2.6	2.4	1.7
High-income Asia	7.9	5.4	4.2	3.2	5.5	3.7	3.4	5.1	3.7	3
China, incl. Hong Kong	18.7	15.2	13.8	11.8	15.3	12.8	11.9	14.7	13	11.1
India	43.8	25.1	19.5	13.5	18.8	5.6	4.2	17	7.4	4.4
Brazil	20.4	11.4	8.1	4.8	9.2	3.2	3	8.6	3.4	2.7
México	8.3	4.6	2.9	1.6	3.5	0.6	0.6	3.2	0.7	0.5
Bangladesh	56.1	0.8	1.3	0.8	0.7	1.5	1.4	0.7	1.5	0.8
Philippines	7.5	2.8	0.9	0.4	2.4	0.8	0.7	2.3	0.7	0.2
Malawi	24.7	6.6	5.4	4.2	6.5	3.7	3.2	6.5	3.1	2.5
Zambia	11.8	0.2	0.2	0.2	0.5	0.3	0.2	0.7	0.4	0.3
Bulgaria	14.4	6.0	3.8	2.6	5.1	1.4	1.2	4.5	1.6	1.3
Rest of South Asia	22.4	11.5	8.8	4.9	9.1	5.9	5	7.8	6	2.9
South-East Asia	11.6	5.6	3.6	2.4	5.2	2.5	2.1	4.3	2.5	1.6
Central America and the Caribbean	20.9	9.4	6.8	3.8	8.7	4.9	4.3	8.7	4.9	2.5
Andean Pact	10.1	4.2	2.9	1.2	3.1	1.1	0.9	2.9	1.1	0.7
Argentina, Chile and Uruguay	13.7	6.7	5.3	3.8	5.5	3.2	3	5.1	3.3	2.8
Middle East and North Africa	15.1	5.8	4.5	3.1	4.4	1.6	1.4	4	1.8	1.4
Sub-Saharan Africa	17.5	3.9	2.4	1.8	3.9	1.6	1.4	3.6	1.6	1.2
All other regions	13.6	3.8	2.7	1.9	3.4	1.8	1.6	3.2	1.8	1.4
Developing countries	15.9	8.5	6.8	7.7	4.8	4.4	7.2	5.0	4.0	
World	**7.7**	**4.6**	**3.9**	**2.9**	**4.3**	**3.2**	**2.9**	**4.1**	**3.2**	**2.5**

Source: GTAP simulations.

For India, the estimated increase in exports following implementation of the Swiss 'ambitious' scenario is 25 per cent, or $16 billion. As with China, the major destinations for the additional exports from India are the EU ($6 billion) and the United States ($3 billion), while China and South-East Asia account for $1 billion each. By sector, the largest components of Indian exports are textiles ($2.2 billion), apparel ($2.4 billion), other manufactures ($2.0 billion), and machinery and equipment ($1.6 billion).

The export gains to some of the smaller countries examined in the case studies in Part II of this book – Bangladesh, Malawi, Zambia and Bulgaria – are generally modest. Bangladesh and Zambia show minimal gains in industrial exports across all scenarios. Bangladesh loses some of its preferential access in the textiles and leather sectors, but gains in sales of apparel, unprocessed agricultural products and business services. In the case of Bangladesh in particular, the distinction between textiles and apparel is somewhat misleading.

Zambia also appears to gain little from liberalization. The increase in exports of processed agriculture to the EU and other manufactures to India does not outweigh the fall in exports of textiles to sub-Saharan Africa and the EU, and non-ferrous metals to the Middle East and North Africa, and South-East Asia. Sub-Saharan Africa imports more of its textiles from the EU and high-income Asia, whereas the Middle East and North Africa region sources more of its imports from the EU and from countries within its own region.

Malawi exports more textiles and apparel to other countries in sub-Saharan Africa and processed agricultural products to the EU.

Finally, Bulgaria enjoys export gains in all sectors, particularly leather, machinery and equipment, and chemicals, rubber and plastics. A reduction in apparel sales to the EU is partially offset by additional exports to the United States, other developed countries and Rest of the World. Leather sales to Japan are also sizeable.

It may be noted that South–South trade would also expand more under the more ambitious scenario This result can be observed by comparing export revenues in the WTO 'ambitious' and 'moderate' scenarios. In these two scenarios, the developed-country tariff reductions are similar, but, in the developing countries, the average tariff is reduced marginally from 11.6 to 6.3 per cent in the 'ambitious' case and 10.4 per cent in the 'moderate' case. For developing countries as a group, exports increase from 4.8 to 7.7 per cent under the 'ambitious' scenario, amounting to an increase of $56 billion. The impact on Sub-Saharan African exports, is an increase of 1.6 per cent in the 'moderate' case and 3.9 per cent in the 'ambitious' case.

1.7.2 Imports

A similar story holds for imports at the regional level: national imports move broadly in line with exports. This reflects our assumption that countries adopt policies aimed at maintaining their balance of trade. The regional changes are shown in Table 1.9. Once again, it is the level of ambition rather than the formula chosen that is important. However, the approaches may have varying sectoral effects, and the bilateral flows will differ from exports. For example, a quarter of China's additional exports go to the United States following the Swiss 'ambitious' scenario, but only 16 per cent of additional imports are sourced from the United States. To supply inputs into its expanding apparel sectors, $11 billion in additional textiles are sourced from Japan and high-income Asia.

1.7.3 Government revenues

The most ambitious (Swiss) scenario modelled here results in a global reduction in tariff revenues of 50 per cent (see Table 1.10). In each case, the harmonizing Swiss formula leads to greater losses in revenue than the alternative WTO or Capped approaches. This applies at the three levels of ambition, and the pattern tends to hold across all regions.

However, all the scenarios indicate a significant variation between regions: from a 5 per cent gain in Malawi to an 83-per-cent fall in the United States. These variations reflect where the tariff cuts fall, the relationship between bound and applied rates, and the relevant import elasticity. For example, cuts in bound rates may have no impact on applied rates if the initial difference exceeds the cut. Imports of luxury goods with a high elasticity may increase sufficiently to offset the tariff reduction, leading to an increase in revenue. The harmonizing Swiss and WTO formulae tend to reduce tariff revenues by the greatest amount in high tariff regions, but the gap between bound and applied rates also matters. For example, the linear approach leads to similar tariff losses for low-tariff China as the harmonizing approaches, but for other developing countries, the tariff revenue losses tend to be lower under the linear Capped formula. In particular, there is a large difference between the Swiss 'moderate' and the other 'moderate' approaches. Developing countries lose 30 per cent of their revenue in the first case yet only 15 and 17 per cent respectively in the WTO and Capped approach. This is most apparent in the double digit declines for developing countries under the Swiss 'moderate' scenario.

Clearly, large falls are more significant in developing countries that are more dependent on tariffs as a source of revenue. The lowest income developing countries tend to be the most dependent on tariffs as a source of revenue.

Table 1.9: Changes in imports relative to base under alternative scenarios

	Free trade (%)	Swiss			WTO			Capped		
		Ambitious (%)	Moderate (%)	Flexible (%)	Ambitious (%)	Moderate (%)	Flexible (%)	Ambitious (%)	Moderate (%)	Flexible (%)
EU	2.6	1.9	1.7	1.3	1.8	1.4	1.3	1.7	1.3	1.1
United States	4.9	3.5	3.4	2.5	3.5	3.6	3.2	3.4	3.4	2.5
Japan	10.3	6.9	6.1	4.3	6.7	5.8	5.2	6.2	5.4	3.9
Canada	2.2	1.5	1.5	1.2	1.4	1.4	1.3	1.4	1.4	1
Rest of OECD	6.8	3.5	3.4	2.4	3	3.1	2.7	3	2.7	1.9
High-income Asia	8.7	6	4.6	3.6	6.1	4.1	3.7	5.7	4.1	3.4
China, incl. Hong Kong	23.3	19	17.3	14.8	19.1	16	14.9	18.4	16.2	13.8
India	47	27	20.9	14.5	20.2	6	4.5	18.2	7.9	4.7
Brazil	18.5	10.4	7.4	4.4	8.3	2.9	2.7	7.8	3.1	2.5
México	9.2	5.2	3.2	1.7	3.9	0.7	0.7	3.6	0.7	0.6
Bangladesh	44	0.6	1	0.6	0.6	1.2	1.1	0.6	1.1	0.6
Philippines	6.7	2.5	0.8	0.3	2.2	0.7	0.6	2	0.6	0.2
Malawi	25.6	6.8	5.6	4.4	6.8	3.8	3.3	6.8	3.3	2.6
Zambia	13	0.3	0.2	0.3	0.5	0.3	0.2	0.8	0.4	0.3
Bulgaria	13.6	5.7	3.6	2.4	4.8	1.3	1.2	4.3	1.5	1.2
Rest of South Asia	22.1	11.4	8.7	4.9	9	5.9	5	7.7	6	2.9
South-East Asia	15.8	7.6	4.9	3.2	7	3.4	2.9	5.8	3.3	2.2
Central America and the Caribbean	13.9	6.3	4.5	2.5	5.8	3.2	2.9	5.8	3.2	1.7
Andean Pact	10.2	4.3	2.9	1.2	3.1	1.1	0.9	2.9	1.2	0.7
Argentina, Chile and Uruguay	14.9	7.3	5.7	4.2	6	3.4	3.2	5.6	3.6	3.1
Middle East and North Africa	14.8	5.7	4.5	3	4.4	1.6	1.4	3.9	1.8	1.4
Sub-Saharan Africa	17.4	3.9	2.4	1.8	3.9	1.6	1.3	3.6	1.5	1.1
All other regions	14.2	4	2.8	1.9	3.6	1.9	1.7	3.4	1.9	1.4
Developing countries	17.5	9.4	7.5	5.6	8.5	5.3	4.8	7.9	5.4	4.3
World	**7.7**	**4.6**	**3.9**	**2.9**	**4.3**	**3.2**	**2.9**	**4.1**	**3.2**	**2.5**

Source: GTAP simulations.

Table 1.10: Initial and change in tariff revenue under alternative scenarios

	$b	Swiss			WTO			Capped		
		Ambitious (%)	Moderate (%)	Flexible (%)	Ambitious (%)	Moderate (%)	Flexible (%)	Ambitious (%)	Moderate (%)	Flexible (%)
EU	27.1	−58	−58	−33	−56	−61	−50	−53	−53	−32
United States	20.0	−79	−79	−49	−79	−83	−72	−78	−77	−46
Japan	17.1	−45	−46	−30	−46	−48	−42	−44	−44	−24
Canada	3.0	−58	−58	−39	−55	−60	−52	−53	−53	−34
Rest of OECD	8.0	−47	−47	−28	−34	−41	−30	−33	−33	−13
High-income Asia	17.7	−55	−37	−30	−58	−31	−29	−53	−33	−30
China, incl. Hong Kong	32.5	−79	−70	−65	−81	−64	−61	−77	−67	−62
India	12.9	−61	−44	−30	−44	−7	−5	−40	−11	−8
Brazil	5.6	−56	−31	−13	−43	0	1	−39	−2	0
México	6.8	−50	−26	−11	−39	−8	−7	−37	−8	−7
Bangladesh	1.7	1	1	1	1	2	2	1	2	1
Philippines	1.2	−32	−2	−1	−27	1	1	−23	1	−1
Malawi	0.1	5	5	3	5	3	2	5	2	2
Zambia	0.1	0	0	0	1	0	0	1	0	0
Bulgaria	0.5	−41	−22	−12	−34	−5	−4	−28	−6	−4
Rest of South Asia	2.5	−38	−20	−9	−18	3	2	−8	2	0
South-East Asia	14.0	−37	−14	−9	−33	−2	−2	−21	−4	−4
Central America and the Caribbean	3.6	−23	−8	−1	−19	3	3	−19	2	1
Andean Pact	4.8	−42	−26	−10	−29	−1	−1	−25	−2	−1
Argentina, Chile and Uruguay	3.3	−40	−19	−6	−29	0	1	−26	0	1
Middle East and North Africa	22.0	−32	−24	−16	−24	−5	−4	−20	−7	−5
Sub-Saharan Africa	10.6	−16	−8	−5	−16	−3	−2	−13	−2	−2
All other regions	15.2	−19	−10	−6	−17	−3	−3	−15	−4	−3
Developing countries	142.7	−44	−30	−23	−38	−15	−14	−34	−17	−15
World	**230.2**	**−50**	**−40**	**−27**	**−45**	**−30**	**−27**	**−42**	**−30**	**−21**

Source: GTAP database and simulations.

1.7.4 Welfare

Static annual welfare effects of the various scenarios, plus free trade, are shown in Table 1.11. The welfare effects tend to be associated with trade flows: an increase in trade generates increased welfare. At a global level the Swiss 'ambitious' scenario generates the greatest potential gains, of almost \$135 billion. This compares with a free trade result of over \$200 billion. As with trade flows, the three Swiss scenarios generate greater welfare effects than the equivalent WTO and Capped approaches.

However, the welfare benefits of greater ambition are relatively modest. Reducing trade-weighted applied industrial tariffs from the initial average of 3 to 0.8 per cent (rather than 1.5 per cent) in developed countries and from 8 to 3.8 (rather than 6.2 per cent) in developing countries generates 25 to 30 per cent more in global-welfare gains. In other words, the initial reductions generate the greatest gains. This is the rationale behind reducing individual tariff peaks.

At a regional level, the distribution of the gains is fairly constant across the scenarios, with 58–67 per cent of the welfare gains going to the developing countries, reflecting the existing trade flows and protection patterns. The share of gains to developing countries tends to rise under the 'ambitious' scenarios in which the applied tariffs of developing countries are reduced compared with their being somewhat sheltered under the flexible formula. For example, in the Capped approach, developing country gains are \$54, \$66 and \$78 billion under the ambitious, moderate and flexible scenarios respectively, but the average tariffs are reduced from 8 per cent to 6.2, 5.9 and 3.8 per cent respectively (Table 1.5B). The moderate scenario seems to generate reasonable gains with modest tariff reductions. This is because under the moderate Capped formula, developed countries' additional tariff cuts are quite significant, with the average industrial tariff being reduced from 1.5 per cent under the flexible formula to 0.8 per cent (Table 1.4B).

1.7.5 Labour use

In these simulations it is assumed that employment of unskilled labour in developing countries would rise as demand for such labour in labour-intensive industries increases. Conversely, employment could fall if, relatively, prices moved unfavourably. Results are shown in Table 1.12 for the three Swiss scenarios and for free trade.[12] In developed countries, with more rigid unskilled labour markets, the real wage, rather than the quantity of labour, is assumed to be flexible. The contribution to welfare gains in developing countries based on the assumption of a flexible unskilled labour force can be seen in Table 1.13, in which welfare under the Swiss

Table 1.11: Changes in welfare relative to base under alternative scenarios

	Free trade ($b)	Swiss			WTO			Capped		
		Ambitious ($b)	Moderate ($b)	Flexible ($b)	Ambitious ($b)	Moderate ($b)	Flexible ($b)	Ambitious ($b)	Moderate ($b)	Flexible ($b)
EU	28.5	22.6	20.1	20.4	21.3	15.8	16.7	20.7	16.8	18.4
United States	11.2	5.8	5.2	7.0	5.9	4.9	5.4	5.9	5.3	7.2
Japan	11.5	9.1	7.7	6.4	8.6	6.9	6.5	7.9	6.5	6.1
Canada	0.5	0.8	0.7	1.0	0.8	0.6	0.8	0.9	0.8	1.0
Rest of OECD	4.9	3.1	3.0	2.8	3.2	3.0	3.0	3.2	3.0	2.7
High-income Asia	8.9	6.5	6.2	4.9	6.1	5.7	5.3	5.8	5.4	4.3
China, incl. Hong Kong	46.1	41.2	40.0	34.8	40.9	38.8	36.7	40.3	38.6	32.7
India	11.7	5.1	4.8	3.5	4.2	2.7	2.1	3.8	3.1	1.8
Brazil	5.4	2.7	2.3	1.6	2.1	1.2	1.1	1.9	1.3	1.0
México	2.8	2.1	1.6	1.1	1.4	−0.2	−0.1	1.2	−0.1	0.2
Bangladesh	1.3	0.0	0.1	0.1	0.0	0.1	0.1	0.0	0.1	0.1
Philippines	0.6	0.4	0.4	0.3	0.4	0.4	0.4	0.4	0.4	0.2
Malawi	0.2	0.1	0.0	0.0	0.1	0.0	0.0	0.1	0.0	0.0
Zambia	0.1	0.0	0.0	0.0	0.0	0.0	0.0	0.0	0.0	0.0
Bulgaria	0.2	0.1	0.1	0.1	0.1	0.0	0.1	0.1	0.1	0.1
Rest of South Asia	2.6	1.5	1.4	0.8	1.3	1.1	0.9	1.1	1.1	0.5
South-East Asia	17.4	10.4	8.6	6.7	10.0	7.6	7.0	9.0	7.6	5.4
Central America and the Caribbean	3.0	1.8	1.7	1.2	1.7	1.4	1.3	1.7	1.4	0.9
Andean Pact	1.1	0.7	0.6	0.4	0.6	0.4	0.4	0.6	0.5	0.3
Argentina, Chile and Uruguay	5.7	3.5	3.2	2.7	3.1	2.5	2.4	3.0	2.5	2.3
Middle East and North Africa	14.1	8.4	7.1	5.9	7.4	3.6	3.2	7.1	4.1	3.4
Sub-Saharan Africa	8.2	2.9	2.2	2.0	2.9	1.7	1.6	2.8	1.7	1.6
All other regions	14.7	5.9	5.0	4.2	5.6	4.2	3.9	5.4	4.2	3.6
Developing countries	135.3	86.9	79.1	65.2	81.7	65.7	61.1	78.4	66.4	54
World	**200.8**	**134.7**	**122.2**	**107.6**	**127.6**	**102.7**	**98.7**	**122.8**	**104.1**	**93.7**

Source: GTAP simulations.

Table 1.12: Changes in unskilled labour use in developing countries relative to base

	Free trade (%)	**Swiss**		
		Ambitious (%)	**Moderate (%)**	**Flexible (%)**
China, incl. Hong Kong	7.0	6.0	5.7	5.1
India	5.7	2.2	1.8	1.2
Brazil	1.9	0.7	0.4	0.0
Mexico	1.8	1.0	0.6	0.4
Bangladesh	7.9	0.0	0.1	0.1
Philippines	3.1	1.5	0.9	0.6
Malawi	11.0	2.7	2.2	1.8
Zambia	6.3	0.2	0.1	0.2
Bulgaria	3.5	1.3	0.9	0.7
Rest of South Asia	4.9	2.1	1.9	1.0
South East-Asia	7.1	3.6	2.5	1.9
Central America and the Caribbean	7.4	3.1	2.2	1.3
Andean Pact	1.6	0.8	0.5	0.3
Argentina, Chile and Uruguay	1.7	0.6	0.3	0.1
Middle East and North Africa	5.3	2.3	1.8	1.4
Sub-Saharan Africa	6.6	1.6	1.0	0.8
All other regions	4.7	1.4	1.0	0.8

Source: GTAP simulations.

'ambitious' scenario is compared under alternative assumptions. Global welfare gains are almost $135 billion with a flexible labour force compared with $74 billion with flexible wages. Most of the gain accrues to China. These results illustrate the importance of utilizing all available resources.

Unskilled labour use in developing countries responds positively to liberalization in every instance. The changes are positive but quite small, and somewhat variable. With the flexible scenario, most of the changes are less than 1 per cent, but under the hypothetical free trade scenario the increases are as high as 11 per cent in Malawi (Table 1.12). The variations depend on the demand for the products that can be produced with unskilled labour. Most unskilled labour is used in the services sectors. Outside of services and agriculture, a significant amount of unskilled labour is used in lumber, leather, paper products, apparel, light manufactures and electronics.

Rising employment at a national level does not imply similar sectoral effects. Some sectors are bound to employ less labour (and capital and

Table 1.13: Changes in welfare with flexible labour and wages under the Swiss 'ambitious' scenario

	Welfare change with flexible labour ($b)	**Welfare change with flexible wages ($b)**
EU	22.6	21.9
United States	5.8	5.2
Japan	9.1	8.8
Canada	0.8	0.7
Rest of OECD	3.1	3.0
High-income Asia	6.5	6.2
China, incl. Hong Kong	41.2	9.3
India	5.1	1.4
Brazil	2.7	1.4
Mexico	2.1	0.8
Bangladesh	0.0	0.0
Philippines	0.4	0.2
Malawi	0.1	0.0
Zambia	0.0	0.0
Bulgaria	0.1	0.0
Rest of South Asia	1.5	0.8
South-East Asia	10.4	5.5
Central America and the Caribbean	1.8	0.7
Andean Pact	0.7	0.0
Argentina, Chile and Uruguay	3.5	2.7
Middle East and North Africa	8.4	2.2
Sub-Saharan Africa	2.9	0.9
All other regions	5.9	2.0
Developing countries	86.9	28.0
World	**134.7**	**73.8**

Source: GTAP simulations.

intermediate inputs). Unemployment in particular sectors is seen as a major adjustment problem, and a serious impediment to reform. To illustrate the potential effects, Table 1.14 shows the use of labour in selected sensitive sectors for the Swiss 'ambitious' scenario.

The results indicate some substantial changes, positive and negative, in specific sectors. The negative effects are of the most interest. For example, in the leather sector, there is a loss of skilled and unskilled employment of over 30 per cent in Japan and nearly 21 per cent in Canada. In developing countries, the losses tend to be less than 10 per cent, one exception being leather in Bangladesh. These data give an indication of the structural adjustment that would be needed. However, the size of the sector should

Table 1.14: Use of labour in selected sectors, Swiss 'ambitious' scenario

	Textiles (%)	Wearing apparel (%)	Leather (%)	Motor vehicles (%)
EU	−1.3	−6.6	−4.7	0.3
United States	−9.2	−9.9	−15.9	0.0
Japan	11.2	−7.2	−29.8	3.0
Canada	−17.9	−19.3	−20.6	0.7
Rest of OECD	−10.5	−10.9	−1.4	−2.5
High-income Asia	17.2	13.4	23.3	1.0
China, incl. Hong Kong	16.3	25.6	20.8	−3.5
India	8.9	38.9	7.3	−3.6
Brazil	−5.1	−1.7	−0.5	−2.7
Mexico	−14.3	−19.7	−10.5	5.0
Bangladesh	−0.8	4.3	−13.5	2.4
Philippines	21.5	58.3	2.3	−5.3
Malawi	42.7	90.9	−11.4	−2.7
Zambia	−9.7	−1.1	−6.9	1.1
Bulgaria	−4.7	−5.0	2.6	2.1
Rest of South Asia	9.4	33.4	−4.2	−35.5
South East-Asia	9.4	20.5	28.2	−3.4
Central America and the Caribbean	28.0	20.2	2.7	1.0
Andean Pact	−6.9	3.4	−6.9	−9.0
Argentina, Chile and Uruguay	−8.1	−6.1	−9.1	9.6
Middle East and North Africa	−11.3	14.1	−7.4	2.6
Sub-Saharan Africa	−6.1	−1.5	−12.8	3.0
All other regions	−2.4	−0.5	−3.6	0.4

Source: GTAP simulations.

also be taken into account (e.g. leather is not a big employer in Japan), and the ability of workers to find jobs in other sectors requiring similar skills.

1.7.6 Output

As might be expected, changes in output tend to move in the same direction as labour use. In percentage terms, the largest falls in output over the partial liberalization scenarios occur under an ambitious application of a Swiss-type formula in sectors such as motor vehicles and electronic equipment for the Rest of South Asia (i.e. other than India) (−36 per cent and −14 per cent), textiles and wearing apparel for Mexico (−15 per cent and −20 per cent) and non-ferrous metals for India (−25 per cent). In the leather sector, there is a loss of output of over 30 per cent in Japan

Table 1.15: Impacts of sectoral tariff elimination on revenues and welfare compared with WTO moderate scenario

	WTO moderate				Sectoral tariff elimination			
	Export revenue (%)	Import revenue (%)	Output (%)	Welfare $million (%)	Export revenue (%)	Import revenue (%)	Output (%)	Welfare $million (%)
EU	1.3	1.4	0.24	15,805	1.5	1.5	0.53	20,736
United States	5.1	3.6	0.03	4,899	3.9	2.7	0	5,897
Japan	5	5.8	1.07	6,920	4.5	5.2	0.86	6,230
Canada	1.3	1.4	−0.36	635	1.2	1.4	−0.06	1,312
Rest of OECD	2.7	3.1	0.72	3,031	2.3	2.6	0.82	3,001
High-income Asia	3.7	4.1	2.16	5,743	4.5	5.0	1.81	5,048
China, incl. Hong Kong	12.8	16	2.19	38,827	13.5	16.8	1.92	38,842
India	5.6	6	1.05	2,703	15.1	16.2	−0.45	3,465
Brazil	3.2	2.9	1.74	1,190	8.0	7.2	0.77	1,641
México	0.6	0.7	−0.7	−172	3.3	3.7	−0.68	1,379
Bangladesh	1.5	1.2	0.86	64	0.7	0.6	0.4	34
Philippines	0.8	0.7	1.68	412	2.2	1.9	1.64	412
Malawi	3.7	3.8	3.57	31	6.5	6.7	6.08	50
Zambia	0.3	0.3	0.22	2	0.9	1.0	0.84	15
Bulgaria	1.4	1.3	0.5	49	4.2	4.0	0.21	55
Rest of South Asia	5.9	5.9	3.41	1,104	7.8	7.7	2.85	1,095
South-East Asia	2.5	3.4	2.71	7,636	4.0	5.4	2.42	8,706
Central America and the Caribbean	4.9	3.2	2.85	1,425	8.6	5.7	2.61	1,711
Andean Pact	1.1	1.1	0.65	424	2.9	2.9	−0.1	610
Argentina, Chile and Uruguay	3.2	3.4	2.94	2,455	4.7	5.1	2.53	2,811
Middle East and North Africa	1.6	1.6	0.47	3,646	3.5	3.5	0.42	6,742
Sub-Saharan Africa	1.6	1.6	0.59	1,694	3.6	3.6	0.79	2,897
All other regions	1.8	1.9	0.88	4,191	2.9	3.1	0.68	5,100
Total	**3.2**	**3.2**	**0.57**	**102,714**	**3.6**	**3.6**	**0.56**	**117,789**

Source: GTAP simulations.

and nearly 21 per cent in Canada. Under the free trade scenario (not shown here) some of the output changes can be quite large, as much as 50 per cent in some specific sectors. These changes are a strong indication of the structural adjustment that would be needed for developing countries. The importance of each sector to the economy or region can be gauged by examining the initial output values.

1.7.7 Sectoral tariff elimination

The large number of variables to be negotiated makes it difficult to identify what is driving the tariff reductions, that is, to determine what countries will have to do and what benefits they will receive. Calculations undertaken at the tariff line level indicate that removing the sectoral elimination of tariffs for developing countries makes a significant difference to their average tariffs, trade and welfare. This is essentially the difference between the various 'ambitious' and 'moderate' scenarios. Removing the sectoral elimination of tariffs for developed countries as well ('flexible' scenario) makes the proposals much less ambitious. To quantify this, we simulated the removal of tariffs in specific sectors (electronics and electrical goods; fish and fish products; footwear; leather goods; motor vehicle parts and components; stones, gems and precious metals; and textiles and clothing) while leaving other industrial tariffs unchanged. The agriculture and service sectors were treated as in most of the other simulations. The results are shown in Table 1.15, along with the WTO 'moderate' scenario for comparison. The elimination of all tariffs in specific sectors alone generates similar revenue and welfare gains as the WTO 'moderate' scenario. The share of developing-country welfare gains for the two scenarios is around 64 per cent. However, individual country or regional shares differ. Comparing the two scenarios, the greatest beneficiary of sectoral elimination among the developed countries/groupings is the EU. Among developing countries/regions, the Middle East and North Africa, South-East Asia, Mexico and India would benefit most from a sectoral elimination approach, but all developing countries would enjoy greater exports at the expense of the United States, Japan, Canada and Rest of OECD. By sector, there are lower impacts on textiles, metals and other manufactures, which are exempt from proposed tariff elimination, and greater impacts on motor vehicles and chemicals, rubber and plastics.

1.8 Implications and conclusions

Negotiators seeking to bring the current round of NAMA negotiations to a close face several challenges: the choice of a formula, the degree of sectoral elimination, the treatment of unbound tariffs, the degree of special and differential treatment for developing countries, and the method of calculating the binding level of currently unbound tariffs.

Reducing tariffs on a non-linear rather than a capping basis would appear to contribute little to the outcome. Non-linear cuts have a harmonizing effect within countries, and, while there are more benefits from reducing high tariffs than low ones, the bulk of the impact can be obtained from a more transparent Capped formula. The linear Capped formula provides similar effects to the more complex harmonizing formulae. For example, the WTO and Capped 'ambitious' scenarios provide similar tariff cuts for developed countries, but the welfare gains are proportional to these cuts.

A further issue is exclusions, both in terms of what should be bound and whether newly bound tariffs should be cut. Allowing countries to bind at twice the simple average of bound tariffs for developing countries provides greater flexibility for sensitive products, and introduces a degree of harmonization across countries. We did not estimate the separate effect of this provision in the simulation exercises. However, experience from previous rounds indicates that exclusion of certain products (e.g. textiles) can lead to significant distortions and disillusionment with the final outcome, leading to greater problems later.

Eliminating tariffs in specific sectors appears to have similar effects as the less transparent and broader based approaches. Global and regional export revenue and welfare impacts are somewhere between the Swiss and WTO 'moderate' approaches. Because of the linkages between sectors, with output in one sector used as an input into another, the output effects from eliminating tariffs in specific sectors are distributed across all sectors. Although dismissed as inadequate in earlier negotiations, this approach is transparent and provides similar gains to more obscure scenarios.

Where to go from here? There is an obvious trade-off between ambition and flexibility, with each of the Members wanting to retain flexibility for themselves without weakening the whole agreement. The simulations indicate that similar outcomes can be obtained from a variety of approaches. The various exclusions and exemptions are as important as the formula itself. Future research could usefully separate out the effects of the various individual exclusions that are not captured in the formula.

Adjustment costs appear to be a major stumbling block to progress in the negotiations. Once the final formula is agreed and implemented, attention will turn to mitigating the adjustment costs. A phased-in adjustment, e.g. over 10 years, should help. Nonetheless, some sectors will experience significant output and employment losses. The simulations presented here help to identify where the losses are likely to occur. Difficulties arise where workers made redundant have skills that cannot be readily transferred to another industry, or if the industry is in a specific location. Appropriate policies need to be in place to help the labour force adjust in these circumstances.

A further stumbling block in the negotiations is the erosion of preferences. However, simulated results indicate that the trade expansion effects of market opening exceed the trade diversion effects of loss of preferential access for the developing-country groups modelled here. It should be noted, however, that these results may not hold for individual countries.

Modelling results need to be interpreted with caution, and policymakers should certainly keep in mind social, political, environmental and other factors of importance. It is also useful to compare the results from different models and to understand what drives any differences. Overall, the results indicate there are gains to be had from further liberalization, and developing countries can obtain a significant share of the benefits, provided policies are put in place to assist the adjustment process.

Notes

1 The use of WTO-consistent non-tariff measures has therefore grown in importance: SPS/TBT, anti-dumping and safeguard measures. In these cases, the options for exporters are, say, to meet the standards or avoid the practice giving rise to the measure. In the long-term, the rules for the application may be renegotiated.

2 For more information on the existing level of protection see Fernández de Córdoba et al. (2004b).

3 Proposal by Argentina, Brazil and India, based on an earlier draft by the Swiss Chairman of the Negotiating Group on Market Access, Ambassador Pierre-Louis Girard, also known as the 'Girard' proposal. TN/MA/W/35/Rev.1.

4 These scenarios are based on on-going WTO negotiations, WTO (2003a; 2003b), WTO (2004) and WTO (2005) and interviews with developed and developing countries interviews carried out in the summer of 2004 in Geneva. See Fernández de Córdoba (2004a).

5 Estimates of protection are obtained from the (Australian) Productivity Commission http://www.pc.gov.au/research/rm/servicesrestriction/index.html.

6 Ambassador Pierre-Louise Girard, Chairman of the Negotiating Group on Market Access, TN/MA/W/35/Rev.1.

7 WTO, *Negotiating Group On Market Access: Report by the Chairman, Ambassador Girard, to the Trade Negotiations Committee*, TN/MA/12, Geneva, 2003.

8 For more information on CGE modelling see J. Francois (2000).

9 The estimates for the EU, just over one per cent, appear deceptively small because the base data includes a large proportion of intra-EU trade. Tariff barriers among the 25 EU members were removed prior to simulation.

10 The Andean Pact includes Bolivia, Colombia, Ecuador, Peru and Venezuela.

11 Unless otherwise indicated EU refers to EU25 Member States.
12 Employment seems to vary with the level of ambition, but less so with the degree of harmonization.

References

GTAP http://www.gtap.agecon.purdue.edu/.

Fernández de Córdoba, Santiago, Laird, S. and Vanzetti, D. (2004a) Trick or treat? Development opportunities and challenges in the WTO negotiations on industrial tariffs. Credit Research Paper, University of Nottingham.

Fernández de Córdoba, Santiago, Laird, S. and Vanzetti, D. (2004b) Blend it like Beckman: Trying to read the ball in the World Trade Organization negotiations on industrial tariffs, *Journal of World Trade*, 38(5).

Francois, J. (2000) Assessing the results of general equilibrium studies of multilateral trade negotiations. Policy Issues in International Trade and Commodities Study Series No. 3. Geneva, UNCTAD.

WTO (2003a) Draft Elements of Modalities for Negotiations on Non-Agricultural Products TN/MA/35 and TN/MA/35/rev.1. Geneva.

WTO (2003b) Preparations for the Fifth Session of the Ministerial Conference Draft Cancún Ministerial Text, Note by the Secretariat – Revision, JOB(03)/150, JOB(03)/150/Rev.1 and JOB(03)/150/Rev.2. Geneva.

WTO (2004) Doha Work Program: July Package WT/L/579. Geneva.

WTO (2005) Doha Work Program: Hong Kong Ministerial Declaration WT/MIN(05)/DEC. Geneva.

Annex Table 1.A1: Possible scenarios

Scenario	Description	Formula	Binding	Sectoral elimination	Elimination of low nuisance tariffs	Coefficients
Free trade	Zero tariffs on all non-agricultural goods		100%			
Swiss formula	Ambitious	$T_1 = \frac{(a \times T_0)}{(a + T_0)}$	100% for all countries **Developed** = twice the applied rate **Developing** = twice the applied rate **'Paragraph 6'** = simple average of bound tariffs for all developing countries (29.4%)	Yes	All tariffs below 2% reduced to zero	Based on average weighted industrial bound tariff by country grouping Developed = 3.4% Developing = 12.5%
	Moderate	$T_1 = \frac{(a \times T_0)}{(a + T_0)}$	**Developed** = 100% **Developing** and **'Paragraph 6'** countries = 95% **Developed** = twice the applied rate **Developing** = twice the applied rate or twice the simple average of bound tariffs for developing countries (29.4% × 2 = 58.8%) **'Paragraph 6'** = twice the applied rate or twice the simple average of bound tariffs for developing countries (29.4% × 2 = 58.8%)	Developed: yes Developing: no	Developed countries only: All tariffs below 2% reduced to zero	Based on average weighted industrial tariff by country grouping Developed = 3.4% Developing = 12.5%

(*continued*)

Annex Table 1.A1: (*continued*)

Scenario	Description	Formula	Binding	Sectoral elimination	Elimination of low nuisance tariffs	Coefficients
	Flexible	$T_1 = \frac{(a \times T_0)}{(a + T_0)}$	**Developed** = 100% **Developing** and **'Paragraph 6'** countries = 90% **Developed** = twice the applied rate **Developing** = twice the applied rate or twice the simple average of bound tariffs for developing countries (29.4% × 2 = 58.8%) **'Paragraph 6'** = twice the applied rate or twice the simple average of bound tariffs for developing countries (29.4% × 2 = 58.8%)	No	None	Twice the average weighted industrial tariff by country grouping Developed = 3.4% × 2 Developing = 12.5% × 2
WTO formula	Ambitious	$T_1 = \frac{(B \times t_a \times T_0)}{(B \times t_a + T_0)}$	100% for all countries **Developed** = twice the applied rate **Developing** = twice the applied rate **'Paragraph 6'** = simple average of bound tariffs for all developing countries (29.4%)	Yes	All tariffs below 2% reduced to zero	B = 1
	Moderate	$T_1 = \frac{(B \times t_a \times T_0)}{(B \times t_a + T_0)}$	**Developed** = 100% **Developing** and **'Paragraph 6'** countries = 95% **Developed** = twice the applied rate	Developed: yes Developing: no	Developed countries only: All tariffs below 2% reduced to	Developed B = 0.5 Developing B = 3

			Developing = twice the applied rate or twice the simple average of bound tariffs for developing countries (29.4% × 2 = 58.8%) **'Paragraph 6'** = twice the applied rate or twice the simple average of bound tariffs for developing countries (29.4% × 2 = 58.8%)		zero	
	Flexible	$T_1 = \frac{(B \times t_a \times T_0)}{(B \times t_a + T_0)}$	**Developed** = 100% **Developing** and **'Paragraph 6'** countries = 90% **Developing** = twice the applied rate or twice the simple average of bound tariffs for developing countries (29.4% × 2 = 58.8%) **'Paragraph 6'** = twice the applied rate or twice the simple average of bound tariffs for developing countries (29.4% × 2 = 58.8%)	No	None	Developed B = 0.5 Developing B = 5
Capped formula	Ambitious	$T_1 = (a \times T_0)$ With a cap on any tariff more than three times the average national applied rate	100% for all countries **Developed** = twice the applied rate **Developing** = twice the applied rate **'Paragraph 6'** = simple average of bound tariffs for all developing countries (29.4%)	Yes	All tariffs below 2% reduced to zero	Developed (a) = 0.5 Developing (a) = 0.666

(continued)

Annex Table 1.A1: (*continued*)

Scenario	Description	Formula	Binding	Sectoral elimination	Elimination of low nuisance tariffs	Coefficients
	Moderate	$T_1 = (a \times T_0)$ With a cap on any tariff more than three times the average national applied rate	**Developed** = 100% **Developing** and **'Paragraph 6'** countries = 95% **Developed** = twice the applied rate **Developing** = The greater of twice the applied rate or twice the simple average of bound tariffs for developing countries (29.4% × 2 = 58.8%) **'Paragraph 6'** = The greater of twice the applied rate or twice the simple average of bound tariffs for developing countries (29.4% × 2 = 58.8%)	Developed: yes Developing: no	Developed countries only: All tariffs below 2% reduced to zero	Developed (a) = 0.5 Developing (a) = 0.666
	Flexible	$T_1 = (a \times T_0)$ With a cap on any tariff more than three times the average national applied rate	**Developed** = 100% **Developing** and **'Paragraph 6'** countries = 90% **Developing** = twice the applied rate or twice the simple average of bound tariffs for developing countries (29.4% × 2 = 58.8%) **'Paragraph 6'** = twice the applied rate or twice the simple average of bound tariffs for developing countries (29.4% × 2 = 58.8%)	No	None	Developed (a) = 0.5 Developing (a) = 0.8

Note: Least-developed countries are exempt from formula reductions and sectoral eliminations.

2
Comment: the Effects of Tariff Liberalizations and Preference Erosion

Joe Francois

The study by Fernández de Córdoba and Vanzetti (Chapter 1) contains a careful, detailed examination of the likely macroeconomic impacts of tariff concessions, as part of the Doha Round, on developing countries. The assessment builds on an analysis of tariff-line data, with the application of possible tariff-reduction formulas. Particular attention is given to the implications of bindings above current applied rates (including unbound tariffs), as well as to the meaning of special and differential treatment in the context of actual application of tariff-reduction formulas. The resulting tariff rates from this exercise then serve as the basis for a set of CGE model scenarios. These scenarios in turn provide estimates of the impact of tariff reductions on developing countries in general, and LDCs in particular, and also on the high-income countries (basically the OECD Members).

I have two sets of comments: one involves the importance of developing-country tariff liberalization for these countries; and a second involves the real scope for preference erosion.

2.1 Developing-country tariffs matter for LDC market access

One message from this study is that all the formulas yield larger cuts, in percentage terms, for the OECD countries, and larger cuts, in absolute terms, for developing countries (at least under the 'ambitious' scenarios). Admittedly, the OECD countries have tariff peaks, but focusing on the pattern of results reported in this study, it is clear that the big issue concerns tariffs in developing countries themselves. In other words, there may be a pay-off from shifting the focus from the OECD countries – where, despite tariff peaks, simple average tariffs are 5.5 per cent – to developing countries, especially middle-income ones – where simple average tariffs are 12.5 per cent, as reported in the study. In the study, we learn that the averages in the OECD countries (excluding those countries that have since joined the EU, and Switzerland) range between 3 and 4 per cent. By contrast, in the developing countries, simple average tariffs of 15 to 20 per cent are not unusual. On a value basis (total duties collected), protection in the developing world is of growing importance to developing countries, and is, arguably, more important than obtaining additional market access concessions from the OECD countries through the NAMA negotiations.

The model results here reflect this fact. Figure 2.1 shows results from the three capping formula scenarios. The left vertical axis plots reductions in tariff rates under the scenarios, while the right vertical axis maps corresponding changes in exports from sub-Saharan Africa (SSA). Moving from the first to the second scenario sees the introduction of flexibility for developing countries, meaning they engage in less ambitious tariff reductions. While the average tariff reduction does not change in the OECD countries, it falls dramatically in the developing countries. The export results show a substantial corresponding fall in export expansion. Moving to the flexible, or third, scenario, which involves a reduction in OECD tariff cuts as well, the impact on the exports of the LDCs is much less dramatic than what happens when developing countries liberalize

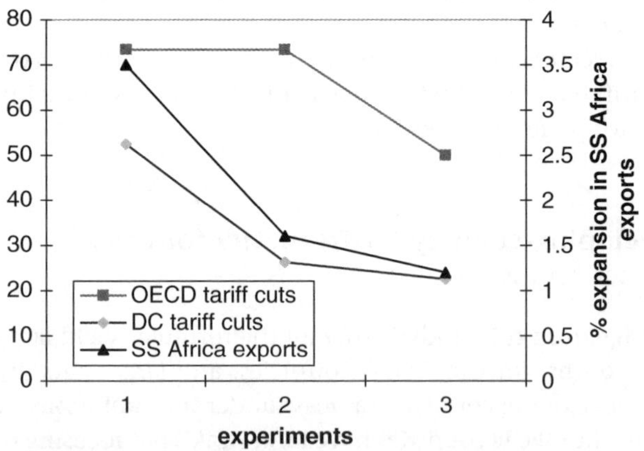

Figure 2.1: Tariff reductions and exports: capping formula
Source: UNCTAD NAMA study; Experiment 1: most ambitious tariff reductions; Experiment 2: moderate tariff reductions; Experiment 3: flexible (and least ambitious) tariff reductions.

less. This result is similar to all recent CGE studies of the Doha Round, including the one by Francois, van Meijl and van Tongeren (2005). If individual developing countries desire improved market access, the strongest export gains actually occur from a collective reduction of average tariffs across other developing countries.

2.2 Preferences and the benefits of NAMA negotiations for LDCs

A message between the lines from this study is that tariff preferences may be a second-order economic issue, despite its high profile as a political one. Turning again to Figure 2.1, it is helpful to recollect that the GTAP data includes OECD tariff preferences (Bouet et al., 2004). The data are based on a thorough and careful effort to include use of preferences in a matrix of global import protection. In particular, they are the product of a joint effort between the United Nations International Trade Centre, the United Nations Conference on Trade and Development (UNCTAD), the WTO and the Centre d'Etudes Prospectives et d'Informations Internationals (CEPII). An important contribution of the project has been an exhaustive coverage of preferential trade arrangements (PTAs) around the world, along with calculations of the ad valorem (or percentage) equivalent (AVE) of specific duties. Combined with differences in the bilateral composition of trade, the results show that protection varies by sector and partner for each importer. Hence the experiments in Figure 2.1 include preferences, and therefore preference erosion. Note that, despite preference erosion, the total effect of OECD tariff reductions is a net expansion of exports of the LDCs (many of which are in the SSA aggregate in the model).

The relevance of preferences is also limited by their limited use. In an early paper, Herin (1986) estimated that the costs of documentation and administration of rules of origin, which constitute the largest proportion of increased costs of preferential trade, impose costs on exporters equivalent to some 3 per cent of the value of the goods traded among the members of the European Free Trade Association (EFTA). For ACP countries, these costs are expected to be even higher, due to information constraints and institutional difficulties, among others. More recently, Manchin (2004) has used sophisticated threshold estimation techniques, in conjunction with detailed data from the EC, to examine preference utilization in the context of EU preferences. Her results suggest that, because of rules of origin and related compliance costs, it costs roughly 4 per cent of the value of trade to qualify for preferences.

Table 2.1: EU-15 imports from the least developed countries, 2001

Sector	Total EU-15 imports ($ '000)	Duty-free imports ($ '000)	Sector's share of LDC total	Duty-free share of sector total	Share subject to specific duties
Agriculture	905,722	611,791	7.6	67.5	14.0
Forestry, fisheries	258,714	174,782	2.2	67.6	0.0
Mining	3,982,709	3,973,127	33.5	99.8	0.0
Processed foods	1,035,968	32,188	8.7	3.1	4.2
Other manufactures	5,720,632	394,087	48.1	6.9	1.4
TOTAL	11,903,744	5,185,974	100.0	43.6	2.1

Source: WTO integrated database.

Table 2.2: Composition of EU-15 processed food imports from LDCs

Product category	Total EU-15 imports ($ '000)	Duty-free imports ($ '000)	Duty-free import share of category total	Share of total processed food imports	EU average rate of protection, all extra-EU trade
Animal products	92	0	0.0	0.0	16.0
Vegetable oils and fats	104,029	26,506	25.5	10.0	37.7
Dairy products	99	0	0.0	0.0	18.4
Processed rice	1,176	0	0.0	0.1	38.6
Sugar	37,818	0	0.0	3.7	36.7
Food Products n.e.c.	891,547	5,287	0.6	86.1	11.6
Beverages and tobacco	1,208	394	32.6	0.1	20.3
TOTAL	1,035,968	32,188	3.1	100.0	15.2

Source: WTO integrated database (trade) and GTAP database (protection).

What does this threshold imply for the actual scope for trade preference erosion? Tables 2.1, 2.2 and 2.3 present EU imports from the LDCs for 2001. They provide estimates of the rate of MFN protection that would be applied to LDC exports to the EU-15, and underlying trade flows, as well as the share of imports by sector, reported as actually entering the EU-15 duty-free in 2001. The following points are worth

Table 2.3: Composition of EU-15 manufactured imports from LDCs, 2001

Product category	Total EU-15 imports ($ '000)	Duty-free imports ($ '000)	Duty-free import share of category	Share of total manufactures in imports	EU MFN tariffs, weighted by LDC trade	Maximum tariff
Textiles	1,838,393	39,012	2.1	32.1	11.5	12.6
Clothing	1,977,100	164	0.0	34.6	12.2	12.6
Leather	325,254	38	0.0	5.7	7.4	17.0
Wood products	104,170	24,665	23.7	1.8	1.7	10.0
Paper products	6,926	2,709	39.1	0.1	1.7	9.8
Petroleum and coal products	27,544	0	0.0	0.5	3.9	4.7
Chemicals, rubber, plastics	84,751	29,399	34.7	1.5	3.7	12.8
Non-metallic minerals	21,430	176	0.8	0.4	9.7	12.0
Iron and steel	6,364	4,218	66.3	0.1	0.7	5.7
Non-ferrous metals	640,473	251,514	39.3	11.2	3.5	10.0
Fabricated metal products	7,671	2,166	28.2	0.1	2.3	8.5
Motor vehicles and parts	3,120	143	4.6	0.1	6.8	22.0
Other transport equipment	587,053	78	0.0	10.3	1.4	15.0
Electrical machinery	16,766	15,003	89.5	0.3	0.6	14.0
Other machinery	41,592	9,546	23.0	0.7	1.6	8.0
Other manufactures	32,025	15,258	47.6	0.6	1.4	9.0
TOTAL	5,720,632	394,087	6.9	100.0	9.0	22.0

Source: WTO integrated database.

making. First, for LDCs the most important exports are manufactures, even when mining activities are included. This is despite the fact that the highest utilization of preferences, as proxied by duty-free imports, was in agriculture. It is obvious that, in the case of agriculture, rates of protection are generally well above the threshold we have identified. In addition, it is much easier to prove origin for food products. It is therefore in manufacturing that we expect rules of origin, and related administration burdens, to be harder to contend with. It is clear that, on average, many European tariffs on manufactures are below the threshold we have identified.

What does this mean for our interpretation of the results of the NAMA study? On the one hand, preference erosion is probably overstated in this study, but also in almost all other literature. On the flip side, however, this reinforces a basic message of the study: NAMA matters. In fact, because of limitations placed on trade preferences, NAMA negotiations matter even more for developing countries than if preferences worked better.

2.3 Concluding comments

The Doha Declaration mandates negotiations on a broad range of issues. This study focuses on an important subset of these negotiations: non-agricultural market access. The authors have done an admirable job, from mapping very detailed and careful analysis of tariff reduction formulas, to the macroeconomic consequences of implementing such reductions. The results tell us something useful, and something policy-makers need to know. One point offered here is that developing-country market access includes access to non-OECD markets, and this should not be forgotten. These markets are important. At the same time, because utilization of OECD trade preferences is often hampered by rules-of-origin compliance requirements, preference erosion is not as much of an issue as one might think. This shifts the cost–benefit calculus towards deeper gains to developing countries from OECD tariff reductions. On balance, therefore, tariff reductions in the context of the NAMA negotiations for both OECD and non-OECD markets are important for developing-country exporters.

References

Bouet, A. et al. (2004) A consistent, ad-valorem equivalent measure of applied protection across the world: The MAcMap-HS6 database. CEPII discussion paper No. 2004, Paris CEPII, 22 December.

Francois, J., van Meijl, H. and van Tongeren, F. (2005) Trade liberalization in the Doha Development Round, *Economic Policy*, 42, April.

Herin, J. (1986) Rules of origin and differences between tariff levels in EFTA and in the EC. Occasional Paper No. 13, European Free Trade Association, Economic Affairs Department, Geneva.
Manchin, M. (2004) Preference utilisation and tariff reduction in EU imports from ACP countries. Discussion paper no. 04-132/2, Amsterdam, Tinbergen Institute.

3
Adjustment Costs and Trade Liberalization

Santiago Fernández de Córdoba, Sam Laird, Jean-Christophe Maur and José María Serena

3.1 Introduction

Trade-induced adjustment costs experienced by developing countries are a matter of growing concern within multilateral negotiations liberalization. While the longer-term benefits of trade liberalization are well accepted, the process of transition and associated costs are not as well understood. The challenge is to identify policies that help developing countries reallocate resources to more productive uses with minimal social disruption. In reviewing the literature on structural adjustment costs, we address questions of timing and sequencing, supporting policies and institutions, especially in developing country situations.

3.2 Definition of adjustment costs

Adjustment costs are generally defined as the short term costs of transition from one state to another. More narrowly, adjustment costs are the costs of transferring resources from one sector to another. It is useful to draw the distinction between gross and net adjustment costs. The gross costs take account of positive and negative changes, including costs arising from the turnover in resources, whereas net adjustment costs refer to the change in level of resource (labour, capital) use after some of the positive and negative effects have offset one another. Essentially, resources such as land, labour and capital may become unemployed, obsolete or may require retraining or reconfiguring. The various forms of adjustment costs are listed in Figure 3.1. A comprehensive definition of adjustment costs includes those borne by both the private and the public sector. The major impact of policy change on the public sector is loss of revenue.

Figure 3.1: Adjustment costs

Private sector	**Labour**	Opportunity costs of unemployed labour Obsolescence of skills and skill specificity Lower wage levels Re-training costs Personal costs such as psychological suffering Other costs (e.g. rent seeking)
	Capital	Opportunity costs of underutilized or unemployed capital Cost of capital rendered obsolete (Capital write-offs) Transition costs of shifting capital from one activity to another
Public sector	Shift tax revenue base Social safety net spending (e.g., unemployment benefits) Erosion of benefits from preferential treatment Efforts to ensure macroeconomic stability Implementation costs of trade reforms Non Trade Concerns: food security, support to rural areas, environmental concerns	

Within the private sector, the costs imposed on labour markets are the most widely studied and documented category of adjustment costs. Labour markets receive the most attention because they bear the highest costs, and can also have considerable political influence. They are particularly important in developing countries that are specialized in labour intensive manufacturing. Costs borne by labour markets in the private sector include forgone earnings, retraining expenses, personal costs and displacement costs.

Capital is also an important input into industrial production. Structural adjustments to the economy can result in underutilized or obsolete capital, as well as shifts in capital from one sector to another. However, in many developing countries, capital mobility may be limited by lack of capital and credit markets, resulting in higher adjustment costs. In agricultural communities, land may be left out of production or abandoned when farmers switch from one crop to another activity. There is a significant adjustment period for tree crops such as coffee, tea or rubber.

The adjustment costs faced by the public sector are mainly losses of revenue. Losses of tax revenue are of major concern to countries in which tariff revenues are a large part of total revenues. The changes in tariff revenues are merely transfers from producers and taxpayers to consumers, but governments must make up for this loss with increases in taxes on income, profits, capital gains, property, labour and consumption, and through non-tax revenue.

Public sector adjustment costs can also include spending on social safety nets, efforts to ensure macroeconomic stability and the implementation costs of trade reforms.

In describing adjustment costs, it is worth noting that economies adjust constantly in response to non-policy effects, such as commodity price changes and technological change. Finally, policy changes occur against the background of the overall macroeconomic situation of the country. This may be positive or negative. For instance, if the economy is growing at say 7% a year, tariff changes implemented over ten years may see a doubling of the size of the economy. In such a situation, the affected industries may experience slower growth rather than an absolute decline.

3.3 The rise in concern about structural adjustment costs

3.3.1 Why adjustment costs matter?

Trade economists tend to place greater emphasis on the long-run effects of trade liberalization, such as those resulting from comparative advantage and shifting trade patterns, and dismiss the short term adjustments costs. As for example noted by Baldwin, Mutti and Richardson (1980) in their pioneer contribution to the trade-induced adjustment cost literature: '*Economists have sometimes dismissed such adjustment costs with the comment that the displaced factors become reemployed in the long-run.*' Labour economists have traditionally been concerned about adjustment costs in the labour market, but the bulk of research has focused on developed economies.

Structural adjustment issues facing developing countries did not receive much attention either from governments or policymakers in earlier rounds of trade liberalization due to the smaller magnitude of the agreements reached and the lack of involvement of developing countries in the negotiations. However, in the light of some recent negative experiences of reform (as discussed in some case studies later in this book) as well as the current WTO negotiations, there is now a growing interest in the costs of trade liberalization faced by developing countries and how to minimize them.

Why might some groups reject trade reforms?

Any policy change generates winners and losers. The benefits from liberalization are diffused among many (mainly consumers), while the losses affect a small number of producers, which thus are more likely to organize themselves against the policy change (Olson, 1965). There are also various dimensions of perception of trade liberalization that might affect how adjustment costs are perceived: the level of aggregation, the time horizon, monetary versus multidimensional measures, and relative versus absolute measures (Verdier, 2004).

Distinguishing between social and private costs helps to explain the sources of opposition to trade liberalization. Social costs are the costs to society as a whole, while private costs are the costs to an individual due to liberalization. Private costs include losses of income through unemployment or lower wages and indirect costs such as losses of monopoly power. The more concentrated losses are among groups within the private sector, the more that they will be likely to oppose trade liberalization. Political opposition depends on the concentration of costs within the economy, and on the size of private costs, which might be augmented by rent seeking or corruption. Even if the gains from reform outweigh losses, and the economy as a whole can still be better off, losers are unlikely to be fully compensated. The fact that private costs are high and that compensation is very difficult to implement and, in some cases, does not occur at all, helps to explain opposition.

It is obvious that the transfers between producers, taxpayers and consumers far exceed the net social welfare gain, and these distributional effects generate powerful political forces that affect the country's ability to achieve the potential benefits of adjustment. For example, if trade liberalization generates annual welfare losses of $9.5 million for the domestic producers and annual welfare gains of $10 million for consumers, policy makers will tend to look more at these two numbers than the $0.5 million net welfare gain. These effects are likely to be compounded by prior uncertainties about who will gain from liberalization, therefore creating a bias in favour of the status quo (Fernandez and Rodrik, 1991). Critiques of trade liberalization will also tend to focus more on individual (private costs) stories than on the global picture.

As the adjustment costs are one-off (but maybe spread over an extended period of years), whereas the benefits are ongoing, the costs of adjustment will have to be borne upfront whereas benefits are delayed to the future and discounted. The policymaking process, which may be biased in favour of the short term, is therefore faced first with the certainty of localized adjustment costs, such as job losses, versus the longer term benefits from liberalization, for instance job creation in exporting competing sectors. Policy makers may also fail to take into account the positive outcomes of adjustment (Hoekman and Smarzynska-Javorcik, 2004).

Two other dimensions might explain the difference between societies' perception about liberalization and the analytical view. Empirical analyses do not include broader and perhaps normative dimensions of welfare (i.e. non-monetary ones), which may matter a great deal to the civil society.

Recent findings

Recent studies have shown that adjustment costs can reduce and in some cases actually outweigh gains from liberalization. Davidson and Matsusz (2000), for example, find that in economies with rigid labour markets, the adjustment costs might offset the gains to a significant extent because of the decrease in output and income associated with unemployment. The major issue is the duration of unemployment. Although most empirical studies on adjustment costs point out that they are a small fraction of total gains, the evidence is inconclusive and varies greatly form one situation to another. Much has still to be learned on the assessment of adjustment costs.

3.3.2 The process of adjustment

Ensuring functioning markets can mitigate the frictional costs of the reallocation process. Markets may not exist or may not perform adequately. For instance, if financial markets are weak and interest rates are high, it might be difficult for private agents to find the capital to move into sectors that benefit from the liberalization. Implementing reforms over a gradual period, and taking other labour market institutions such unions and unemployment benefits into account, can help to reduce the short run costs. The objectives are essentially short term since evidence shows that a large share of the adjustment on factor markets takes place upfront (Harrison and Revenga, 1998; Hammermesh and Pfann, 1996).

Equity issues are important. Classical economic theory predicts substantial redistribution effects affecting factor markets. However, this need not always to be so: in the presence of increasing returns to scale, and when intra-industry trade is the dominant source of gain these distribution effects are small.[1] The objective in the context of equity issues is to guarantee that appropriate transfers are in place to redistribute more equally the gains from trade liberalization. In recent times the poverty impacts of trade liberalization are increasingly integrated into the policy debate in developing countries. The objectives of such policy is different from the other concerns as it focuses on redistributing the long-term gains from liberalization. However, short term considerations will apply to the poor and vulnerable in the very short term.

Political economy motives arise from the desire to accommodate opponents to liberalization. The issue here is how to offset the private costs of trade liberalization on specific sectors and agents. The most direct way to achieve this is of course by postponing trade liberalization itself, but this can be at the expense of the objective of efficiency gains (Bown and McCullock, 2004). Compensating opponents to the liberalization process may seem counterproductive but may be necessary to implement the liberalization reform.

3.3.3 Why adjustment costs matter for developing countries

The challenge of adjustment to policy change is much more significant for developing countries for several reasons: a) they are starting from more protected situations (nominal tariff levels in some sectors in some LDCs are as high as 100 or even 200 per cent), and therefore the required adjustment is greater; b) developing countries economies are less diversified (with lower opportunities to expand into other sectors), and therefore the relative impacts are higher; c) factor markets are less deep and efficient, and less able to cope with adjustment; d) administration lacks adequate capacity to put the necessary policies in place; and e) some small economies are very trade dependent.

If factor markets work imperfectly, political intervention (this often means de-regulation or re-regulation) is necessary to facilitate adjustment. However, even with government intervention, the nature and size of short term adjustment costs will be highly specific, depending on industry characteristics such as the proportion of the assets that are specific and/or sunk, and hence difficult to move to another use.

The same applies to labour, where moving from one job to another is favoured by transferability of skills, flexible and transparent labour and housing markets. This calls for policies aimed at correcting factor market imperfections, in particular ensuring that such market exists, and that informational barriers are tackled.

In addition, close attention needs to be paid to channels of transmission of trade liberalization shocks. A frequent cause of failure of reform in developing countries is the imperfect functioning of these channels. Winters (2002) gives the example of trade reform in the maize sector in Zimbabwe, where trade liberalization and the withdrawal of the government from the sector led to the disappearance of markets supplying of inputs for crops. McMillan, Rodrik and Welch (2002) make a similar point about the liberalization of the cashew nut sector in Mozambique, arguing that imperfect market structure stole away some of the benefits from liberalization from the poor farmers and that higher export prices benefited traders and external buyers.

For factor markets, the environment in which firms evolve matters crucially. This is not only because firms are the principal users of labour and capital, but also because they play a central role in distribution channels, and provision of ancillary services such as finance. Therefore, they play an important role in facilitating adjustment. Firms in developing countries also often provide basic and unique services to the local economy, such as credit, or supply of inputs, but also housing, or education (the sugar industry in Jamaica, for instance). If these services disappear because of liberalization, these services are not compensated by price increases of the output (Winters, 2002). Rama (1999) also warns of the risk of 'company-town' externalities, when liberalization affects sectors that are a large source of local employment.

Redistributing resources to more productive uses is obviously a worthy objective. However, distributional concerns may be more important if the losses adversely affect the poor in society. Thus equity considerations are especially important in developing countries. Achieving equitable outcomes necessarily involves some additional mechanism of redistribution. From a policy perspective, the objectives of efficiency and equity need not be in conflict when carefully designed compensation is implemented (a review of this question is provided by Verdier, 2004). Simple re-distribution mechanisms such as lump-sum transfers or tax and subsidies enable gains for all while preserving the efficiency gains for the economy.[2] However, simple theoretical solutions are not necessarily feasible: it is widely acknowledged that lump-sum transfers are difficult to realize. Second, some policies favouring efficiency gains also lead to a more equitable distribution of gains. This only requires that consumers are initially poorer than the protected producers. Supporting factor mobility helps the diffusion of the gains and losses from trade liberalization throughout the economy. Nonetheless, Winters (2002) finds in the survey of trade liberalization that its impacts are unequally shared. This is probably explained by the segmentation of labour markets in these countries and that displaced workers will have difficulty finding jobs in other sectors other than closely related to their original one. A generalization from this argument is that poverty arises essentially from workers being unable to sell their labour. Given this observation, some argue that redistributive policies generate political economy benefits by insuring against economic insecurity and creating long-term support for reforms. Rodrik (2000) quotes Argentina's reforms in the 1980s as an example of failure in this regard.

The vulnerability of poor people in developing countries calls for greater attention to be given to equity issues. As discussed above, even small shocks can have disproportionate effects on the poor, because their lack of ability to accommodate risks. Although unskilled people are not hindered by skill specificity, they find it harder to find jobs outside their sector of origin, as labour markets in developing countries are segmented (Winters, 2002). In particular, a lack of information and access to any means of smoothing out consumption such as credit and future markets or insurance policies implies that unskilled workers in developing countries are less able to cope with the adverse effects of unemployment. This explains for instance why farmers are often particularly vulnerable, because of a very limited ability to sell their labour in alternative markets or switch to alternative products (what about land specificity?). Restricted access to efficient channels of distribution mean also that the poor receive less benefits and incentives from trade liberalization. A corollary of this is that because their share of consumption on imported goods is low, the poor are less likely to benefit from the lower prices of imported goods (Ravaillon and Loskin, 2004).

3.4 The nature of structural adjustment costs

Adjustment costs arise from a wide range of causes, such as technological change, change in demand/tastes, regulatory changes, weather/natural conditions, political (in)stability or change in international agreements, such as trade agreements. There is no agreement on whether it is feasible or desirable to try to separate the causes of adjustment costs. Bacchetta and Jansen (2003) underline the importance of separating adjustment costs produced by trade agreements from other costs of adjustment. Rama (2003) objects that it is neither feasible nor desirable to disentangle adjustment costs, arguing that it is globalization as a whole and not trade agreements by themselves that cause adjustment pressures. Bhagwati and Srinivasan (1983) has also argued that it is difficult to predict the impact of trade liberalization, since it affects many sectors and various trade barriers at the same time. Despite these complications, it would seem desirable to the extent possible to try to understand the likely extent of adjustment arising from trade liberalization in order to prepare adequate support and transitional measures. Whether originating from trade liberalization or another shock, the ultimate question is how to deal with adjustment. The policy makers need to focus on factor markets and channels of transmission, irrespective of the cause. They need to know what trade liberalization entails as this may constrain the policy options available, and have specific bearings on particular sectors. The question of the source of adjustment needs to be addressed at the policy making stage, so as to be able to perform a cost/benefit analysis of the policy choice.

Winters (2002) identifies four broad groups of institutions through which the trade liberalization shocks are transmitted: households, distribution channels, factor markets and government. Paying attention to these channels contributes to a better understanding of the adjustment process, in particular at the policy-design stage. In particular, the household and distribution channels are often overlooked, as policymakers tend to focus on firms (factor markets) and government revenues while ignoring the household dimension, yet this is critical when tackling poverty issues and understanding how poverty levels respond (or not) to change in prices resulting from trade liberalization. For consumers, imperfect distribution channels, because for instance of lack of competition, infrastructure and inadequate regulation result in portions (sometimes none) of the price reduction transmitted into retail prices. Likewise for exports, faulty distribution limits access to external markets. Price changes induced by trade liberalization may not be fully transmitted to economic agents. The fact that most research focuses on the adjustment of firms to liberalization should not hide that the most acute costs are likely to be faced by households, and any attempt to identify and measure costs should take these into account.

3.5 Measuring structural adjustment costs

The methods used to estimate costs of adjustment have evolved since earlier studies that focused on more narrow definitions of structural adjustment costs. Magee (1972) looked only at labour markets and estimated the number of workers who had lost their jobs due to trade reforms and the duration of unemployment. He estimated that adjustment costs represent 12 per cent of gains from trade during the first few years after liberalization. Unlike Magee, Baldwin, Mutti and David Richardson (1980) take both capital and labour into account, although they use a similar approach to compute labour adjustment costs which are estimated at some 4 per cent in the longer-run. These findings, i.e. 12 per cent in the short term and 4 per cent in the longer term, taken together support the intuition that adjustment costs are front loaded. De Melo and Tarr (1990) use a CGE model to study the effects of the removal of quantitative restrictions in the United States, estimating adjustment costs of 1.5 per cent of overall gains.

There have also been various approaches to measuring the duration of unemployment. Takacs and Winters (1991) in their study on the British footwear industry take into account the natural turnover of the sector, and they later estimate the duration of unemployment produced by the removal of quantitative restrictions. Bale (1976), in his study on the trade displacement costs for US workers, interviewed the workers and found unemployment duration of about 31 weeks.

Another cost to consider is the lower wages obtained by workers in their new jobs. Some studies try to assess the percentage reduction in the earnings of workers, with perhaps the most illustrative study being that by Rama and MacIsaac (1999), who find that the average earnings of workers displaced from the Ecuadorian Central Bank were only 55 per cent of their previous earnings.

There is a growing body of literature on the trade-induced structural adjustment costs borne by developing countries. These studies face challenges such as lack of available data and smaller sample sizes due to relatively lower levels of trade flows (compared to developed countries). Table 3.1 provides an indication of the range of relevant work that has been completed in the past.

Table 3.1: Research on trade-induced adjustment costs in developing countries

Author	Countries	Main features
Papageorgiou, Choksi, Michaely (1992)	19 countries including Argentina, Brazil, Chile, Korea, Peru, Philippines, Singapore, Sri Lanka, Turkey	Employment in manufacturing
Thomas and Nash (1991)	Bangladesh, Columbia, Ghana, Jamaica, Madagascar, Mauritius, Pakistan, Chile, Korea, Panama, Philippines, Thailand, Turkey, Ivory Coast, Guyana, Malawi, Senegal, Togo, Yugoslavia, Zambia, Zimbabwe	Import tax revenue Inflation, fiscal and trade balance
Parker, Riopelle, Steel (1995)	Ghana, Malawi, Mali, Senegal, Tanzania	SME employment
Harrison and Revenga (1995)	16 countries Costa Rica, Czechoslovakia, Peru, Poland, Romania, Uruguay	Employment
Milner and Wright (1998)	Mauritius	Positive effects of trade liberalization on employment.
Ghose (2000)		Manufacturing Employment
Rama (2003)	Developing countries, in general	
McMillan Rodrik and Welch (2002)	Mozambique	Employment in cashew nut processing
Ebrill, Strotsky and Gropp (1999)	Ghana, Kenya, Senegal, Malawi	Tariff revenue

Milner and Wright (1998) studied the economy of Mauritius after liberalization. As noted earlier, Rama (1999) examined the experience of employees at the Ecuador Central Bank highlighting the loss of earnings of the displaced workers. Rama (1994) has also explored the effects of trade liberalization on the Uruguayan economy. All of these studies listed in Table 3.1 try to assess ex-post the effect of trade liberalization. Other studies on developing countries are those by Harrison and Revenga (1995), which observe increasing unemployment following liberalization in Costa Rica, Peru and Uruguay, and McMillan, Rodrik and Welch, (2002) on the reforms of Mozambique. Although this list does not exhaust the available studies on developing countries,[3] the amount of literature dealing with developing countries is relatively small compared to that dealing with developed countries. In general, the available studies try to assess ex-post effects of implemented policies, and many studies provide only descriptive and informal assessments. Broadly these empirical studies conclude that benefits are higher than costs even in the short run. The implication is that policy makers should proceed with liberalization but give attention to reducing the adjustment costs. However, these studies are relatively weak in coming up with detailed policy prescriptions.

3.6 Policy implications

Governments can reduce the costs of structural adjustment following trade liberalization by providing unemployment benefits, information or training courses.[4] However, there is a vast literature within labour economics showing the difficulties of implementing policies of this kind, and there is a growing concern about how different labour markets institutions affect adjustment costs. In the case of developing countries, there are concerns that trade liberalization may reduce the government capacity to conduct redistribution programmes. Trade liberalization (and WTO rules) constrain the government in its *choice* of instruments and, because of informational constraints, re-distribution is often less efficient under an open regime (Verdier, 2004 offers a review of these arguments). Some authors go as far as to suggest that the best policy governments can implement is to restrict their interventions to ensuring macroeconomic stability and promote private initiative (Matusz and Tarr, 1999).

3.6.1 Timing and sequencing

A key conclusion from the literature is that timing matters. It is often argued in this respect that the speed of liberalization is key. The debate is mainly between proponents of a rapid opening of trade barriers and those advocating a gradual approach. The arguments against rapid opening essentially pertain to the potentially disruptive effects on the overall economic environment and the macroeconomic imbalances that such a process would involve (Blanchard and Kremer, 1997).

The main benefit of a gradual introduction of reforms is that labour and capital markets can adjust by natural attrition. As capital depreciates it can be replaced in a different location or configured to perform a different function. Likewise, entrants into the labour force can train for rapidly expanding sectors rather than retraining displaced workers. A gradual approach also helps to build a capital base to compensate for lack of access to credit. On the other hand, to opt for a gradual process means bearing the cost of protectionism for longer and might create incentives to invest in uncompetitive sectors during the transition period.

Sequencing of different reforms is the other aspect of the dynamic dimension of policy making. The debate is still open on the question of whether trade liberalization should precede, follow or complement other policies such as provision of adequate physical and social infrastructure such as roads, ports and the development of an educated workforce. The broadening of the tax base is also useful before the phasing-in of tariff policies that may reduce tariff revenues.

Subsequent to liberalization, contingent protection tools, such as anti-dumping, and safeguard mechanisms, may also provide temporary (or not so temporary) relief. There is relatively large empirical evidence that such tools do not achieve the expected outcomes of shielding the industry from decline, and often end up benefiting those with vested interests (Bown and McCullock, 2004). Limited examples of successful safeguard of an industry exist (OECD, 2004a reports the story of Harley Davidson in the US) but the cost of such successes is often not known.

The evidence suggests that gradual implementation should be over a limited period of time, and that it is evenly spread across time and goods, so as to avoid back-loading of reform and raising effective rates of protection (Matusz and Tarr, 1999).

3.6.2 Complementary domestic measures

Firms

For firms, Hoekman and Smarzynska-Javorcik (2004) advocate for policies supporting competitive firm conduct. Fostering the contestability of markets is now often underlined as a desirable policy paradigm, with implementation of competition policy regimes, the reliance on import competition, and policies facilitating the establishment of new businesses.

On the other hand the significance of policies permitting exit of inefficient firms, and transfer of the assets of failing ventures, such as bankruptcy laws is often neglected. The importance of exit is underlined by recent findings that in the UK it contributed to 50 per cent of overall productivity growth (Criscuolo, Haskel and Martin, 2004).

Second, access to technology and know-how is crucial, as technical change is largely recognized as the main driver of export growth following the opportunities generated by tariff reform. To assist domestic firms becoming internationally competitive, government intervention may be necessary in the knowledge market, due to the presence of market failure. Government actions can be numerous, ranging from active subsidization of research and development to policies encouraging foreign direct investment and regulatory institutions guaranteeing the appropriation of knowledge such as intellectual property rights. This point is also emphasized in the findings of the case studies conducted by OECD (2004b), in which successful adjustment is associated with smart policies of technology transfer.

Third, Hoekman and Smarzynska-Javorcik (2004) underline enabling foreign market access to foster numerous spillovers from trade. This is a difficult challenge for firms, especially small ones, in particular as informational barriers in developing markets are high. Government intervention can help mitigate many of these barriers to entry with export promotion strategies (tax exemption, provision of market information, etc.).

Government intervention in this sector should, however, take care not to subsidize inefficient producers. Policies of direct assistance to industry or firms does not have a good track record (Hoekman and Smarzynska-Javorcik, 2004). Therefore horizontal type policies that aim primarily at addressing market failure, instead of firm failure, and not coupled to specific sector performance, are preferable.

Credit markets and services

In order to cope with inter-temporal adjustment, recourse to credit markets is crucial. Addressing the reasons for lack of depth of credit market and credit availability should therefore help the adjustment process. Policies impeding the development of efficient credit markets are common in developing countries, ranging from restrictions over entry and over-regulation of interest rates, to crowding out of the private sector by (inefficient) public sector borrowing. Evidence shows quite clearly that small operators are the most vulnerable to this lack of access to credit (Bacchetta and Jensen, 2003), and therefore suggests that policies should be directed at them in particular. Subsidized credit schemes has been tried out, but face the difficulty of identifying suitable borrowers where there are no credit histories. An element of training of private sector agents is therefore part of the policy (as for instance in micro-credit schemes).

Horizontal infrastructure services providers play a central role in the economy and to the process of adjustment (OECD, 2001). The spillovers of efficiency gains in these sector accrue to the economy as a whole. Collier and Gunning (1999) demonstrate how the lack of transport, communication, or electricity have impacted on Africa's performance. Policies aimed at developing trade-related services such as access to communication matter a great deal. Fink, Mattoo and Neagu (2002) for instance demonstrate that access to good telecommunication services has a significant impact on trade.

Labour and welfare policies

Discussion about the so-called adjustment policies directed at labour markets often do not make the distinction between efficiency, equity and political economy objectives. Most policies are generally designed with compensation in mind. This is probably because policies trying to achieve efficiency and to favour mobility are more difficult to design. In this respect, as pointed out by Rama (2003), the most important policies are probably outside of the labour market, on enabling economic agents to adopt optimal behaviour. This does not, however, mean that labour policies are not needed to mitigate the impact of job losses.

Training schemes have proven to be of limited utility, notably because overestimation of the effectiveness of classroom training as compared to on-the-job-learning. There are also problems identifying the appropriate training to provide. Finally, skill upgrading is often not necessary for re-employment, as other sectors may need to employ low skill jobs, or already highly skilled people may not need further training. Other job-search support programmes include employment services, offering placement information, and counselling. Such programmes can be very efficient in developing countries where markets are very segmented and information about other geographical or sectoral markets may not be available to the poorest. In particular, participatory approaches should be advised as a means to improve information sharing (OECD, 2004b).

Unemployment insurance, income support programmes, mandatory saving schemes, minimum wages and compulsory severance payments could possibly generate efficiencies, enabling individuals to maintain their wages and letting them afford to look for new jobs in a more secure environment. They also contribute to reduce opposition to liberalization. A common criticism of unemployment insurance is, however, that when too generous, it generates perverse incentives to stay unemployed for longer. Likewise, compulsory severance payments gives firms an incentive to hire less and contribute to reduced employment. Minimum wages combine both drawbacks.[5] These schemes benefit the employed at the expense of the unemployed. Finally, the effectiveness of income support programmes is not proven (Rama, 2003), while compulsory saving does not address the problem of the poorest.

Recent thinking on redistribution tools suggest that they may have to be focused on building incentives to reward individual initiatives. Subsidies to mobility have been suggested by economists, along with taxes on commodities, before being adopted in some countries, notably in the shape of wage-insurance schemes (Kletzer, 2004). A relatively new tool, an insurance wage works on the premise that when a displaced worker finds a new job, part of the wage gap with their previous job is subsidized for some time. The mechanism is also compensatory, but with a built-in incentive to find a new job rapidly. Mobility can also be impaired by the cost of exiting a job. Bacchetta and Jensen (2003) draw the attention on the portability of fringe benefits, for instance in existence in Mexico.

3.6.3 Policies directed at the poor

From a poverty point of view, labour issues matter, in particular in relation to employment of unskilled workers (Winters, 2002). Harrison and Revenga (1998) find that employment in the manufacturing sector rises again in half the episodes of liberalization that they study. In other cases, where employment did not recover so well, other conditions prevailed-Harrison and Revenga conclude that trade shocks should not pose a problem in most cases as workers were already very poorly paid before liberalization. There are, however, three situations where poor workers might be significantly at risk: huge shocks (one company town), high prior protection, and specificity of factors. These conditions are unfortunately not uncommon and policy intervention should be devised in such cases.

3.6.4 Fiscal and financial policy issues

Policies to manage government revenue along with trade liberalization require two main components: revenue-efficient tariff reduction and domestic tax reform. OECD (2004a) offers a review of these policies in the context of the NAMA negotiations. Switching from trade taxes to domestic ones is generally viewed as efficient, since the former apply to a narrower tax base and distort consumption and production decisions (Ebrill, Stotsky and Gropp, 1999). Many developing countries have already started applying this prescription and moving away from trade taxes.

Indirect taxes on consumption are viewed as superior to direct taxes on factors of production (capital and labour): less costly to maintain (than direct taxes, but more expensive than international trade taxes) and incentive-compatible. However, they also present specific difficulties for developing countries. First, there is debate on the capacity of low-income country to implement some of the reforms that developed countries have made, such as value added taxation. Baunsgaard and Keen (2005) show that middle income countries have only recovered between 35–55% of their previous tax revenue when implementing VAT, and low income countries almost nothing, when high income countries have not had such difficulty. This could mean than when confronted with a potentially large adjustment effort, as discussed above, developing countries may also have less policy options at hand when switching from trade taxes to domestic ones. Secondly, indirect taxation tends not to be progressive and hence biased against lower income groups, which would go against poverty reduction objectives. To counter this, products such as food or fuel could be taxed at a lower rate or exempted altogether.

Developing countries are constrained by a lack of funds to aid the adjustment process (Bhagwati, 2003).[6] Financing the fixed costs of setting up institutions enabling efficient and equitable outcomes is beyond the capacity of many poor countries. As long as such institutions are not in place, the gains from trade liberalization will be limited. This is where external assistance can help, by providing the financial basis for institution building. Many of the adjustment costs are borne upfront: government revenues are diminished in the short term, while adjustment costs associated with restructuring the use of resources in the economy need to occur before the benefits can be obtained.

3.7 Concluding comments

The possibility of sizable adjustment costs following liberalization is commonly cited as sufficient reason not to proceed with tariff reform, and the current WTO negotiations are being held back as a result of these concerns. This is not entirely surprising in the light of the evidence that is now becoming available about the extent of short run adjustment costs. While most studies conclude that aggregate trade-induced adjustment costs are relatively small compared to the long run gains from trade liberalization, the divergence between social and private adjustment costs helps to explain the concerns about adjustment costs. Policy makers are concerned about the political effects of unemployment or social unrest in specific sectors of the economy, particularly in the short run, even though the long run economy wide benefits, although uncertain in timing and magnitude, are likely to be positive.

The current round of WTO negotiations, which is focused on development, is fuelling a need for greater understanding of the short term consequences of trade liberalization in developing countries. Certainly, there is a role for government, and perhaps the first objective should be to identify the location and magnitude of the likely adjustment costs. A second task is to facilitate adjustment by making capital and labour markets work better. While sound capital market policies are more obvious, the labour market policies can have adverse or counterintuitive effects if incorrect incentives are provided. More research is needed to explore the dynamic relationships within the labour markets in developing countries.

Finally, addressing adjustment problems directly, by making markets work better and through redistributive mechanisms as well as by providing adequate, well directed finances and transition periods, would enable developing countries to opt for policies that would allow them to capture the larger long-term gain from trade.

Notes

1 Developing countries are arguably less likely to be concerned by this situation, although intra-industry trade has grown significantly in sectors like textile. This consideration has two implications in terms of our overall study: the results from the general equilibrium simulation with regard to distribution effects need to be interpreted with some caution, and the distribution effect will vary by country and industry depending on the specific characteristics of it.
2 A review of the arguments is provided by Facchini and Willmann (2001).
3 For a more comprehensive list of studies on developing countries see Matusz and Tarr (1999).
4 On this Baccheta and Jansen (2003) provide a good insight of how governments can facilitate the adjustment process.
5 This of course depends on the level of the minimum wage. Minimum wage policies are fairly widespread in developing countries (see Bachetta and Jensen, 2003).
6 Prowse (2005) reviews the main reasons why additional international support for trade liberalization is needed.

References

Bacchetta, Marc and Jansen, Mario (2003) Adjusting to trade liberalization, the role of policy, institutions and WTO disciplines, WTO Special Study 7, World Trade Organization.

Baldwin, Robert, Mutti, John and David Richardson, J. (1980) Welfare effects on the United States of a significant multilateral tariff reduction, *Journal on International Economics*, 10, 405–23.

Bale, Malcolm D. (1976) Estimates of trade-displacement costs for US workers, *Journal of International Economics*, 6, 245–50.

Baunsgaard, Thomas and Keen, Michael (2005) Tax revenue and (or?) trade liberalization, International Monetary Fund Working Paper no. 05/112 (June), Washington, DC: IMF.

Bhagwati, Jagdish (2003) *In Defense of Globalisation*, Council of Foreign Relations, Oxford: Oxford University Press.

Bhagwati, J. and Srinivasan, T. N. (1983) Trade policy and development, in R. Dornbush and J. A. Frankel (eds), *International Economic Policy Theory and Evidence*, Baltimore: John Hopkins University Press.

Blanchard, Oliver and Kremer, Michael (1997) Disorganization, *Quarterly Journal of Economics*, 111, 1091–126.

Bown, Chad P. and McCullock, Rachel (2004) U.S. trade policy and the adjustment process, mimeo, Brandeis University.

Clarete, Ramon (2005) Trade gains and transaction costs: making trade work for the poor, mimeo, University of the Philippines.

Collier, Paul and Willem Gunning, Jan (1999) Explaining African economic performance, *Journal of Economic Literature*, American Economic Association, 37(1), 64–111.

Criscuolo, C., Haskel, J. and Martin, R. (2004) Productivity, restructuring and globalisation, *Oxford Review of Economic Policy*, 20: 393–408.

Davidson, Carl and Matusz, Steven J. (2000) Globalisation and labour market adjustment: how fast and at what cost?, *Oxford Review of Economic Policy*, 16(3), 42–56.

Ebrill, Liam, Strotsky, Janet, and Gropp, Reint (1999) Revenue implications of trade liberalization, IMF Occasional Paper. No 180, Washington DC: International Monetary Fund.

Facchini, G. and Willman, G. (2001) The political economy of international factor mobility, Stanford Institute for Economic Policy Research (SIEPER) Working Paper 00–20, Stanford: Stanford University.

Fernandez, Raquel and Rodrik, Dani (1991) Resistance to reform: status quo bias in the presence of individual-specific uncertainty, *American Economic Review*, 81(5), 1146–55.

Fink, Carsten, Mattoo, Aaditya and Neagu, Ileana Cristina (2002) Assessing the impact of communication costs on international trade, Policy Research Working Paper 2929, Washington DC: World Bank.

Ghose, Ajit K. (2000) Trade liberalization and manufacturing employment, International Labour Organization Employment Paper 2000/3.

Hamermesh, Daniel S. and Pfann, Gerard A. (1996) Adjustment costs in factor demand, *Journal of Economic Literature*, 34(3), 1264–92, September.

Harrison, Ann and Revenga, Ann (1995) Factor markets and trade policy reform, World Bank Manuscript as cited in Matusz and Tarr (1999).

Harrison, Ann and Revenga, Ann (1998) Labour markets, foreign investment and trade policy reform, in J. Nash and W. Takacs (eds) *Trade Policy Reform: Lessons and Implications*, Washington DC: World Bank.

Hoekman, Bernard and Smarzynska-Javorcik, Beata (2004) Policies facilitating firm adjustment to globalisation, Policy Research Working Paper 3441, Washington: World Bank.

Kletzer, L. G. (2004) Trade-related job loss and wage insurance: a synthetic review, *Review of International Economics*, 12(5), 724–48.

Magee, Stephen P. (1972) The welfare effects of restriction on US trade, *Brookings Papers on Economy Activity*, 3, 645–701.

Matusz, S. J. and Tarr, D. (1999) Adjusting to trade policy reform, World Bank Working Paper 2142, Washington DC: World Bank.

McMillan, Margeret, Rodrik, Dani and Welch, Karen H. (2002) When economic reform goes wrong: cashes in Mozambique, CEPR Discussion Paper.

de Melo, Jaime and Tarr, David (1990) Welfare costs of US quotas in textiles, steel and autos, *Review of Economics and Statistics*, 72: 489–97.

Milner, Chris and Wright, Peter (1998) Modelling labour market adjustment to trade liberalization in an industrializing economy, *Economic Journal*, 108 (March), 509–28.

OECD (2001) *Open Services Markets Matter*, Paris: Organization for Economic Cooperation and Development.

OECD (2004a) Impact of changes in tariffs in developing countries' government revenue, Organization for Economic Cooperation and Development, Paris, TD/TC/WP(2004)29/REV1.

OECD (2004b) Trade and structural adjustment. Organization for Economic Cooperation and Development, Paris, TD/TC(2004)10.

Olson, Mancur (1965) *The Logic of Collective Action: Public Goods and the Theory of Groups*, Harvard Economic Studies, Cambridge MA: Harvard University Press.

Papageorgiou, Demetrios, Choksi, Armeane and Michaely, Michael (1992) *Liberalization Foreign Trade: The Lessons of Experience in the Developing World*, Washington DC: World Bank.

Parker, Ronald L., Riopelle, Randalle and Steel, William F. (1995) Small enterprises adjusting to liberalization in five African countries, Washington DC: World Bank.

Prowse, S. (2005) 'Aid for Trade' – Increasing support for trade adjustment and integration – a proposal, mimeo, DFID, London (May).

Rama, M. (1991) Economic growth and stagnation in Uruguay, in M. Blomstrom and P. Meller (eds), *Diverging Paths: a Century of Scandinavian and Latin American Economic Development*, Baltimore: Johns Hopkins University Press.

Rama, Martin (1999) Public sector downsizing: an introduction, *World Bank Economic Review*, 13(1).

Rama, Martin (2003) Globalisation and workers in developing countries, World Bank Working Paper 2958, Washington DC: World Bank.

Rama, Martin and MacIssave, Donna (1999) Earnings and welfare after downsizing: Central Bank employees in Ecuador, *World Bank Economic Review* 13(1), 1–22.

Ravaillon, Martin and Loskin, Michael (2004) Gainers and losers from agricultural trade reform in Morocco, Policy Research Working Paper 3368, Washington: World Bank.

Rodrik, Dani (2000) Institutions for high-quality growth: what they are and how to acquire them, NBER Working Paper 7540, Cambridge MA: National Bureau of Economic Research.

Rodrik, Dani (2004) Getting institutions right, CESifo DICE Report, Harvard University, April.

Takacs, W. and Winters, L. A. (1991) Labour adjustment costs and British footwear protection, *Oxford Economic Papers*, 43(3): 479–501.

Thomas, Vinod, Nash, John and Associates (1991) *Best Practices in Trade Policy Reform*, Washington DC: World Bank.

Verdier, Thierry (2004) Socially responsible trade integration: a political economy perspective, CEPR Discussion Paper No. 4699.

Winters, L. Alan (2002) Trade, trade policy and poverty: what are the links?, *The World Economy*, 25(9).

Part II
Adjusting to Trade Reforms: Country Studies

4
Bangladesh

Nurun N. Rahman

4.1 Introduction

4.1.1 Main features of the Bangladesh economy

The rate of growth of GDP in Bangladesh has picked up in recent years. During the period 1980–1990, it grew at an average annual rate of 3.7 per cent, barely exceeding the population growth rate; but subsequently, during the period 1999–2004, it exceeded an average annual rate of 5 per cent, to reach about $54 billion in the fiscal year 2003–2004. The investment/GDP ratio increased from 17 per cent to 23 per cent; within this, the ratio of public investment to GDP remained stagnant, at around 7 per cent, while that of private investment increased from 10 per cent to 17 per cent.

Bangladesh's economy has undergone important structural transformations over the past three decades. At independence in 1971, agriculture was the dominant sector, accounting for over half of total GDP. The industrial sector was small, contributing less than 10 per cent of GDP. However, following remarkable growth in the ready-made garments sector, the contribution of industry to GDP had almost doubled to over 20 per cent by 1990, while the share of agriculture fell to 29 per cent, and services rose to nearly 50 per cent. By 2004, the industrial sector accounted for 27 per cent of GDP, while the share of agriculture dropped to 23 per cent, and that of the services sector remained steady around 50 per cent. Within the manufacturing sector, textiles and clothing alone accounted for one-third of the total manufacturing value added in 2002, followed by food, beverages and tobacco at 22 per cent, machinery and transport equipment at 16 per cent and chemicals at 10 per cent.

4.2 Role of foreign trade

Today, exports are dominated by manufactures, compared to the early 1980s when jute and jute products were the principal export items.

Textiles and clothing (ready-made garments and knitwear) accounted for nearly 75 per cent of total merchandise exports in 2003–2004 indicating an exceptionally high export concentration in this sector. Given the predominance of textiles and clothing in Bangladesh's exports, the expiry of the WTO Agreement on Textiles and Clothing (ATC) at the end of 2004, has serious implications for the trading prospects of the country.

Remittances by expatriate workers amounted to $3 billion in 2003/03, which, on a net basis, is more important than from textiles and clothing exports, because the latter reflects 'export illusion' caused by the high import content of those exports. From this standpoint, it is not difficult to appreciate the importance attached by Bangladesh to WTO negotiations on services, particularly on the temporary movement of natural persons supplying services (Mode 4).

Nearly 75 per cent of Bangladesh's exports in 2002 went to developed countries/regions. In particular, the EU accounted for 43 per cent of the country's exports, followed by the United States and Canada, which together absorbed 29 per cent. On the import side, Bangladesh sourced nearly 18 per cent of imports from Indonesia, Malaysia, Singapore and Thailand – and 11 per cent each from China (excluding Hong Kong) and India (Bangladesh Bureau of Statistics, 2002). However, official figures tend to underestimate the true magnitude of imports from India due to the existence of illegal cross-border trade.

As a least-developed country (LDC), Bangladesh enjoys duty- and quota-free access to the EU market. However, to avail itself of preferential market access, it needs to meet the EU rules of origin. This puts Bangladesh at a disadvantage compared to certain other developing countries with relatively better-developed backward linkages. Another difficulty relates to the high tariffs faced by Bangladesh's ready-made garment exports in the United States market. Nearly half of its clothing exports to the United States face an ad valorem duty of 15 to 20 per cent, while another 13 per cent are subject to tariffs in excess of 25 per cent (Government of Bangladesh, 2004b). This high tariff puts Bangladesh exports at a serious disadvantage vis-à-vis more than 70 African and Caribbean countries that are eligible for duty-free treatment under the Trade Development Act, 2000.

4.3 Reform and liberalization policies

4.3.1 Historical background

Over the last three decades, Bangladesh's economic and policy orientation has evolved considerably, from a highly interventionist regime with widespread control on trade, the exchange rate and investment, to a substantially liberalized economic regime. At independence in 1971, Bangladesh faced the daunting challenge of rehabilitating its economy, which had suffered serious dislocation and devastation during a bloody war. Faced with very low foreign exchange reserves, a shallow export base and rising import prices, the government resorted to severe import controls, ranging from extensive use of non-tariff barriers (NTBs) to high and even prohibitive import duties.

4.3.2 Initial phases of reforms

The beginnings of policy reform and liberalization can be traced to deregulation measures starting in 1976 under a new government, which increasingly distanced itself from the earlier socialist approach. However, initial reform efforts had neither a clear direction, nor a broad time frame for implementation. Four notable features of policy during this period of greater market orientation were: reduction of restrictions on investment; gathering momentum of denationalization of public sector enterprises; limited reduction of tariffs and NTBs; and incentive packages for the emerging ready-made garments sector. During the latter half of the 1980s, a more coherent picture of reforms began to emerge under structural adjustment policies (SAPs). In the area of tariff reforms, SAPs emphasized rationalization of the import regime, simplification and reduction of effective protection, elimination of negative and restricted lists of industrial imports, and facilitation of imports of raw materials and intermediate and capital goods, including the imports needed for direct and indirect exporters. However, political commitment to policy reforms remained problematic and there were also concerns over the design and implementation of the SAPs.

4.3.3 Recent reforms and liberalization policies

The policy reform process gained substantial momentum following the restoration of democracy in 1991. The main political parties embraced a liberal economic agenda, which augured well for genuine and sustained political commitment to reform and liberalization. Since then, wide-ranging reforms and liberalization measures have been initiated and implemented, which have virtually transformed the policy landscape. These measures include tariff reductions, the elimination of a large number of quantitative restrictions (QRs), a flexible exchange rate regime, and the provision of a range of fiscal and financial incentives for export promotion.

The import policy for 2003–2006 aims at the following objectives: (a) further simplification of the import regime to respond to globalization and to facilitate increased liberalization in the light of the WTO agreements;

(b) strengthened provisions for technology imports to enable the widespread dissemination of modern technology; (c) provision of simplified import procedures for export-oriented industries to enable the development of a robust export supply capacity; and (d) gradual removal of import protection to make available industrial raw materials and enhance competitiveness, competency and efficiency (Government of Bangladesh, 2003). At the same time, the overall trade policy emphasizes regional economic and trade cooperation. The key aspects of recent reforms and liberalization measures are discussed below.

4.3.4 Tariff reform

Throughout the 1990s, Bangladesh consistently reduced its import duties. The average unweighted customs duty fell from 47 per cent in 1993 to less than 16 per cent in 2004 (Table 4.1). During the same period, the average weighted import customs duty fell from 23 per cent to 12 per cent. The share of bound duties remained unchanged between 1997 and 2003, at 13.2 per cent, while the share of duty-free tariff lines increased nearly fourfold in a decade, from 4 per cent in 1992 to over 15 per cent in 2002. The maximum import duty was reduced drastically from 350 per cent in 1992 to 30 per cent in 2003. The 2004/2005 budget provided a further reduction of the maximum tariff rate. The percentage of tariff lines with duties over 15 per cent fell from 80 per cent in 1992 to 42 per cent in 2002.

However, due to the application of a number of other charges, such as supplementary duties and surcharges on imports, the average unweighted

Table 4.1: Impact of tariff reforms on average customs duty rates

Financial year	Unweighted average (%)	Import weighted average (%)
1992–93	47.4	23.6
1993–94	36.0	24.1
1994–95	25.9	20.8
1995–96	22.3	17.0
1996–97	21.5	18.0
1997–98	20.7	16.0
1998–99	20.3	14.1
1999–00	19.5	13.8
2000–01	18.6	15.1
2001–02	17.1	9.7
2002–03	16.5	12.4
2003–04	15.6	11.5

Source: Government of Bangladesh (2004a).

customs duty does not reflect the true extent of nominal protection. According to World Bank estimates, if these charges are taken into account, the average nominal protection rate stood at 27 per cent in 2002 (Ahmed and Sattar, 2004). Moreover, the enterprise-level effective protection rate was 78 per cent for the same year.

4.3.5 Elimination of QRs

There has been a substantial phasing out of quantitative restrictions, which took place in three stages since the early 1990s, to the extent that there may not be much room for their further removal. The first major slashing of QRs took place under the import policy order for 1991–1993, which reduced the number of items on the import control list from 325 to 193. During the period 1993–1997, the number of restricted items was cut to between 111 and 120. The import policy order for 2003–2006 reduced the number further, to 63, of which only 23 are for trade reasons (Table 4.2). As a result, the share of total Harmonized System (HS) 4-digit tariff lines subject to QRs fell more than threefold, from over 6 per cent in 1993 to less than 2 per cent in 2003. Further removal of controls will not be easy: if the current restriction on salt imports were removed, it could threaten the employment and livelihoods of nearly 40,000 raw salt producers.

4.3.6 Exchange rate management

There have been significant improvements in exchange rate management since the 1990s, with the introduction of a flexible exchange rate policy. The multiple exchange rate system gave way to a unified rate in 1992, to be followed up by making the taka convertible for the current account in 1994. Adjustments in the rate of exchange have been undertaken from time to time, taking into account the rates of inflation, movement of exchange

Table 4.2: Progressive reductions of import restrictions

	IPO 1991–93	IPO 1993–95	IPO 1995–97	IPO 1997–02	IPO 2003–06
Number of items in the control list at the HS4-digit level	193 (15.65%)	111 (9.0%)	120 (9.7%)	122 (9.8%)	63 (5.1%)
Number of trade-related items in the control list at the HS 4-digit level	79 (6.4%)	19 (1.5%)	27 (1.9%)	28 (2.2%)	24 (1.9%)

Source: World Bank (2004).

rates and trade weights with partner countries. Finally, in May 2003 Bangladesh opted for an open market exchange rate policy by free float of the taka.

4.3.7 Export facilitation measures

To support export expansion, a number of incentives have been in place, such as lower interest rates on bank loans, duty-free imports of machinery and intermediate inputs, cash incentives, duty drawback and certain tax exemptions. The ready-made garments sector, in particular, has derived substantial benefits from a range of facilitation measures, comprising three main elements: (i) back-to-back letters of credit, whereby ready-made garment exporters are allowed to import their required inputs on a deferred payment basis against a master letter of credit; (ii) bonded warehouse facilities under which the ready-made garments exporters are allowed to import their required materials duty and tax free; and (iii) a mix of miscellaneous measures such as tax holidays, export credits and repatriation of profits by foreign investors.

4.3.8 Regional cooperation

Bangladesh is currently a member of two regional trade agreements (RTAs): the South Asia Free Trade Area and BIMSTEC, an economic cooperation arrangement between Bangladesh, India, Myanmar, Sri Lanka and Thailand. These agreements are due to become operational in 2006. To what extent they will open up trade among participating countries will depend upon the outcomes of ongoing negotiations, including the depth and breadth of tariff cuts, disciplines on NTBs, the scope of negative lists, rules of origin and contingency provisions.

4.4 Implications of the reforms and liberalization

The policy reforms and trade liberalization policies pursued by Bangladesh have had manifold implications for the economy in general, and trade in particular. The impact of the reforms and trade liberalization appears to be mixed: an improved, but not strong enough growth performance; the expansion of trade, but without adequate diversification; a reduction of poverty, but an increase in inequality.

4.4.1 Increased openness of the economy

As reform and liberalization measures were being pursued, the economy also became increasingly open to the world. In particular the trade–GDP ratio increased from over 26 per cent in 1990 to 42 per cent in 2000.

4.4.2 Growth performance

A comparison of GDP data in constant prices between the 1980s and the 1990s indicates that there was an increase in growth rates. The average growth rate in the 1990s was 4.8 per cent compared with 3.6 in the 1980s. Also, the growth rate was higher during the period 1996–2000, at 5.2 per cent, than during 1990–1995, at 4.4 per cent. It reached the highest point at 5.9 per cent in 2000, but fell back to an average of 5 per cent in the early years of the present decade. While there can be many causes for this rise in the growth rate, reforms and liberalization played an important role through greater openness of the economy and improved macroeconomic management. However, the increase has been modest with growth remaining significantly below the 7 per cent target of the Programme of Action for the LDCs for the current decade. The relatively weak supply response also raises the question as to whether the reforms are enough to address underlying structural, institutional and related constraints on growth and diversification.

4.4.3 Competitiveness: inflation and the real effective exchange rate

Keeping inflation low has been an important factor in maintaining macroeconomic stability and competitiveness. In this Bangladesh enjoyed a good measure of success. For every year during 1990–2000, except 1999, inflation in Bangladesh was lower than in other countries in the region, which faced double-digit inflation at some point during the decade, while Bangladesh managed to keep inflation at single-digit levels, and in some years below 4 per cent.

An important result of exchange rate reform, liberalization and price stability is that the real effective exchange rate (REER), another important indicator of competitiveness, has remained quite stable (Islam, 2003). For much of the 1990s the Central Bank seems to have opted for a stable REER. Since the floating of the exchange rate in 2003, the currency has depreciated in nominal and real terms, with a positive impact on competitiveness.

4.4.4 Impact on government revenue

Despite a substantial reduction in tariffs, overall revenue receipts from customs duties almost doubled between 1997–98 and 2003–2004, when they reached Taka 28.3 billion. This can be explained by a rising level of imports, coupled with improved revenue collection. Customs duties continue to account for a substantial share of total government revenues. However, the impact of further substantial cuts in tariff rates in the future may not be offset by any increase in the quantity of imports, and could consequently reduce the overall level of revenue. A more broad-based revenue structure, along with greater efficiency in collection, would be needed to address the possible revenue implications of further tariff liberalization.

4.4.5 Levels of employment

In the absence of reliable statistics, it is difficult to obtain an aggregate picture of the employment implications of reform efforts. However, in the case of the ready-made garments sector, the number of workers employed has increased nearly tenfold during the last 15 years (Ahmed and Sattar, 2004). Most of the increase took place in the 1990s when liberalization gathered serious momentum. Even as the expiry date of the ATC drew nearer, the number of ready-made garments factories and the number of workers employed by the sector continued to increase. The significance of employment in the ready-made garments sector does not concern merely numbers; it also has social implications, as nearly 90 per cent of ready-made garment workers are women from the poorer strata of the society.

Nevertheless, despite rapid growth in the RMG sector employment, overall manufacturing employment has fallen in relative as well as absolute terms (Muqtada, 2003). This may have been caused by deindustrialization, or a rise in productivity, or a combination of the two. In particular, reform of public sector enterprises witnessed job losses in varying degrees. On the other hand, the rise in the manufacturing sector's contribution to GDP concurrently with the reduction in its share of employment point to an improvement in productivity. This is further supported by the fact that there were increases in manufacturing wages relative to agriculture throughout the 1990s.

4.4.6 Implications for poverty

Available estimates indicate that during the 1990s Bangladesh succeeded in reducing poverty on average by 1 per cent per annum (Government of Bangladesh, 2004b). According to World Bank estimates, the poverty headcount index declined from 58.8 per cent in 1991–1992 to 49.8 per cent in 2000. Compared with a headcount index of 88.15 per cent in 1972–1975, this represents a substantial reduction in the incidence of poverty over the past three decades (Ahmed and Sattar, 2004). It is difficult to say the extent to which policy reforms and liberalization have contributed to this decline in poverty, because a variety of factors, policies and institutions have combined to produce this result, and their respective contributions are difficult to isolate. Nonetheless, a general equilibrium analysis indicates that the reforms and liberalization efforts of Bangladesh have been pro-poor in general, although the resulting gains have been small and distributed unevenly across different households, with relatively well-off households gaining more and the extremely poor less (Mujeri and Khondker, 2002).

This raises the question of the links between liberalization, poverty reduction and income distribution. Available evidence indicates that income inequality increased during the 1990s and reached a relatively high level (Government of Bangladesh, 2004b). The Gini coefficient for urban areas rose from 0.33 per cent in 1991–1992 to 0.44 per cent in 2000, and for the rural areas, from 0.26 per cent to 0.36 per cent over the same period. This growing income disparity has particular relevance for poverty reduction in the context of the current GDP growth rate, which is not strong enough to lift the incomes of the poorer segments of the population, given the rise in inequality.

4.5 Adjustment costs arising from trade agreements

The realities of the external sector and related domestic compulsions have raised concerns and interest among policy-makers with regard to the adjustment implications of trade agreements in three key areas: textiles and clothing, food, and remittances by expatriate workers.

4.5.1 Textiles and clothing

The ready-made garments sector has grown from an infant industry to become the dominant player in the merchandise trade sector. This was facilitated by external market conditions, particularly by quotas under the Multi-Fibre Arrangement (MFA), as well as by domestic support measures. This sector plays a central role in the economy and in society because of its contribution to manufacturing output, exports, imports, investment, business development and employment – including female employment – and because of the variety of linkages it has created with the rest of the economy. The possible implications of the expiry of the ATC are not yet completely clear. An IMF paper (Mlachila and Yang, 2004) warned that as much as a quarter of Bangladesh's garment exports, along with a sizeable share of employment in ready-made garments could be lost within a year of the ATC's expiry. A WTO study also warned that Bangladesh may lose up to 50 per cent of its market in the United States (Nordas, 2004).

However, early evidence suggest that in the short-term, there may not be pronounced changes, as the global market needs time to adjust to post-MFA conditions. However, in the longer term, all this might change, and policy-makers need to formulate a strategic approach that aims not merely at the survival of the sector, but also at strengthening Bangladesh's export presence on a longer-term basis, with an emphasis on progressively enhancing participation throughout the value chain and increasing domestic value added, including by entering into more dynamic segments of the textiles and clothing sector. Meanwhile, the international community could help by offering duty-free access to Bangladesh's exports. Other areas of assistance could include infrastructure support, facilitation measures to reduce transaction costs, and capacity building assistance to improve productivity and the quality of decision-making.

4.5.2 Agriculture

Bangladesh has combated its chronic food shortages rather well, and famine appears to be a thing of the past. However, occasional and localized food shortages do occur because of natural disasters and inefficiencies in food distribution. As noted earlier, agricultural productivity remains low, and its substantial improvement could reduce import dependence, at least as far as the main cereals are concerned. However, a major difficulty is that of securing regular water supply. A solution to this issue is not entirely in the hands of policy-makers since much depends on how the issue of sharing the water resources of the major common rivers with India is resolved.

Should domestic support and export subsidies by developed countries to this sector materialize as a result of the Doha Round negotiations on agriculture, there might be increases in the prices of agricultural items during the adjustment period. This is a source of disquiet as far as food security for Bangladesh is concerned. On the other hand, an increase in output prices could possibly change the current cost–price balance and make agricultural production more profitable.

4.5.3 Temporary movement of natural persons supplying services (Mode 4)

The experience of Bangladesh shows that foreign market access for service provision by natural persons through temporary movements can have important positive effects in terms of improved availability of scarce foreign currency, improving the current-account balance, financing of higher levels of imports, economic growth, employment generation and poverty reduction. Improved access for the temporary movement of labour (Mode 4 of the General Agreement on Services, GATS) in the WTO negotiations could provide an important opportunity for Bangladesh for substantial development gains from services exports. However, the initial offers by developed countries are yet to involve any significant liberalization of Mode 4 in respect of categories of particular interest to developing countries. At the domestic level, Mode 4 needs to be better linked with human resource development policies and strategies to improve the skills profile. It is also important to improve the capacity to closely monitor offers under Mode 4 for access to major markets and to identify opportunities.

4.5.4 Potential new and dynamic sectors

Trade agreements can have implications for the participation of countries in dynamic and new sectors of world trade. For example, the exemptions for Bangladesh from obligations under the WTO Agreement on Trade-related Aspects of Intellectual Property Rights (TRIPs), arising from its status as a least-developed country (LDC), as well as the WTO Decision on TRIPs and Public Health. The country has a long-established pharmaceutical base with over 200 licensed manufacturing units, employing an estimated 50,000 skilled workers (Anwar, 2003). It exports high quality pharmaceutical products to over 50 developing countries at what are reported to be competitive prices (Chakraborty, Anwar and Ahmad, 2003). A major difficulty is that the active ingredients of these pharmaceutical products are externally sourced. To become competitive on a sustainable basis, the sector needs to establish strong backward linkages.

Other possible export sectors and products include leather goods, high value-added textiles and clothing, information, communication and technology (ICT) products and ICT-enabled services, specialized and niche products (including those of interest to expatriate Bangladeshi and other South Asian nationals), and agro- and marine products. Besides identifying potentially new export opportunities and formulating appropriate strategies and policies, Bangladesh needs to carefully monitor and effectively participate in the NAMA negotiations, since their outcome will not only have important implications for its future global trade, but also affect its international competitiveness in existing and potential export sectors. There is also a need to rationalize the incentives structure, which currently focuses mainly on the ready-made garments sector, by making the incentives more coherent and broad-based so that they can effectively respond to the requirements of other sectors with export potential.

References

Ahmed, S. and Sattar, Z. (2004) *Trade Liberalization, Growth and Poverty Reduction: The Case of Bangladesh*, Washington, DC, World Bank.

Anwar, S. F. (2003) Pharmaceutical sectors of Bangladesh: Trade prospects with Nepal and the impact of TRIPs, in F. E. Cookson and A. K. M. S. Alam, *Towards Greater Sub-Regional Economic Cooperation*, Dhaka: University Press Limited.

Bangladesh Bureau of Statistics (2002) Statistical pocketbook 2002.

Chakraborty, P., Anwar, S. F., and Ahmad, M. (2003) Strategies under the WTO regime: the pharmaceutical sector of Bangladesh, *Journal of Bangladesh Studies*, 5(2), Pennsylvannia State University, 2003.

The Daily Star (2004) International agencies sceptical about Bangladesh's RMG future, 24 December, 2004 issue, Dhaka.

Government of Bangladesh (2003) Bangladesh Economic Review 2003.

Government of Bangladesh (2004a) Bangladesh Economic Review 2004.

Government of Bangladesh (2004b) Unlocking the potential: national strategy for accelerated poverty reduction.

Islam, M. A. (2003) The impact of exchange rate changes on selected economic indicators in Bangladesh, in *Centre for Policy Dialogue, Employment and Labour Market Dynamics: A Review of Bangladesh's Development 2002*, Dhaka: University Press Limited.

Mlachila, M. and Yang, Y. (2004) The end of textiles quotas: A case study of the impact on Bangladesh, IMF Working Paper WP/04/108, Washington DC, International Monetary Fund.

Mujeri, M. and Khondker, B. (2002) Poverty implications of trade liberalization in Bangladesh: a general equilibrium approach, Globalization and Poverty Globalization and Poverty Programme funded by DFID, UK, 2002.

Muqtada, M. (2003) Promotion of employment and decent work in Bangladesh: macroeconomic and labour policy considerations, in *Centre for Policy Dialogue, Employment and Labour Market Dynamics: A Review of Bangladesh's Development, 2002*, Dhaka: University Press Limited.

Nordas, H. (2004) The global textile and clothing industry post the agreement on textiles and clothing, WTO Discussion Paper No. 5, Geneva: World Trade Organization.

Oxfam (2004) Stitched up: how rich-country protectionism in textiles and clothing trade prevents poverty alleviation, Oxfam Briefing paper, April 2004.

Rahman, A. and Razzaque, A. (2003) Informal border trade between Bangladesh and India: an empirical study in selected areas, in F. E. Cookson and A. K. M. S. Alam, *Towards Greater Sub-Regional Economic Cooperation*, Dhaka: University Press Limited.

UNCTAD (2002) Least Developed Countries Report, 2002.

World Bank (2004) *Trade Policy in South Asia: An Overview*, Washington, DC, World Bank, September 2004.

5
Brazil

Lia Valls Pereira

5.1 Introduction

In the 1960s and 1970s, Brazil displayed GDP growth higher than the world average, but, under the reform programme, economic growth slowed to an average annual rate of only 1.4 per cent in 1980–90 and in the 1990s. Real GDP per capita has remained relatively stagnant, rising only from $4,527 in 1980 to $4,626 in 2000. Thus, the poor performance during the 1990s has created some doubts as to the wisdom of commitments to undertake further liberalization.

5.2 Overview of the Brazilian economy

5.2.1 Main features of the economy

Brazil is the 12th largest economy in the world, and possesses vast natural resources. About 81 per cent of Brazil's 170 million inhabitants live in urban areas. In 2001, the contribution of agricultural value added to GDP was 9.3 per cent, while for industry and services it was 33.9 per cent and 56.8 per cent respectively.

Brazil is a major exporter of mineral ores, soybeans, frozen orange juice and processed meat, in all of which the country has a relatively natural comparative advantage. Brazil is also one of the two leading exporters of small/medium aircraft, the other being Canada. However, overall, in terms of world competitiveness, Brazil's exports to world markets suggest a relatively poor performance.

Brazil ranked 72nd in the Human Development Index (HDI) in 2002. The country had a high Gini coefficient of 0.55 in 1999, showing a high degree of inequality in income distribution. According to the WTO (2004), a quarter of the population lives on less than $2 a day. However, some social indicators have been improving. According to the World Bank (2003) the indicators of gross school enrolment suggest a progressive improvement from 1980 to 2000, especially in primary and secondary enrolment. Moreover, the illiteracy rate of the population aged 15 years and over has fallen. Infant mortality dropped from 48 per thousand to 35 per thousand, between 1990 and 2000, and average life expectancy is about 68 years.

A series of factors has contributed to Brazil's poor economic performance over the last two decades, its poor institutional framework, macroeconomic instability and external shocks, among others. Investment in physical and human capital, a major driver of growth, has also been declining over the last 20 years. Indeed, the lack of adequate investment in physical infrastructure is perceived as one of the major constraints on a new cycle of economic growth.

5.2.2 Economic developments, 1980–2003

During the 1970s, Brazil experienced a period of rapid growth. Low interest rates, following the oil shock of 1973, allowed this petroleum-importing country to move forward with its development plans and to diversify its industries. However, the second oil shock and a rise in interest rates led to an alteration of the priorities of economic policy. The main issues during the 1980s were the constraints imposed by the adverse external conditions and the rising inflation rate. A package of import and exchange control measures were implemented and new subsidies were offered to increase exports of manufactures. A 'heterodox plan' to curtail inflation was implemented in 1986, but without success.

In 1994, a stabilization plan, *Plano Real*, was implemented, which succeeded in reversing the inflationary bias of the Brazilian economy. Inflation fell from 27.08 per cent in 1993 to 14.8 per cent in 1995. The general perception of the government was that macroeconomic stability and economic reforms would allow a new cycle of economic growth. The economic results of the mid-1990s, however, did not fulfil all the expectations associated with the new economic policies. Three periods can be distinguished:

- *1995–1998*. The use of an overvalued exchange rate as an anchor of the stabilization plan between 1994 and 1998 led to an increasing trade deficit. However, the Asian crisis in 1997 followed by the Russian debt moratorium obliged the government to devalue its currency in 1999 and adopt a flexible exchange rate regime. The main success of this period was the control of the inflation rate.

- *1999–2001.* The government's main goals were to keep inflation in check, reduce external vulnerability and ensure fiscal discipline. The exchange rate anchor was replaced by a programme of inflation targeting to calm inflationary expectations. The adoption of a flexible exchange rate regime also helped to improve the trade balance. An attempt was made to curtail the increasing public debt. The net reduction of foreign capital inflows – portfolio investment fell from $6,955 million in 2000 to only $77 million in 2000 – and the global economic crisis led to a fall in the growth rate to just 1 per cent in 2001.
- *2002–2003.* The new government maintained a commitment to a stable macroeconomic environment. However, interest rate remains high under the burden of increasing public debt. Improvements in the external conditions, together with the devaluation of the currency, led to a trade surplus amounting to $24.8 billion. By the end of 2003, the positive expectations of economic growth were realized, and in 2004 the economy achieved a growth rate of 4.9 per cent

5.3 Trade liberalization

At the end of the 1980s, a consensus was developing to promote some kind of trade liberalization process, and a broad trade policy reform was introduced in 1990. Quantitative controls affecting more than 1,200 import products that had either been prohibited or had their import licence suspended were removed. Moreover, nearly all the special import programmes that caused the legal tariff to differ from the effectively applied tariff on imports were terminated.[1]

A timetable for tariff reductions was established, with the goal of arriving at a tariff range of 0–40 per cent and an average and mode tariff of 20 per cent by 1994. Under the reforms, tariffs were also substantially rationalized, reducing the spread in rates. However, there was no substantial change in terms of the structure of protection; the most protected sectors in the periods before (1970/1990) continue to be protected: transportation equipment, clothing, and electrical and communications equipment, had the highest rates of effective protection even in 1994.

In March 1991, the Brazilian government along with the governments of Argentina, Paraguay and Uruguay signed the Treaty of Asuncion to form the Southern Common Market, MERCOSUR. During the period 1991–1994, intraregional trade was subject to linearly reduced tariffs, and a common external tariff (CET) was negotiated. This was followed, in January 1995, by the creation of a customs union, encompassing around 85 per cent of the tariff lines.

The main features of the CET approved in December 1994 (*Protocolo de Assunção*) were:

(i) A simple average nominal tariff of 12 per cent – varying from 0 to 20 per cent – and a tariff mode of 10 per cent;
(ii) An import tariff structure differentiated by the final use of goods (demand categories): intermediate goods (0 to 12 per cent); agricultural products (10 to 12 per cent), capital goods (12 to 16 per cent) and consumer goods (18 to 20 per cent);
(iii) A list of exceptions, which was needed in order to take into account different production structures and protectionist demands of the member countries.[2] To accommodate these differences it was decided to negotiate special deadlines for the CET in respect of some products.

The idea was that the CET would impose discipline upon ad hoc changes in tariffs, and therefore lock in the trade liberalization programme in respect of tariffs. However, when the trade deficit deteriorated following the *Real Plan* of July 1994, a series of changes in the tariff structure were introduced. Import tariffs were increased, and safeguard measures were introduced, including for toys and coconuts, and for textiles and clothing under the Agreement on Textiles and Clothing (ATC) of the WTO. Moreover, the Asian crisis and capital flight, which jeopardized the stabilization plans of Argentina and Brazil, led all members of MERCOSUR to agree in 1997 on an increase of the CET by 3 percentage points. In December 2003, this measure was abolished.

Figure 5.1 shows the behaviour of the simple average nominal tariff and weighted tariff from 1989 to 2003 during the three periods of tariff reform. The first is related to the reforms of 1990 and the adoption of the CET by MERCOSUR. The simple average fell from 44.02 per cent to 12.75 per cent between 1989 and 1994. After that there was a minor reversal of the liberalization process, with the average rising to 15.94 per cent in 1998, but again falling in 2003 to 13.45 per cent.

Abreu (2004) has analysed the political economy of protection in Brazil and concludes that the interests of specific groups have an important influence on trade policy. The most notorious case is the automobile sector, which was able to get the nominal rate of 20 per cent agreed in 1994 increased to 70 per cent, on a temporary basis; thereafter it was to settle down at a 35 per cent tariff, which corresponds to the maximum

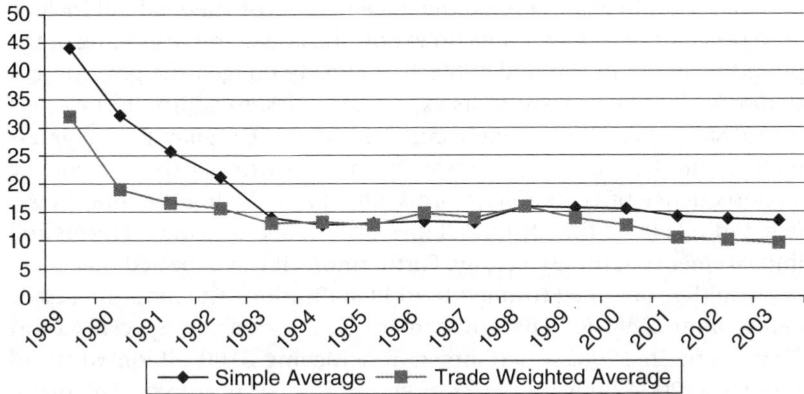

Figure 5.1: Nominal import tariffs: 1989/2003

bound industrial tariff of Brazil in the Uruguay Round. Similarly, when the exchange rate became overvalued, tariffs were increased on automobiles, motorcycles, bicycles and trucks, and some electronic consumer goods and toys (safeguard). Some import restrictions (e.g. safeguards of some textile and clothing products and coconut products), were justified on the grounds that imports of these products had grown during the second half of the 1990s. In addition, anti-dumping investigations had increased after 1994.[3]

While the liberalization process has not suffered a significant reversal, it is also true that Brazil's trade agenda lacks the impetus for further unilateral liberalization. The debate about tariff changes is strictly linked with MERCOSUR CET, except, of course, for possible offers related to the WTO negotiations. The devaluation of the Brazilian currency and the Argentine crisis has led to a proliferation of exceptions in respect of the CET and intra-regional free trade, and there is no formal commitment to revise the CET in the direction of a more open trade regime.

Nonetheless, Brazil has signed various bilateral agreements since the mid-1990s. As a member of MERCOSUR, it negotiated a free trade agreement (FTA) with Bolivia and Chile in 1996, and with the Andean Community in 2004, and negotiations for a possible FTA with Mexico and South Africa are under way. A short list of fixed preferences is being negotiated with India, and there is also a project to deepen the margin of preferences. An FTA with the European Union (EU) has not been realised. Negotiations for a Free Trade Area of the Americas (FTAA) are effectively in abeyance.

With regard to export policy, the trade reforms of 1990 did not include any special or new programme on export subsidies. The worsening of the public accounts in the mid-1980s had already obliged the government to drastically reduce most of its export subsidies. In addition, the scope for subsidies had been severely curtailed by the Uruguay Round agreements. Thus the general belief was that any growth of exports would be a consequence of economic reforms aimed at reducing the 'Brazil cost' (e.g. indirect taxes that distort relative prices, labour market reforms and improvements in infrastructure). Furthermore, it was expected that benefits would be obtained through tariff liberalization. The mounting trade deficit after 1994 led the government to announce a Special Export Programme in 1998, which aimed at achieving $100 billion worth of exports in 2002,[4] but it did not offer any special incentives. The major mechanism to support Brazil's exports are associated with special conditions of financing offered by the government and export promotion agencies that support the participation mainly of small and medium-sized enterprises in foreign trade.

5.4 Economic impact of trade liberalization

As mentioned earlier, the post-liberalization period has been characterized by relatively low rates of economic growth, influenced by adverse external conditions, especially after 1997. The rate of investment declined; having peaked at 21.4 per cent of GDP in 1995, it fell to 17.3 per cent in 2003.

The overall performance of imports was influenced by the movements of the exchange rate and domestic growth. During the first period of the liberalization process (1990–1994), imports grew at an average annual rate of 12.5 per cent. In 1995–1999, even with an overvalued exchange rate, the low rates of economic growth led to negative growth rates of imports, averaging −0.3 per cent. Export performance was relatively good in the first period (7.6% (1995–98)) until it was adversely affected by the exchange rate, which slowed down growth to 0.8 per cent per annum in the period 1995–1999. After devaluation, export growth resumed and imports continued to decline, given the low level of activity of the economy. In 2004, exports increased by 32 per cent driven by world demand, while imports increased by 30 per cent as the domestic economy picked up.

Under the impact of trade liberalization, the share of imports in apparent domestic consumption (output and imports exports) rose from 3.2 per cent to 11.9 per cent between 1990 and 1999. Huge increases were registered in electronic equipment (9.6 per cent to 50.8 per cent), parts and components of vehicles (6.9 per cent to 33.5 per cent), electrical equipment (6.5 per cent to 30.6 per cent) and pharmaceutical products (5.5 per cent to 20.0 per cent). Moreover, it was high even for traditional industries such as footwear (2.8 per cent to 8.2 per cent) and textiles (1.6 per cent to 8.9 per cent). In addition, import penetration for automobiles increased from 0.2 per cent to 13.9 per cent. These increases led to a demand by some sectors, such as automobiles, textiles, chemicals and some food industries, for protectionist measures to alleviate the competition from imports, resulting in a slight reversal of the liberalization process during the 1990s.

Following the liberalization some sectors that registered high import growth rates, such as machinery and chemicals, also saw high export growth rates. However, growth in manufactured exports linked with imported inputs is not a guarantee of an increase in the domestic value added, and in fact there was a significant decline of the value added in the manufacturing sector between 1994 and 1999 (from 26.8 per cent to 20.4 per cent).[5] Thereafter, it increased, but remained lower than in 1990.

The overall results for the Brazilian economy after the liberalization process have provoked an intense debate about its benefits. One of the main issues concerns the observed increase in productivity growth and its apparently weak effect on economic growth. As Bonelli (2002) points out, there is no overall agreement concerning the magnitude of the gains, as methodologies and data sets differ. However, all the studies show that Brazil's productivity growth was negative in the 1980s and became positive in the 1990s.[6]

Since the beginning of the 1990s, unemployment has increased in Brazil; the unemployment rate grew from 5.7 per cent in 1992 to 7.6 per cent in 1999. Even after the devaluation of the currency and the improvement of the trade balance, the unemployment rate did not decrease. The low GDP growth rates during the period 2001–2003 could explain the continuous upward trend in unemployment. Nonetheless, how much can be attributed to trade reforms is not clear.

All sectors except commerce, transportation, public administration and services registered negative annual growth rates in the period 1999–2003. As Bonelli (2002) has pointed out, this result poses a problem for improving the structure of employment in Brazil. Two of the largest employment sectors – services and commerce – experienced negative annual productivity growth rates in the period 1991–2000. Agriculture, the second major employer in Brazil, experienced a decline in its share of labour absorption, from 25.5 per cent to 18.8 per cent between 1991 and 2000.

Manufacturing registered a total decline in employment of 6.9 per cent in the period 1990–2003, but in some sectors (steel products, electrical equipment, electronic equipment, rubber, chemicals, petroleum refining and vegetable oils) it was over 30 per cent. The greatest employment losses were in textiles, which saw 174,700 jobs lost, while the wearing apparel industry, which is the biggest employer in the manufacturing sector, lost 12,000 jobs. On the other hand, the greatest increase in the number of employed workers was in machinery and tractors, with 120,000 jobs added.

Soares, Servo and Arbache (2001) surveyed various studies on the impact of liberalization on employment in Brazil. They concluded that the openness of the economy did have an impact on employment in the manufacturing sector. Ribeiro et al. (2003), concluded that greater openness destroyed jobs, but that the devaluation of the exchange rate after 1999 created jobs. Sarquis and Arbache (2001) concluded that it was not completely clear how liberalization had affected income distribution in Brazil. Increased openness destroyed jobs in the manufacturing sector, partly due to competition and partly to an increase in productivity through the adoption of new technologies and/or greater management efficiency.

Some studies based on general equilibrium models have simulated the impact on poverty reduction in Brazil due to liberalization. Hertel et al. (2003), assuming a scenario of total elimination of tariffs and agricultural subsidies, found a reduction in the proportion of families living below the poverty line (less than $1 a day) would be 13 per cent. Nonetheless, the result is not uniform across all sectors. The level of poverty increases among the population whose family income depends upon wages, 95 per cent of which, in the model, come from non-agricultural activities, mostly from manufacturing. The increase in poverty is due to an increase in the price of agricultural products. Harrison et al. (2003) estimated that the poorest income groups experienced larger gains and that income distribution did not change. They explained the improvement in income by the increase in production in the labour-intensive sectors.

There is little information on the issue of labour adjustment costs related to the loss of jobs due to the liberalization process in Brazil. One of the consequences of the reduction of employment in manufacturing seems to have been an increase in the informal labour market. According to Ramos and Ferreira (2004), informal employment grew from 40 per cent in 1990 to 46 per cent in 1996, and reached 51 per cent in 2000. However, the authors observe that thereafter it has remained more or less stable, suggesting that the bulk of the adjustment process has been completed.

Brazil has an unemployment insurance scheme, but it lasts for only 6 months and covers only those workers who have been employed for at least one year in the formal market. Therefore unemployed workers do not have a good social safety net to guarantee reasonable living conditions for their families during extended periods of unemployment.

Finally, does the direction of trade matter? Castilho (2004) explores the possible impact of trade agreements on employment for the years of 1999–2001. On the basis of a simulation exercise of the impact of a proposed FTAA and an agreement with the EU, it is expected that a MERCOSUR-EU agreement will provide relatively more jobs to unskilled workers, but the difference is not very significant for a similar agreement with the United States. The total effect on the employment rate of both the agreements together is relatively small: about 0.4 per cent. From Castilho's analysis, it may also be inferred that as a result of multilateral negotiations, the winners will be the less skilled workers, as against skilled workers, if the labour content (in terms of educational level) of Brazil's global trade flows is considered.

In sum, it is tempting to conclude that liberalization will help Brazil's less skilled workers. In part this might be true, but as the experience of Brazil shows, openness is followed by pressure to modernize, which involves the use of new technologies. This would eventually hurt the less skilled workers as well.

5.5 Conclusions, policy lessons and implications of the Doha Negotiations

The experience of the Brazilian liberalization process of the 1990s underlines that there are risks in using trade liberalization as part of a stabilization programme. In the Brazilian case, the combination of trade reforms with an overvalued exchange rate after 1994, in order to help control domestic prices, exacerbated the effects on employment in manufacturing. The overvalued exchange rate exacerbated the impact of tariff cuts on imports and hindered export growth. It is also clear from this study that trade liberalization per se cannot assure growth. Part of the increase in productivity of the manufacturing sector in Brazil was achieved by a process of downsizing. But this also created an environment of uncertainty, which was accentuated by the macroeconomic conditions of the 1990s. The positive effect on productivity, associated with the introduction of new technologies and a new wave of investment, was not a widespread phenomenon in Brazil, since the investment rate did not increase. It is possible that this was due to the absence of a climate of positive expectations concerning demand growth.

In conclusion, Brazil has a diversified economy and in this sense it can, in principle, cope 'more easily', relatively speaking, with changes related to trade reforms. Nonetheless, this depends on its ability to pursue sustained growth – still a major challenge for the country. Moreover, the low level of literacy imposes an additional challenge, given the pressure stemming from the liberalization process to modernize production. The reduction of adjustment costs in terms of employment requires a short- and medium-term strategy, which is on Brazil's domestic agenda. In the multilateral negotiations, more flexibility is needed, with a possible timetable for tariff reductions; improved market access for agricultural products and manufactures that still face relatively high tariffs in developed countries is important. Indeed, developing countries should concentrate on making the issue of market access a priority in the negotiations. Proposals to include new issues, or requests for the creation of new rules of investments, government procurement or services, for example, should wait.

Notes

1 The difference between the legal tariff and the one actually levied (the ratio between the import tax collected over the import value) was very high. In 1985, the legal tariff for the transformation industry reached 83 per cent (although the tariff change was considered temporary) and the tariff actually applied was 7.9 per cent.

2 During the negotiations, for example, Argentina had zero tariffs on capital goods. The value added of such goods had fallen from 23.14 per cent in 1985 to 17.7 per cent in 1990. Brazil, however, as the largest producer of capital goods in MERCOSUR, and with a relatively diversified production structure, did not accept a common zero tariff.

3 Legislation on dumping and countervailing duties entered into force in 1988. Between 1994 and 2002, 132 anti-dumping investigations and 7 subsidies investigations were initiated; in 2002, 63 anti-dumping measures and 6 countervailing duties were in force.

4 It was only in 2004 that Brazil's exports reached $96.5 billion.

5 Instituto Brasileiro de Geografia e Estatísticas (www.ibge.gov.br).

6 See, for instance, Bonelli and Fonseca (1998), Muendler, Servén and Sepúlveda (2001), Muendler (2002) and López-Córdova and Moreira (2003).

References

Abreu, M. P. (2004) Trade liberalization and the political economy of protection in Brazil since 1987, INTAL-ITD Working Paper SITI 08B. Buenos Aires: Inter-American Developing Bank.

Bonelli, R. (2002) Labour productivity in Brazil during the 1990s. Discussion paper no. 906, Rio de Janeiro: Institute of Applied Economic Research (IPEA).
Bonelli, R. and Fonseca, R. (1998) Evolução da competitividade da produção manufatureira no Brasil. Discussion paper no. 574, Rio de Janeiro: IPEA.
Castilho, M. (2004) Integração Regional E Conteúdo de Trabalho do Comércio Exterior Brasileiro, Discussion Paper no. 1028, Rio de Janeiro: IPEA.
Harrison, G. et al. (2003) Regional, multilateral and unilateral trade policies of MERCOSUR for growth and poverty reduction in Brazil (mimeo), Washington, DC: World Bank.
Hertel, T. W. et al. (2003) OECD and non-OECD trade liberalization and poverty reduction in seven developing countries, in Jonathan Brooks (ed.), *Agricultural Trade and Poverty. Making Policy Analysis Count,* Paris: OECD.
López-Cordova, E. and Moreira, M. M. (2003) Regional integration and productivity: the experiences of Brazil and Mexico, INTAL-ITD Working paper no.14, Buenos Aires: Inter-American Developing Bank.
Muendler, M. (2002) Trade, technology and productivity: a study of Brazilian manufactures 1986–1988 (mimeo), Berkeley, CA: University of California.
Muendler, M., Servén, L. and Sepúlveda, C. (2001) Productivity growth in Brazilian industry, in *Brazil: The New Growth Agenda,* Vol. II, Report No. 22950-BR, Chapter 3. Washington, DC: World Bank.
Ramos, L. and Ferreira, V. (2004) Geração de empregos e realocação espacial no mercado de trabalho Brasileiro, 1992–2002. Texto Para Discussão No. 1027, Rio de Janeiro.
Ribeiro, E. R. et al. (2003) Trade liberalization, the exchange rate and job flows in Brazil, available at: www.iadb.org.
Sarquis, S. J. B. and Arbache, J. S. (2001) Openness and external effects of human capital (mimeo), London: London School of Economics.
Soares, S., Servo, L. M. and Arbache, J. S. (2001) O que (não) sabemos sobre a relação entre abertura comercial e mercado de trabalho no Brasil, Discussion Paper no. 843, Brasília: IPEA.
World Bank (2003) World Bank Development Indicators 2003, Washington DC.
WTO (2004) *Trade Policy Mechanism Review of Brazil,* Geneva: World Trade Organization.

6
Bulgaria

Victor Ognivtsev

6.1 Introduction and overview of the country[1]

Bulgaria has been undergoing almost 15 years of profound reforms in the process of transition to a market economy from a previously centrally planned system. Trade liberalization and integration into the multilateral trading system have been among the top priorities of the reform strategy. The country is also pursuing its strategic goal of joining the European Union (EU) by 1 January 2007. Its accession to the World Trade Organization in December 1996 was an important milestone.

6.1.1 Economic and trade environment

Main features of the economy

Following negative real GDP growth in 1996 and 1997, the Bulgarian economy grew steadily between 1998 and 2003, by around 4 per cent on average. Real GDP growth in 2003 was estimated at 4.3 per cent. In the earlier stage of transition, GDP fell almost steadily through 1997, when it was 40 per cent below its 1990 level. Real GDP per capita of €6,280 ($7,059) at purchasing power parity (PPP) is only 27.9 per cent of the average per capita GDP in the EU. At the market exchange rate, its GDP per capita was $1,986 in 2002.[2] The population was just under 8 million in 2001.

One of Bulgaria's main assets is a relatively well-educated and trained workforce, in particular, in engineering and natural sciences, although there is a shortage of skills in social sciences and management.

The employment rate of the working age population fell from 54.5 per cent in 1997 to 49.7 per cent in 2001, but increased again to 52.5 per cent in 2003. The unemployment rate in 2003 was back to its 1997 level of 13.6 per cent, after climbing to 19.2 per cent in 2001. The unfavourable unemployment dynamics, although improving in 2002–2003, is mainly associated with the restructuring of State-owned enterprises.

The agricultural sector's share in gross value added more than halved, from 26 per cent in 1997 to 11 per cent in 2003, due to both negative developments in the agricultural sector and positive developments in the non-agricultural sectors. The share of industry remained at between 28 per cent and 30 per cent over this period, but services expanded rapidly, from 44 per cent in 1997 to 59 per cent in 2003. This sectoral shift has been much less pronounced in terms of employment: employment in agriculture increased from 25 per cent to 28 per cent and in services from 43 per cent to 45 per cent, while there was a decline in industrial employment, from 32 per cent to 28 per cent.[3]

The savings rate in Bulgaria amounted to 14.2 per cent of GDP in 2003, remaining below the average for the euro area, while the fixed investment-to-GDP ratio has gradually increased, from 11 per cent in 1997 to nearly 20 per cent in 2003. The savings-investment gap is mainly filled by foreign direct investment (FDI), which represented an average of about 6 per cent of GDP from 1998 to 2003.

Overview of recent economic developments

Following the severe economic crisis in 1996–1997, a currency board arrangement (CBA) was introduced in July 1997. A conservative fiscal policy was adopted as well as a sharp acceleration of structural reforms encompassing agriculture, energy, privatization, further price and trade liberalization, reform and restructuring of the social sectors, and financial discipline in the private sector. Inflation has generally been kept below single digits. However, notwithstanding the achievements of the economic transition, real GDP and consumption in 2002 were still below their pre-transition (1989) levels by 17 per cent and 13 per cent respectively.[4]

Substantial progress has been made in restructuring the economy. A large number of State-owned enterprises have been sold or liquidated, but several major enterprises remain to be privatized. The financial sector is now almost entirely in private hands, and to a large extent foreign-owned. Private ownership, including by foreigners, together with a tight fiscal policy and competition rules have been largely responsible for creating a competitive environment, especially in industries and the services sector. Thus conditions for doing business in Bulgaria have improved, although substantial efforts are still required to enhance the efficiency of the public administration, the judicial system and the regulatory environment, and in particular to improve the prospects for small and medium-sized enterprises.

Accession to the European Union (EU)

Negotiations on accession to the EU were opened in February 2000 and became a major factor influencing Bulgaria's economic and trade environment. On accession, Bulgaria will be required to align its tariffs with those of the EC. Bulgaria's applied most-favoured-nation (MFN) tariffs in 2004 were, on average, 12 per cent for all products. According to Eurostat, applied tariffs on agricultural products were 24.9 per cent on average, while tariffs on fishery and industrial products remained stable at 11.7 and 8.7 per cent respectively. By comparison, EC tariffs currently stand at 6.3 per cent on all products, 16.2 per cent on agricultural products, 12.4 per cent on fishery products and 3.6 per cent on industrial products.[5]

Bulgaria benefits from several pre-accession instruments that were established by the European Union to assist the applicant countries of CEE: the *Phare* programme; the Special Accession Programme for Agricultural and Rural Development (*SAPARD*); and the Instrument for Structural Policies and Pre-Accession (*ISPA*), which finances infrastructure projects relating to the environment and transport. For the period 2000–2004, total financial assistance to Bulgaria amounted to about €178 million annually from Phare, €57.6 million from SAPARD, and between €93 and €127 million from ISPA.[6]

In its first 1997 Opinion on Bulgaria's Application for EU Membership, the Commission concluded: 'Bulgaria's progress in the creation of a market economy has been limited by the absence of a commitment to market-oriented economic policies; it would not be able to cope with competitive pressure and market forces within the Union in the medium term.' However, in its 2003 Regular Report, the Commission noted that: 'Bulgaria is a functioning market economy. It should be able to cope with competitive pressure and market forces within the Union in the near term, provided that it continues implementing its reform programme to remove remaining difficulties.' This conclusion was reconfirmed in 2004.

On 25 April 2005, the Treaty concerning the accession of the Republic of Bulgaria and Romania to the European Union was signed in Luxembourg. Its main objective is to achieve the EU accession of both countries by 1 January 2007.[7]

6.1.2 Role of trade in Bulgaria's economy

As a small country with a relatively open trade regime, Bulgaria is highly dependent on foreign trade, as reflected in the high share of imports and exports of goods and services in the GDP (over 80 per cent in recent years). Total external trade increased by 40.1 per cent in the period

1996–2002. Export growth, which averaged 12.5 per cent a year over the period 2000–2002, was the main contributor to GDP growth in 2000 and 2001, and the second largest contributor in 2002 after domestic consumption. Annual growth of imports averaged 12.8 per cent over the same period.[8]

Bulgaria has undergone a rather dramatic reorientation of its trade. Before the transition, over half of Bulgaria's foreign trade was with members of the Council for Mutual Economic Assistance (CMEA). In 2003, the EU accounted for 52.4 per cent of Bulgaria's total trade, up from 38.5 per cent in 1995. Other preferential partners – the European Free Trade Area (EFTA), Central European Free Trade Area (CEFTA) and Turkey – together accounted for some 16.5 per cent of Bulgaria's exports and 13.6 per cent of its imports in 2002; the Russian Federation accounted for 1.6 per cent of its exports and 14.5 per cent of its imports, and the United States' share was 4.7 per cent of exports and 2.2 per cent of imports.[9]

In 1989, before the transition, Bulgaria's exports were estimated at $8.3 billion, of which $5.1 billion went to the CMEA and about $3.2 billion to other countries. The collapse of the CMEA led to a drastic fall in the value and volume of exports, to the extent that by 1992 total exports were estimated at $3.9 billion. Since the beginning of transition reforms in 1991, export values have in general fluctuated in accordance with the performance of the economy. In the period 1992–1994, they averaged at around $3.9 billion; after increasing to about $5 billion in 1995, they fell back to $4 billion in 1999. Recent estimates show a rising trend: in 2001 exports were estimated at $5.1 billion and in 2002 at $5.7 billion.[10]

Similarly, the value of total imports has fluctuated considerably since the pre-transition period. In 1989, their total value was about $9 billion, of which the CMEA accounted for $4.6 billion. By 1992, total imports had fallen to $4.5 billion, mainly due to the drastic fall in real incomes that occurred during the early transition period. They then rose to $5.3 billion in 1995, but, as with exports, this trend was curtailed by the 1996–1997 economic crisis which resulted in imports falling to about $4.9 billion in 1997. Since the resumption of economic growth, imports have resumed their rising trend. In 2001 and 2002 total imports were estimated at $7.3 billion and $7.9 billion respectively.[11]

In the pre-transition period, Bulgaria was a major exporter of capital goods and processed food to the CMEA, but is now a net importer of these products; it is proving competitive in exports of footwear, textiles and apparel. Prior to the 1990s, agricultural products were a major export, especially to the former Soviet Union. Today, agricultural exports have shrunk substantially, although Bulgaria traditionally had a distinct comparative advantage in agriculture. There are several reasons for this. First, Bulgaria has almost completely lost its large markets in the countries that made up the former Soviet Union, as they have reoriented their trade to the EU and other countries (e.g. the United States and Latin American countries). Second, Bulgaria's agricultural exports, like those of many developing countries, continue to face protectionist policies of the EU (even though the EU is Bulgaria's trade preferential partner) and other countries of Europe and elsewhere. In general, the evolution of Bulgaria's trade structure reveals a movement in comparative advantage towards labour- and resource-intensive manufacturing products; it also reflects a measure of deindustrialization as a result of reforms.

Bulgaria has recorded a positive balance on its service account since 1994. In 2002, this amounted to $598 million.[12] Tourism is the main service industry, making a valuable contribution to the positive balance of trade in services.

6.2 Trade liberalization and its economic impacts

6.2.1 Trade liberalization process

Prior to the reforms, the Bulgarian economy, like other former socialist countries, had been dominated by State ownership and was governed by centralized planning. A large part of Bulgaria's GDP was created and realized within the framework of the CMEA. Following the disintegration of this regional arrangement in 1989–1990, the country's export revenues drastically declined, and in March 1990 the government declared a unilateral moratorium on external debt service payments.

In 1990, Bulgaria joined the IMF and concluded its first stand-by agreement, which provided some resources to initiate the reform process. At the end of 1993, Bulgaria signed the Europe Agreement with the EU member States, a preferential trade agreement that was probably the most important initial catalyst for trade policy reforms. However, as mentioned above, the 'asymmetric' liberalization of trade regimes under this Agreement appeared to be insufficient for substantially expanding Bulgarian exports to the EU.

The period 1990–1997 was characterized by a stop-go transformation towards a market economy, which caused the GDP to shrink by 40 per cent in real terms, while consumer prices soared almost 20 times relative to 1990. Inflation averaged 233 per cent a year, and turned into hyperinflation from late 1996 to early 1997, at the height of a major banking and exchange rate crisis.[13] This in turn led to the collapse of real incomes and wealth, and to a growth in poverty levels. Thus Bulgaria's transition started and initially proceeded under more difficult, and even dramatic, circumstances than in most other CEE countries.

The National Economic Development Plan of the Republic of Bulgaria for 2000–2006 (NEDP) addressed a number of longer-term issues concerning Bulgaria's socioeconomic development, including further trade liberalization. The Plan, which was updated between September 2002 and April 2003, also sets a vision for the country's future development in line with the identified national priorities, the progress achieved in negotiations with the EU and the changes in the economic and external environment since 1999. The NEDP also provides the basis for the programming of assistance through the EU pre-accession funds for 3–4 years. In addition to trade liberalization, the NEDP sets as a key national priority, improvement in the competitiveness of the national economy with the aim of attaining sustainable and balanced growth and development.

During the transition process, Bulgaria's overall trade policy objective was geared to the gradual liberalization of its trade regime. This was pursued at multilateral, regional and bilateral levels. However, its main trade liberalization efforts have been implemented through a network of regional and bilateral free trade agreements (FTAs).

Bulgaria acceded to the WTO on the 1 December 1996. It managed to negotiate ceiling bindings as its tariff concessions, both in agricultural and industrial goods, i.e., WTO bound tariff levels were generally higher than the applied levels. Such ceiling bindings can be considered as convenient 'safety nets' for the future (in case urgent protection might be required, without the need to initiate complex and expensive safeguard and anti-dumping investigations), but also to facilitate transition to the EU trade regime and to ensure that Bulgaria has an adequate negotiating basis for eventual multilateral trade liberalization on a reciprocal basis with its MFN trading pernters.

On accession to the WTO, Bulgaria bound all its MFN tariffs under GATT 1994 (see Tables 6.1 and 6.2 below). The simple average tariff on agricultural products is 47.6 per cent, while on non-agricultural items it is 22.7 per cent. However, applied most favoured nation (MFN) tariff rates were reduced to a simple average of less than 12 per cent in 2003 (and 17.2 per cent in 1996): the applied simple average MFN rates were 21.7 per cent for agricultural products and 8.6 per cent for industrial products. Applied duties range from 0 per cent to a maximum of 40 per cent for industrial products and 80 per cent for agricultural products. Bulgaria applies ad valorem duties of a specific rate to all industrial products, with the exception of one tariff line, and to 83.9 per cent of agricultural products.[14] Average applied MFN tariff rates are well above preferential

Table 6.1: Bulgaria: bound and applied tariffs, 2003

By tariff lines	**Bound**	**Applied**
Number of tariff lines	10,606	10,606
Unweighted average	28.2	11.6
Minimum	0.0	0.0
Maximum	200.0	80.0
By stage of processing		
Stage 1 (raw materials)		
Average	29.1	9.6
Minimum	0.0	0.0
Maximum	200.0	80.0
Stage 2 (semi-manufactures)		
Average	21.6	8.8
Minimum	0.0	0.0
Maximum	128.0	50.0
Stage 3 (finished products)		
Average	31.4	13.4
Minimum	0.0	0.0
Maximum	200.0	74.0
By Harmonized System chapter		
HS 01–24		
Average	47.6	21.7
Minimum	0.0	0.0
Maximum	200.0	80.0
HS 25–97		
Average	22.7	8.6
Minimum	0.0	0.0
Maximum	128.0	40.0

Source: WTO Secretariat calculations.

rates; average preferential rates for all products range between 2.5 per cent to 5.9 per cent. As in most OECD countries, a few maximum MFN tariffs (both bound and applied) are concentrated on several domestically produced agricultural products (mainly, dairy products, cereals, vegetables and tobacco).

On the basis of the International Standard Industrial Classification (ISIC), the Bulgarian tariff structure shows tariff escalation; the first and semi-processed stages of manufacturing attract average rates of 7.8 per cent and 8.8 per cent, respectively, and fully processed products attract an average tariff of 13.4 per cent. Tariff escalation appears to be relatively

Table 6.2: Structure of MFN tariffs in Bulgaria

	1998	2002	2003
1. Bound tariff lines (% of all tariff lines)	100.0	100.0	100.0
2. Duty-free tariff lines (% of all tariff lines)	5.2	15.0	14.6
3. Non-ad valorem tariffs (% of all tariff lines)	3.6	3.6	3.7
4. Tariff quotas (% of all tariff lines)	2.4	2.2	2.1
5. Non-ad valorem tariffs with no AVEs (% of all tariff lines)	3.6	3.6	3.7
6. Domestic tariff 'spikes' (% of all tariff lines)[a]	0.7	5.1	5.1
7. International tariff 'peaks' (% of all tariff lines)[b]	39.7	25.3	25.3
8. Overall standard deviation (%)	11.7	10.9	11.0
9. 'Nuisance' applied rates (% of all tariff lines)[c]	0.4	0.7	0.7

[a] Domestic tariff spikes are defined as those exceeding three times the overall simple average applied rate.
[b] International tariff peaks are defined as those exceeding 15 per cent.
[c] Nuisance rates are those greater than zero, but less than or equal to 2 per cent.
Source: WTO Secretariat calculations, based on data provided by the Bulgarian authorities.

marked in the food, beverages and tobacco, textile and leather, wood and furniture, and chemicals sectors.

Bulgaria also provides more favourable market access to 118 developing and least developed countries under the Generalized System of Preferences (GSP). It applies preferential duties on a large number of goods originating from developing countries, at the rate of 70 per cent of the MFN duty rate, and for imported goods originating from least developed countries it applies zero duty.

On WTO accession, Bulgaria made commitments across all major service sectors and in more than 90 out of 155 sub-sectors.

The Europe Agreement establishing an Association between the European Union and its members States (EAA) and the Republic of Bulgaria was signed in March 1993 and entered into force on the 1 February 1995. Bulgaria also has a free trade agreement (FTA) with the member States of EFTA, and it acceded to CEFTA on 1 January 1999. In 2000–2002, it concluded bilateral FTAs with Estonia, Israel, Lithuania, Latvia, the former Yugoslav Republic of Macedonia and Turkey. Estonia, Latvia and Lithuania are now EU members. In 2001, Bulgaria signed a Memorandum of Understanding on Trade Liberalization and Facilitation between countries of South-eastern Europe within the framework of the Stability Pact. In accordance with the obligations under this Pact, Bulgaria finalized negotiations on FTAs with Bosnia and Herzegovina and Serbia and Montenegro. The FTA with Albania was signed on 26 March

2003 for entry into force in 2005. In all these FTAs, trade in industrial goods is duty-free, while agricultural trade is partially liberalized.

6.2.2 Other trade policy measures

Imports

Bulgaria applies a 20 per cent value-added tax on most goods and services, including imports. Excise duties are levied on a limited number of products for mainly health and environmental reasons.

On 1 January 1997, the customs clearance fee of 1 per cent ad valorem was abolished. On 1 July 1998, the temporary import surcharge introduced for balance-of-payments purposes was reduced, and on 1 January 1999 it was completely eliminated, ahead of schedule and in spite of a negative trade balance.

Bulgaria currently does not apply any automatic licences on imports. Remaining non-automatic licences are maintained in conformity with Bulgaria's commitments under various international agreements related to trade in arms, and protection of human, animal and plant life.

During the process of its accession to the WTO, Bulgaria introduced new anti-dumping, countervailing and safeguard legislation in conformity with WTO disciplines. It has so far initiated one anti-dumping action, and six safeguard investigations, two of which have resulted in increased duties.

National standards are being harmonized gradually with international and regional standards, in particular with those of the EU. Some 2 per cent of standards in force are mandatory technical regulations. In 2002, 52 per cent of Bulgaria's standards were harmonized with those of the EU, and it intends to achieve 80 per cent harmonization by 2005.[15]

Exports

Bulgaria no longer imposes any duties, taxes or other charges on exported goods. At the time of its WTO accession in 1996, it applied a range of export taxes for the purpose of preventing or relieving critical shortages of foodstuffs and other essential products. However, it undertook to minimize the use of such measures upon accession. In 1998, export taxes were eliminated on 24 products, including wheat, barley and maize and in 1999 on live cattle, skins, wool, paper waste, metal scrap and metal products. In January 2000 the remaining export taxes, on unprocessed wood products, were abolished.

Since January 2000, Bulgaria has liberalized its export licensing procedures. Currently, non-automatic export licences are required in a limited number of cases, slinked to obligations under international treaties.

In 2003–2004, Bulgaria's exports of textile and apparel products were subject to quota restrictions only in the United States and Canada.

Bulgaria does not apply any export subsidies.

Domestic supports

In line with the government's conservative fiscal stance, the amount of State aids (i.e. subsidies) has declined, both in absolute and relative levels in recent years. As a percentage of GDP, State aid declined from 3.3 in 1999 to 0.7 per cent in 2001. Similarly, direct subsidies declined from 2.5 per cent of GDP in 1999 to 0.6 per cent in 2002. The mining and transport sectors have benefited the most from State aid: assistance for the production of coal (29.5 per cent of value) and provision of transport services (29.0 per cent of value) accounted for almost 60 per cent of the total subsidies in 2001.[16]

6.2.3 Development impact

The transition process and the more open economy has resulted in high and persistent unemployment, with a large proportion of long-term unemployed. On the other hand, since 2001 unemployment has been decreasing, but was nevertheless still high, at 14.3 per cent at the end of 2003. Unemployment among young people, ethnic minorities and other disadvantaged groups remains high.

Living standards in Bulgaria are lower than in other EU new member or applicant states, and poverty indicators have deteriorated over the years of transition and reform in terms of average monthly incomes, proportion of the poor (with incomes under 60 per cent of the average monthly income) and the poverty threshold (60 per cent of the average monthly income). However, income inequality in Bulgaria is lower than in the EU and even lower than in most other transition economies, although the Gini coefficient grew slightly over 1992–2001 (UNDP, 2003).

6.3 Policy lessons and implications

Significant macroeconomic and structural reforms implemented in Bulgaria since 1997, its membership of the WTO in 1996 and the process of accession to the EU have all contributed to the transition process. Major reforms implemented included trade and investment liberalization and wide-scale privatization. These have contributed to relatively high rates of economic growth in 1998–2002. However, problems of widespread poverty and high levels of unemployment remain major challenges, although there are signs of improvement in the social indicators.

The persistent current-account and trade deficits are another major challenge, reflecting the relatively low level of competitiveness.

The process of accession to the EU has also contributed to improving the competitiveness of the economy and its recovery, including increased trade on a regional basis. The EU continues to provide significant financial support to Bulgaria's accession process, having raised the amount of its assistance by an average of 30 per cent for the period 2004–2006. Bulgaria receives around €400 million per year, which amounts to 2 per cent of its GDP.[17] Such significant assistance undoubtedly serves as an important safety net for trade liberalization and structural adjustment process.

As noted, Bulgaria's trade liberalization strategy has been carried out predominantly at the regional and bilateral levels through preferential FTAs on a reciprocal basis. As a result, more than 70 per cent of Bulgaria's trade is now with its FTA partners, including the EU, EFTA and CEFTA. At the multilateral level, Bulgaria's process of accession to the WTO, proceeded in a rather cautious manner, with ceiling binding intended to enable a smoother adaptation to the EU bound tariffs, and to provide a safety net in trade.

Notes

1 The analysis of Bulgaria's experience in economic transition was handicapped by the almost complete lack of statistical data on the pre-1989 period of central planning, especially in such areas as employment, education, savings and investment, government consumption, competitiveness and monetary indicators.
2 EU Commission (2002–2004).
3 European Union (2004).
4 WTO (2003).
5 EU Commission (2002–2004).
6 Ibid.
7 EU doc. AA2005/NDX, April 2005, Brussels.
8 World Bank (2002).
9 WTO (2003).
10 Stefanov (2001).
11 Pirinski (2001).
12 WTO (2003).
13 IMF(2004).
14 WTO (2003).
15 EU Commission (2002–2004).
16 WTO (2003).
17 EU Commission (2002–2004).

References

Economic Commission for Europe (2004) *Economic Survey of Europe, No.1–2*, Geneva.

EU Commission (2002–2004) Annual reports on Bulgaria's progress towards accession, Brussels.

European Union (2004) *External and intra-European Union Trade, Statistical Yearbook, Data 1958–2003*, Brussels.

IMF (2004) Bulgaria: 2004 Article IV consultation and ex post assessment of longer-term program engagement, *IMF Country Report* No. 04/176, Staff Reports, Staff Statement, and Public Information Notice on the Executive Board Discussion, Washington, DC: June 2004.

Pirinski, G. (2001) Bulgaria's experience with WTO accession and the first years of membership, in *WTO Accessions and Development Policies*, UNCTAD/DITC/TNCD/11, New York and Geneva: UNCTAD

Stefanov, S. (2001) The competitiveness of the Bulgarian economy, *South-East Europe Review*, 3.

UNDP (2003) *Millennium Development Goals: Bulgaria*, Sofia.

World Bank (2002) Memorandum of the President of the International Bank for Reconstruction and Development and the International Finance Corporation to the Executive Directors on a country assistance strategy of the World Bank Group for Bulgaria, Report No. 23927-BUL, Washington, DC.

WTO (2003) WTO trade policy review of Bulgaria. Report by the Secretariat, WT/TPR/S/121. Geneva,15 September 2003.

7
India

Veena Jha

7.1 Introduction

With a population of over 1 billion people, India is the second most populous country in the world. However, prior to the reforms of 1991, the economy had only grown at some 3.6 per cent a year over the previous 30 years. The 1991 economic reforms were intended to put the Indian economy on a path to sustainable growth and to address long-standing fiscal and current-account imbalances. The reforms encompassed liberalization in areas such as the exchange rate regime, foreign investment, industrial policy, external borrowing, import licensing, import tariffs and export subsidies. The sequencing of the reform process, whereby fiscal and monetary reforms preceded trade liberalization has been said to explain India's 'soft landing' (Stiglitz, 2003). The unilateral liberalization also coincided with the Uruguay Round of Trade Negotiations (1986–1994), which, inter alia, resulted in binding non-optional agreements on a comprehensive array of issues such as goods (including agricultural goods), services, trade-related investment measures (TRIMs) and trade-related aspects of intellectual property rights (TRIPS).

7.2 Overview of the trade and economic reforms

There is general recognition that industrial policy and investment reforms in India preceded trade policy reforms. Moreover, the freeing of the exchange rate regime provided another cushion from the effect of the trade reforms. These changes paved the way for trade policy initiatives that included the progressive removal of quantitative restrictions so that tariffs, substantially rationalized and reduced, now constitute the main trade policy instrument.

7.2.1 New industrial and investment policy

The new industrial policy that began in 1991 did away with much of the industrial licensing and myriad entry restrictions on investment and expansion. It also ended public sector monopoly in many sectors, and initiated a policy of automatic approval for FDI of up to 51 per cent. The 1991 policy statement also limited public sector monopoly to six sectors selected on security and strategic grounds.

FDI policy in India has been made considerably more investor-friendly, particularly by virtue of the provisions incorporated under the Foreign Exchange Management Act ('FEMA') regulations, which replaced the infamous Foreign Exchange Regulation Act (FERA). Nodal agencies such as the Foreign Investment Promotion Board (FIPB), and the Foreign Investment Implementation Authority (FIIA) facilitate realization of approved FDI and provide a 'proactive', one-stop service to foreign investors by helping them obtain the necessary approvals and acting as a single point interface between the government and governmental authorities. All these steps are significant improvements over the tightly regulated import-export regime of the 1980s and early 1990s.

7.2.2 Exchange rate policy

The economic reforms of the 1990s were also accompanied by the lifting of exchange controls that had been another layer of restriction on imports. The rupee was devalued by 24 per cent in July 1991 as part of the initial stabilization programme, and a dual exchange rate was introduced briefly from March 1992 to March 1993. In March 1993, the dual exchange rate was unified, and the unified rate was allowed to float. As early as in 1994, many current account transactions, including all current business transactions, education, medical expenses and foreign travel were also permitted at the market exchange rate. These steps culminated in India accepting IMF Article VIII obligations, which made the rupee officially convertible on the current account (WTO, 1996).

7.2.3 Trade policy

India's trade policy regime was highly complex until the early 1990s. Protective measures have taken three forms: tariff barriers that limit imports, non-tariff quantitative restrictions (QRs) and outright prohibition of imports. There were also various categories of importers, import licences and methods of importing. As much as 93 per cent of India's local production of internationally tradable goods was still protected by some type of QRs on imports in 1990/91. The export and import (EXIM) policy in effect from 1992 to 1997, significantly reduced trade restrictions and liberalized the import of capital goods and raw materials. The 1991 economic reforms also made a break from the earlier approach by replacing the positive-list approach of listing licence free items on the open general licence (OGL) with a negative-list approach. However quantitative restrictions, including import-licensing requirements, were maintained on a number of products on balance-of-payments grounds. These items were listed in the 'negative list' of imports in India's official Export and Import Policy (EXIM Policy). Items in the negative list were highly regulated and fell into three broad categories: banned or prohibited items; restricted items requiring an import licence, and 'canalized' items, that could be imported only by government trading monopolies. The import licences were non-automatic in nature and were also subject to other conditions such as limited coverage (for instance, the special import licence included 10 per cent of the HS lines, subject to restrictions) and an 'actual user' stipulation. The major changes included an expansion of the list of products eligible for import under special licences.

Although the 1991 reforms first did away with import licensing on virtually all intermediate and capital goods, consumer goods, which accounted for nearly 30 per cent of the tariff lines, remained subject to import licensing (WTO, 1996). The government's view was that Indian exports were subject to supply constraints, and thus unresponsive to price changes resulting from altering the exchange rate. Essential imports were similarly considered price-inelastic, but 'luxury' imports were not. Given that the import basket would contain some of both, it was argued that the targeted QR system was the most efficient way of managing large volumes of luxury imports. In this respect the QR regime operated successfully to discourage imports of a number of products such as meat, fish, cereals, malt and starches, cocoa, chocolate, nuts, fruit juices, wine, beer spirits and vinegar. It was only after a successful challenge by the United States and others at the WTO dispute settlement body (DSB) that these goods were released from QRs in two phases, culminating in April 2001.

7.2.4 Tariff policy

One element of the trade liberalization was the lowering of import tariffs. In 1990/91, the highest tariff stood at 355 per cent, with a simple average of 113 per cent and the import-weighted average of tariff lines of 87 per cent. This was further reduced to 71 per cent in 1993/94 and to 41 per cent in 1995/96. The average applied rate remained at 17 per cent in 2004, and is expected to be further lowered. Import tariffs were reduced gradually by lowering the top tariff rates while rationalizing the tariff structure through a reduction in the number of tariff bands. By 1992/93, the applied rates for protective tariffs and total imports had fallen to 33 per cent and 38 per cent respectively.

India's economic reforms in the 1990s continued to focus on the manufacturing sector. In Uruguay Round (UR) of multilateral trade negotiations, India increased its binding coverage in industrial goods to 69.8 per cent of its tariff lines, from 6 per cent.

Notwithstanding trade liberalization, India still has high tariffs compared with the rest of the world. Some two per cent of the tariff lines have peak rates of duty. Examples include edible oils, alcoholic beverages and motor vehicles. The structure is also characterized by tariff peaks and tariff escalation. The average MFN tariff rates, during 2001/02 for raw materials, semi-manufactured and finished goods were 23.6 per cent, 32.4 per cent and 31.4 per cent respectively.

7.2.5 Policy measures for encouraging exports

While the pre-reform period was characterized by policies that promoted import substitution, important initiatives have subsequently been introduced to promote exports. Motivated by the success of China's special economic zones (SEZs) and the Shannon Free Trade Zone in Ireland, among others, the government of India introduced SEZs under its Export-Import Policy of 2000. Since then, the establishment of 12 SEZs has been approved. In addition, some of the existing export processing zones are expected to be converted into SEZs. This new policy aims to provide an internationally competitive environment for exports.

In a major initiative to boost export-led growth, the new five-year Foreign Trade Policy of 2004–2009 lifted all quantitative restrictions on exports, and announced additional incentives for SEZs as well as schemes such as the Duty Entitlement Pass Book (DEPB), advance licensing, and Export Promotion Capital Goods (EPCG). The policy also provides an incentive package for the computer hardware sector and simplifies procedures to reduce transaction costs, besides adopting a new commodity classification for imports and exports.

7.2.6 Medium-term export strategy, 2002–2007

The Medium Term Export Strategy (MTES) of the Department of Commerce forms part of the government's Tenth Five Year Plan. Its principle aim is to increase India's share of world exports from 0.8 per cent in 2002 to 1 per cent by 2007, which implies a substantial growth in export volumes from current levels. Among the many recommended policy changes designed to achieve this goal, the MTES includes criteria for judging the usefulness to India of non-WTO trade agreements, be they bilateral or regional (see Box 7.1).

Box 7.1: India and regional trade arrangements

India is a member of four different regional groupings. The oldest is the Bangkok Agreement, signed in 1975, and comprising Bangladesh, China, India, the Lao People's Democratic Republic, the Republic of Korea and Sri Lanka. Under this arrangement, India provides tariff concessions averaging about 5 per cent below MFN rates on 188 products at the HS 6-digit level.

India is also a member of the South Asian Association for Regional Cooperation (SAARC), a regional grouping of seven countries. This association signed the South Asian Preferential Trade Agreement (SAPTA) in 1993. India's concessions under this agreement are considerably greater than those in the Bangkok Agreement: concessions of between 5 and 10 per cent were granted to SAPTA signatories on 2,565 tariff lines at the HS 6-digit level.

A third regional arrangement is the Bangladesh, India, Myanmar, Sri Lanka, Thailand Economic Cooperation (BIMST-EC), a forum established in 1997 aimed at trade and investment facilitation. It was originally conceived as a way to link SAFTA (South Asian Free Trade Area) and the Association of South-East Asian Nations (ASEAN). Members signed a framework agreement in 2004, and it is intended to become a free trade agreement (FTA) in its own right at some time in the future (http://commerce.nic.in/india_rta.htm#b6).

The Indian Ocean Rim Agreement for Regional Cooperation (IOR-ARC) is a fourth group in which India is involved.

India also participates in bilateral trade agreements or transit arrangements with eight partners, all of which are on or in close proximity to the subcontinent. Two other major initiatives include India's framework agreements with the Southern Common Market (MERCOSUR) involving Brazil, Argentina, Paraguay and Uruguay; and the declaration of intent for a comprehensive economic cooperation agreement with Singapore. Initiatives with ASEAN and Thailand include provisions to negotiate trade in goods, services and investment, and 'other areas of cooperation' such as trade facilitation. The India-Thai framework agreement was scheduled to be concluded by March 2005 and the time frame for a full FTA in normal track goods is set at 2010. The ASEAN negotiations are due to be fully concluded by 2007 and the time frames for the completion of sensitive and normal track reductions are set at 2011 and 2016.

Source: UNCTAD.

7.2.7 Anti-dumping – a reversal of trade liberalization?

With the removal of QRs, tariffs and trade defence measures remain the main policy instruments to protect the domestic industry from any surge in imports and unfair trade practices. Concerns have been expressed that increasing resort by India to anti-dumping and safeguard actions has reversed the process of trade liberalization. Given India's imposition of certain taxes, in addition to applicable customs duty on imports, its continued commitment to trade liberalization could be called into question.

With the reduction of tariffs and the removal of QRs, India began resorting to anti-dumping beginning in 1994, and by current statistics it is one of the three most active users of this instrument in the world. While anti-dumping actions could have adverse economic consequences, what is material is not the number of such actions, but the impact, measured in terms of the fall in value of imports consequent to the filing of an anti-dumping action and any resultant trade diversion (Tianshu Chu and Prusa, 2004). In the absence of any study regarding the extent of trade affected by India's anti-dumping actions, it may be difficult to conclude that trade liberalization is indeed being reversed by such action. Furthermore, since 2004 India's rate of use of anti-dumping actions has slowed down.

India has also initiated 18 safeguard actions since then, although some of these actions did not result in the imposition of safeguard duties, reflecting a cautious and measured approach on the part of the government. No safeguard duty is currently being levied by the government of India. Thus the resort to safeguard measures by India may not have reversed the process of trade liberalization.

An increase in average tariffs during the period 1998/99–2001/02 was due to the protective import taxes levied on top of customs duties: initially a 'special duty', then a 'surcharge' and later a 'special additional duty'. These additional duties have now been abolished. It is also reported that tariffs on a few products increased, further to Article XXVIII of the General Agreement on Tariffs and Trade (GATT). This was mainly because of the elimination of QRs and the consequent introduction of certain tariff barriers in their place. For instance, the tariffs on tea, coffee, coconut and desiccated coconut were raised from 35 per cent to 70 per cent. On the whole, there has not been any marked departure from the general direction towards liberalization aimed at reducing the tariffs to ASEAN levels by 2010.

7.3 The development impact of trade liberalization

After growing at the so-called 'Hindu-rate' of growth of 3.6 per cent during the 30 years between 1950 and 1980, India's GDP growth accelerated to 5.6 per cent in the 1980s; and in the period 1992/93–2003/04 it averaged an unprecedented 6 per cent. Per capita income rose from Rs.464 in 1990/91 to Rs.842 in 2001/02.[1] There has been an appreciable improvement in the basic indicators of human development (such as life expectancy, literacy and infant mortality rates). A time-series-based regression analysis of per capita income (PCI) has shown that the PCI has consistently recorded higher growth during the post-reform period as compared to the pre-reform period. Most of the variables that affect PCI have also shown a higher contribution to it during the post-reform period, including the growth of per capita consumer expenditure.

According to NSS data, poverty head-count ratios have been declining both in the rural and urban areas, but more sharply in the urban areas, as expected. In the rural areas, per capita consumption expenditure of the lowest 20 per cent of the population has risen, from Rs.91 in 1987/88 to Rs.325 in 2002. In the urban areas, the corresponding figures are Rs.123 and Rs.491. This shows the overall positive effects of reforms (Chaturvedi and Upadhyay, 2004). However, in the initial period of economic reforms poverty may have increased marginally. Inter-state poverty differentials may have been widening during the post-reform period, not on account of growth, but rather because of changes in the redistribution policies and human capital development.

However, while the standard of living of the population as a whole has improved, the incomes of the educated and those in the knowledge-based industries have increased much faster, leading to a worsening of the Gini coefficient from 0.3 in 1991 to 0.33. in 2003. According to the World Bank (Deolalikar, 2005), India in the 1990s showed high poverty reduction, high growth and rising inequality. Several studies on India and other economies have confirmed this (see, for example, Wu, 1999; and Tsui, 1996).

The head-count ratio[2] of poverty and consumption appear to positively link trade and growth with poverty reduction; the states with a higher share of exports have also shown higher rates of decline in poverty. However, employment indicators show the reverse trend. To reconcile these divergent trends, one explanation could be that trade liberalization and consequent growth have generated a large informal sector, the employment and incomes of which may have gone unrecorded. Thus employment figures may underestimate the actual levels of employment (Jha et al., 2005). Further, export growth has been mainly in capital-intensive sectors.

7.3.1 Savings and investment

Riding high on the booming economy and growing attractiveness of India as an investment destination, foreign institutional investments in the country exceed $9 billion in 2004, the highest in the history of the Indian capital markets. This, together with other capital inflows, boosted the foreign exchange reserves by nearly $20 billion. Foreign direct investment also increased, to $4.5 billion in 2004, from an average of $3.5 billion throughout the 1990s.

There has been a noticeable shortfall in public investment during the late 1990s and early 2000s. Savings accounted for almost 24 per cent of GDP in 2003 (Government of India, 2004). However the Planning Commission of India (2004) has noted that private investment in India is still not sufficiently robust to sustain the estimated annual rate of growth of 6.5 per cent. It had projected public investment to grow to around 33.5 per cent of total investments, which would have made up for the shortfall in private investment. However, it is estimated that, contrary to these expectations, the share of public investment during the Ninth Plan period (1997–2002) declined even below its level of the previous period. The current rate of investment is about 25.2 per cent. These figures indicate that raising investment resources will be an important concern for the Indian economy.

7.3.2 Sectoral distribution of GDP

India's economic growth has been characterized by a decline in the share of agriculture in GDP and an increase in the shares of industry and services. Between 1950 and 2001, the share of agriculture fell from 58 per cent to 25 per cent, while that of industry increased from 15 per cent to 26 per cent, and the share of services increased from 27 per cent to 49 per cent.

7.3.3 Impact on industrial growth

Overall, the manufacturing sector has grown following liberalization, but it continues to account for only about 27 per cent of India's GDP. Available evidence suggests that while the 1980s saw import-competing industries gaining importance over export-promoting industries, the opposite trend occurred in the 1990s.

An examination of the registered manufacturing sector, according to a use-based classification at the three-digit level, shows that labour-intensive industries diminished in importance during the 1980s and 1990s, although most of the change occurred during the period 1980/81–1988/89. The share of resource-intensive industries showed a marginal increase during the first half of the period, but thereafter decreased. Scale-intensive industries grew in importance throughout the period, accounting for 41 per cent of manufacturing output by 1996/97.

Five subsectors – beverages and tobacco, textile products, leather and leather products, chemicals and chemical products, and rubber, plastics, petroleum and coal – benefited from the reforms, with steady growth even after the onset of recession in 1997/98. Most of the traditional manufacturing and capital goods industries experienced declining growth trends after 1997/98. However, the economy revived after 2002, and, as stated earlier, exports increased continuously at an average rate of over 20 per cent per annum throughout the post-liberalization period.

7.3.4 Foreign trade

India's share of world exports fell from 2.2 per cent in 1948 to 0.5 per cent in 1983. However, over the past 20 years, exports plus imports have grown by over 600 per cent with the most dramatic changes in foreign trade flows taking place since 2000 – the period known as the second phase of trade reforms – following the removal of quantitative restrictions.

India has diversified its exports and imports, but still relies largely on traditional sectors such as textiles, gems and jewellery, and chemicals, despite expectations of a recovery of the manufacturing sector. In 2002/03 there was an increase in agriculture and allied products, while 2003/04 saw an upswing in leather and manufactures, complemented by a strong upsurge in ores and minerals, and engineering goods. However, slower growth in exports was recorded due the bottlenecks caused by policy change in prices, limited stocks and poor infrastructure, all of which resulted in a decline in exports of primary products, iron ore and marine products. Nevertheless, the volume of exports and imports doubled between 1998 and 2003.

The growth of exports of non-factor services, accompanied by large inflows of private transfers, has been responsible for bringing the trade account out of deficit. There has been a steady upward trend in non-factor services since 2000/01. Under non-factor services, miscellaneous services is the largest contributor, of which software services have emerged as the second largest item in the invisible receipts. Earnings from software services exports amounted to $9 billion in the first three quarters of 2003/04, representing a 72 per cent increase over earnings for the same time period in 2002/03; there was a 50 per cent increase in the first quarter of 2004/2005. Its highly skilled labour force in this sector gives India a comparative advantage. Apart from the miscellaneous services, travel and transportation also experienced a major upswing in the first three quarters of 2003/04.

7.3.5 Balance of payments

Under the reforms, India's balance-of-payments situation has improved considerably. The deficit in the invisible account in the early 1990s became a surplus as the market-determined exchange rate of the rupee encouraged inward remittances through legal channels. The increased foreign currency assets of India's central bank, the Reserve Bank of India (RBI), which stood at $46.5 billion in January 2002, reflect the steep fall in the current-account deficit as well as large net capital inflows. The composition of these inflows has changed significantly towards equity and away from debt. External assistance, external commercial borrowing, IMF loans, and non-resident Indian (NRI) deposits declined progressively, from 85.8 per cent of net capital inflows in 1990/91 to 40 per cent in 1993/94 and to a further 23 per cent in 1999/00. The debt–GDP ratio declined steadily from its high of 38.7 per cent in March 1992 to 21 per cent at the end of September 2001.

7.3.6 Employment

The total labour force in India is around 406 million. Between the years 1991 and 2001, 65 to 70 per cent of the workforce was engaged in agriculture (National Census 2001), but just under 1 million workers are moving out of the agriculture sector every year. However, the organized industry and services sectors account for only 27 million jobs, of which just 7 million are in the services sector. It is estimated that the organized services sector has generated 760,000 new jobs over the past decade, while employment in organized manufacturing has remained almost unchanged, with only 350,000 new jobs created between 1993/94 and 1999/2000. Growth in total manufacturing employment (organized and unorganized) in India averaged only about 2 per cent a year during the period 1994–2000, the unorganized sector accounting for the bulk of this growth.

Although the effects of tariff cuts on employment are difficult to establish, it is believed that tariff liberalization contributed to dramatic productivity increases leading to long-term efficiency gains (Pandey, 2004), as discussed later.

The services sector has acted as a buffer to the slack in industrial and agricultural growth and employment. Thus, in spite of declining trends in the overall growth rate of employment, both organized and unorganized sectors, services sectors such as electricity, gas and water supply, real estate and insurance provided the required replacement employment. This has resulted in an overall positive trend in both organized and unorganized employment growth rates (albeit slower than in the previous decade).

7.3.7 Attaining the United Nations Millennium Development Goals

India is one of the few countries on track for reducing poverty, and is also likely to achieve the target for enrolment in primary education and access to water resources. However, there are several areas of concern. A detailed analysis of the attainment of the five major human-development-related Millennium Development Goals (MDGs) – child and infant mortality, child malnutrition, school enrolment and completion, gender disparities in schooling, and hunger (reflected in inadequate calorie intake) – by states and local authorities in India reveals some important facts (World Bank, 2003). There are very large disparities across different states and regions, with the indicators being much worse for the northern states – Bihar, Uttar Pradesh, Orissa, Rajasthan and Madhya Pradesh – than for the southern and western states. The attainment of the MDGs will be challenging for the northern states and yet critical if the country as a whole is to succeed in attaining the MDG targets. There is significant regional inequality of development, and underdevelopment has tended to be disproportionately concentrated in certain pockets. Expenditure on education and health, in particular, will have to be optimally managed and the quality of such spending improved if the country as a whole is to attain the various MDGs.

Overall, in the post-reform period, wages do not appear to be increasing and the wage share in value-added has declined. Evidence on productivity in manufacturing appears to be mixed. Some researchers (Srivatava, 2001; Kumari, 2001; Das 1999) believe that the growth of total factor productivity (TFP) in the manufacturing sector was higher during the 1980s than in the post-reform period of the 1990s. On the other hand a study by Unel (2003), suggests that total factor productivity growth in Indian manufacturing accelerated after the 1991 economic reforms. The evidence also seems to suggest that labour productivity in unorganized manufacturing industry showed an overall growth rate of 4.76 per cent during the period 1994–2001 (Pandey, 2004). This increase in labour productivity, in the unorganized manufacturing sector, in conjunction with the overall annual growth rate in the output of capital goods of over 9 per cent in the 1980s and 1990s, suggests a move towards increased capitalization of Indian manufacturing. This conclusion is reinforced by the fact that profitability in the manufacturing sector has also risen, though the share of labour in total value added has fallen.

7.4 Possible effects on Indian industry of further trade liberalization under NAMA

At the WTO Ministerial Meeting in Doha (2001), it was agreed to launch negotiations to cut tariffs and reduce non-tariff barriers on all non-agricultural products. The Framework Agreement on Non-Agricultural

Market Access (NAMA) negotiations, part of the July Package, outlined the 'initial elements for future work on modalities'.

The Global Trade Analysis Project (GTAP) model has been used to examine the possible effects of a 25 per cent cut in applied tariffs for all countries across the board. It was also assumed in a second simulation that all the countries/regions completely eliminate tariffs on imports of minerals n.e.c., textiles, wearing apparel, leather, leather products and footwear, wood and paper products, chemical, rubber and plastic products, metals n.e.c., and manufactures n.e.c. multilaterally.

Under the assumption that all countries reduce tariffs by 25 per cent, India's welfare is estimated to increase by $2.6 billion, and by $3.5 billion when countries eliminate completely their tariffs on selected industrial goods. However, it is estimated that India's gains from liberalization would be much higher in the sectoral liberalization scenario, when trade is expected to expand by nearly 20 per cent.[3]

The terms of trade for India turn negative under both scenarios, as after the reduction in tariffs, India's exports become more competitive than its imports. India's exports and imports increase by $3.5 billion and $4.5 billion, respectively, under the 25 per cent cuts, and by much more (i.e. $9.4 billion and $11.7 billion respectively) under the sectoral elimination. The real returns to skilled labour and capital also show an improvement.

Under the 25 per cent global tariff cut the exports of all the sectors register a positive increase. Sectors such as mining and quarrying, wearing apparel, metal n.e.c., manufacturing n.e.c., electronic equipment, and machinery and equipment register an increase of over 10 per cent. Mining and quarrying exports increase by as much as 45 per cent. This could be because of improved comparative advantage and a higher demand for raw materials due to tariff reductions, as well as a low initial base. Where there is also sectoral tariff elimination on a multilateral basis exports increase for almost all sectors, particularly for textiles and wearing apparel, chemical and rubber products, metals, electronic equipment, and machinery and equipment.

Under the 25 per cent tariff cut, the output of sectors such as textiles and wearing apparel expands; the activity level in the remaining sectors marginally changes. Nine out of 19 sectors see a decline in output, which, as explained above, reflects immiserizing export growth. In the sectoral elimination scenario, it is estimated that there would be an increased output of the order of: textiles −5.6 per cent, wearing apparel −32.5 per cent, electronic equipment −7.9 per cent, motor vehicle and transportation equipment −3.3 per cent, metals and metal products −2.8 per cent, and machinery and equipment −7.3 per cent. Significant falls in output are seen in other metals and other manufacturing.

The gains in output and labour use for textiles and wearing apparel under both simulations appear significant. As these gains are likely to accrue over a broad initial base, tariff liberalization in this sector under the NAMA could provide an overall balance for India.

NAMA negotiations would not be trade neutral or universally beneficial to India. In the worst-case scenario, it is clear that India would gain in some sectors and lose in others. Production of raw materials would decline, while that of finished products is likely to increase, with a few exceptions. Overall, a sectoral negotiation framework is likely to generate greater gains for India. Therefore, even if sectoral negotiations do not take place, India's negotiating strategy should focus on peak tariff reductions in sectors of interest to it. The choice of sectors should not be determined merely by considerations of which ones would benefit from an increase in exports; other variables, such as output and employment, should also guide India's negotiating strategy. Overall, the effects of future tariff cuts are likely to be more significant for India than the entire period of trade reforms.

7.5 Conclusions

Has India become worse off after the reforms? Since the start of the reforms, the growth of GNP and per capita GNP has been higher than in the pre-reform period and poverty has declined, but income disparity has also widened. The economy seems to have acquired a remarkable degree of resilience; it has not only withstood supply shocks but also coped with both domestic and external shocks with minimal adverse consequences. Moreover, a foundation has been laid, particularly in the financial and external sectors, for accelerated growth.

Though the pre-reform era and the initial years of the reform period were characterized as one of 'export pessimism', in the light of significant export growth in recent years there is a general air of optimism concerning India's export performance. Exports recorded a growth rate of 24 per cent in 2004/05. Ways are being considered to improve the export growth rate, such as leveraging the growing imports to push exports by working out quid pro quo arrangements for market access. Free trade agreements being negotiated with a large number of key trading partners could also have a major impact. Agreements being negotiated with groupings such as the ASEAN, the Gulf States and various Latin American countries might also help increase India's integration into the global economy. Growing exports have helped progressively reduce the current-account deficit in recent years, turning it into a modest surplus in 2001/02. While these developments reflect the success of external sector management, they must be regarded as transient in the context of a developing country aspiring for higher rates of growth, given its traditional resource constraints.

There do not appear to have been significant adjustment costs in the post-liberalization era. Scale-intensive industries have grown in significance, while the importance of labour-intensive industries has diminished. Overall, the efficiency of firms may have improved, but the effect of export intensity on firm efficiency has been mixed. Wages, as a proportion of total value added, have fallen for all manufacturing because of increased capitalization and use of higher technologies, attributable to the lowering of tariffs on capital goods. It could also be because of more rapid growth of the informal sector and increased casualization of labour. However, the counterfactual, in terms of a reduction in the head-count ratio of poverty, suggests that the informal sector absorbed unemployed labour, thus contributing to a reduction in poverty, even though inequalities may have increased. This in turn suggests the need for poverty alleviation programmes, rural employment schemes and carefully sequenced trade liberalization, particularly in the textiles and garments sector, in response to future challenges.

The outcome of the WTO NAMA negotiations is difficult to predict while a formula remains to be agreed. However, the estimates suggest that the effects of future tariff cuts are likely to be more significant for India than the impact of roughly 15 years of trade: the GTAP analysis shows that 8 out of 18 sectors could experience a fall in output and labour use. India's negotiating strategy should focus on peak tariff reductions in sectors of interest to it. The choice of sectors should not be determined merely by those that will benefit from increased exports; variables such as output and employment should also guide India's negotiating strategy. As gains in the textiles and garments sector are likely to accrue over a broad initial base, tariff liberalization in this sector could provide the overall balance, if any, to India under any of the possible outcomes of the NAMA negotiations.

Managing further trade adjustment would require a comprehensive set of domestic safety nets. An example is the proposed National Rural Employment Guarantee Act which promises to guarantee 100 days of employment to every household. It could bring enormous rural welfare benefits and go a long way in reducing rural underemployment, an important contributing factor in rural poverty. The programme involves the development of infrastructure, which has recently been neglected, thereby playing a crucial role in regenerating the rural economy. The revival of rural employment opportunities would also reduce migration to urban centres, and help ease problems in those areas.

Finally, the pace of India's reforms has been slower than advocated by many pro-reform economists who favour gradualism over shock therapy, but this is attributable not so much to a conscious choice as to the country's democratic political process, which demands consensus that is slow to build. In one area – capital account convertibility – India has deliberately chosen to move slowly, and even many pro-globalization and pro-reform economists have explicitly advocated such a pace. Growth since 1992/93 has been more robust, with foreign exchange reserves crossing the $140 billion mark. According to some economists, reforms have not failed India; instead, India has failed to reform enough. If it were to undertake deeper and faster reforms without giving up its essentially gradualist approach, India might well be able to push the growth rate up to double-digit levels.[4]

Notes

1 Data reported by the National Sample Survey (NSS), 2003.
2 The head-count ratio is computed on the basis of National Sample Survey (NSS) data on consumption expenditure; people with an income below the poverty line are 'poor', and the proportion of the poor to the aggregate population is the head-count ratio.
3 For details, see Jha (2005).
4 A. Panagariya, *Financial Times,* 31 December 2003.

References

Chaturvedi, Arvind and Upadhyay, V. (2004) India's economic reforms: impact on poverty, Paper presented at the 18th European Conference on Modern South Asian Studies (6–9 July 2004) at University of Lund, Sweden.

Das, D. (1999) Productivity growth in Indian manufacturing: an application of Domer Aggregation, presented at the Workshop on Measurement of Productivity in India, Institute of Human Development, New Delhi, 9–10 July.

Deolalikar, A. B. (2005) Attaining the Millennium Development Goals in India: reducing infant mortality, child malnutrition, gender disparities and hunger-poverty and increasing school enrollment and completion, Oxford University Press for the World Bank.

Government of India, Economic Survey of India (2004).

Jha, Veena, Gupta, S., Nedumpara, J. and Karthikeyan, K. (2005) *Trade Liberalization and Poverty in India,* Macmillan India.

Kumari, A. (2001) Productivity growth in Indian engineering industries during pre-reform and post-reform period: an analysis at company level, in *Proceedings Examining Ten Years of Economic Reforms in India,* Canberra, Australia: ANU.

Ministry of Finance, Government of India, Economic Survey 2004–05.

Pandey, M. (2004) Impact of trade liberalisation in manufacturing industry in India in the 1980s and 1990s, ICRIER Working Paper No. 140.

Planning Commission of India (2004) Approach to the Mid-term Appraisal of the Tenth Plan 2002–07.

Srivatava, V. (2001) The impact of India's economic reforms on industrial productivity, efficiency and competitiveness: a panel study of Indian companies 1980–97, New Delhi: National Council of applied Economic Research.

Stiglitz, Joseph (April 2003) *Globalisation and its Discontents,* New York: W.W. Norton & Co.

Tianshu, Chu and Prusa, Thomas J. (April 2004) 'The reasons for and the impact of antidumping protection: the case of People's Republic of China' East West Centre Working Paper, http://www.eastwestcenter.org/stored/pdfs/ECONwp069.pdf

Tsui, Kai Yuen (1996) Economic reforms and inter-provincial inequalities in China, *Journal of Development Economics,* 50(2), August.

Unel, B. (2003) Productivity trends in India's manufacturing sector in the last two decades, IMF working paper WP/03/02; Unel (2003) has concluded that total factor productivity (TFP) growth in Indian manufacturing accelerated after the 1991 economic reforms.

WTO (1996) Committee of Balance of Payment Restrictions, Report on the Consultation with India, WT/BOP/R/11 23 January.

Wu, Yanrui (1999) *Income Inequality and Convergence in China's Regional Economies,* University of Western Australia.

8
Jamaica

Michael Witter

8.1 Introduction and overview of the country

Jamaica is a small island economy with a population of approximately 2.6 million. Per capita income is estimated at $2,171 in 2001. Real GDP has been growing only moderately after some 20 years of reforms, reaching 1.7 per cent a year in 2001. Services is now the dominant sector in the economy, making up some 63 per cent of GDP, while industry contributes 31 per cent and agriculture 6 per cent.

Jamaica has a relatively well-educated workforce, but also has an emigration rate of over 20,000 people a year. Their remittances make an important contribution to the balance of payments. In September 2004, the government received the report of a task force on educational reform, *A Transformed Education System*, that was commissioned in response to mounting criticism of the education system and the weak performance of many of its graduates. The low rate of output of top quality graduates together with the high migration rate will inevitably constrain economic growth and the development process in an era when knowledge has become so crucial to economic success. Despite progress, there is widespread concern about the high level of illiteracy.

Up to the Second World War, the Jamaican economy was based primarily on agriculture, organized around large British-owned plantations, oriented to the production of food for the domestic market and sugar and bananas for export to the United Kingdom. The other subsector of agriculture comprised small farmers, located mainly in the mountainous interior, who produced primarily foodstuffs for the domestic market, but they also began coffee and banana production, which became important exports carried out by a multinational: Elders and Fyffes.

In the 1950s, an economic development strategy was developed that aimed at the promotion of industrialization through State incentives offered to investors, particularly foreign investors.[1] This strategy succeeded in stimulating the highest economic growth rates on record: more than 7 per cent per annum.

Jamaica gained political independence in 1962 when the process of diversification of the economy was well under way, with rapidly growing mineral (bauxite and alumina), manufacturing, construction and tourism sectors. Demand for aluminium by the United States military and space programmes and by the automobile and other consumer goods industries created a lucrative market for bauxite and alumina. Tourism, originally at the high end of the market, also began diversifying steadily as a result of the post-war growth in household incomes in the United States.

There was a decade of rapid economic growth throughout 1962–1972, but at a slower rate (5–6 per cent) than in the 1950s. There was mounting pressure for social reform from sections of the working class whose expectations of economic opportunities following the end of colonial rule remained unrealized. At the same time, the investment cycle of the multinational bauxite mining companies, the main driving force behind the growth of the economy, began tapering off as the decade of the 1960s drew to a close.[2]

The 1970s has come to be seen as a watershed in the history of the Jamaican economy because of the government's attempts to chart an alternative path to economic development[3] in its bid to redress the colonial legacy of social inequalities. A central element of its development strategy was an increasing role for the State as a senior partner in an alliance with local and foreign private business interests. However, the record of Jamaica's economic performance during this decade was poor. In the minds of the majority of Jamaican voters in 1980, the perceived economic failures of the 1970s, together with the fear of violence induced by the sharp ideological struggles, outweighed the gains in social policy. Consequently, they elected a new government committed to a free market, export-led approach to economic development.

Following this economic and political re-orientation, real GDP grew at an average annual rate of 1.5 per cent from 1981 to 2001, and real GDP per capita grew at an average annual rate of 0.5 per cent. The first period (1981–1986) and the last period (1996–2001) recorded the slowest growth, and per capita GDP declined.

However, despite the weak growth record, the unemployment rate was almost halved, declining from 27 per cent to 15 per cent, over the two decades, 1980–2000. Productivity, as measured by the GDP per employed person, increased in the 1980s, but declined in the 1990s (WTO, 2004), with a net marginal gain over the two decades reviewed.

International trade and payments

Given its narrow production base, Jamaica has been dependent on a narrow range of primary product exports sold in the United Kingdom, the United States, and a few other developed-country markets. Bauxite and alumina replaced sugar and bananas as the leading exports after the Second World War, but since the 1980s tourism has become the leading gross foreign exchange earner.

In the last 20 years, the ratio of imports of goods and services to GDP rose sharply, indicating that Jamaica has been buying more goods and services on the international market than it has been selling. Without a large reserve account (savings) to draw upon, the relative rise in imports could only be financed by external debt. Indeed, the principal features of the Jamaican balance of payments in the reform period are the growth of the current-account deficit, enhanced inflows of private investment, and inflows of government loans.

The increase in the merchandise trade deficit since 1999 is mainly explained by the rise in oil prices. However, there has also been a deterioration in prices for Jamaica's two main export commodities (alumina and sugar) on the one hand, and (imported) oil, as well as a contraction of apparel exports.

Over the last two decades, both the surplus on the services account and the current transfers, particularly the inflow of remittances, grew, but together they were not large enough to offset the burgeoning trade deficit. As a result, the current account has experienced a growing deficit since the middle of the 1990s reaching the $1 billion mark in 2003.

The deficit has been partly financed by the rapid growth of private investment inflows (primarily in bauxite mining and alumina processing, information technology and communications, and agriculture, manufacturing and distribution) (WTO, 2004) in the form of FDI and portfolio investment in search of interest rate differentials. During much of the 1990s, private capital inflows were so robust that the government was able to build up its reserves, while the high interest rates attracted capital inflows, they also discouraged investment in productive activity, especially the production of exportable goods and services.

The other source of financial inflows has been government loans. The government of Jamaica borrowed heavily throughout the 1990s, both internationally and domestically, resulting in the domestic debt exceeding the external debt. Almost all of the external borrowing was market loans, with the proceeds being used to build up net international reserves. The debt burden in 2004 exceeded 145 per cent of GDP, but the government's ability to maintain primary budget surpluses of 12–15 per cent for several years has kept investors relatively confident in its capacity to service its debt.

8.2 Trade liberalization

8.2.1 Process of trade liberalization

The process of trade liberalization began with the stabilization programmes of the IMF in the late 1970s, and accelerated in the 1980s with the structural adjustment programmes advocated by the World Bank. Between 1977 and 1990, Jamaica signed eight agreements with the IMF and six with the World Bank. In the 1980s too, the loan programmes of the United States Agency for International Development (USAID) played a supporting role to the IMF and the World Bank by way of cross-conditionalities of its financial assistance programmes that were enshrined in what was called the tripartite approach (1987) to Jamaica's adjustment process. In the 1990s, the trade liberalization process continued with reform of the common external tariff (CET) of the CARICOM, pressure to comply with the WTO's international trade regime, the restructuring of trade relations with Europe embodied in the Cotonou Agreement (the successor to Lomé IV), and the commitments made in the context of the process to establish a Free Trade Area of the Americas (FTAA). In Jamaica's case, the process of trade liberalization was complemented by far-reaching financial liberalization undertaken in 1991 in the context of a loan programme with the Inter-American Development Bank (IDB).

Because of the context in which trade liberalization proceeded, it is difficult to separate its impact from the impact of fiscal reform, financial liberalization, exchange rate policy and divestment of public enterprises. Indeed, it may well be that the demand management policies that constituted the stabilization programmes of the IMF, with the support of the World Bank, raised the price of imports through the devaluation of the Jamaican dollar while reducing the purchasing power of Jamaicans. In this way, there was no surge of imports following the lowering of trade barriers. What is more, the fall in prices of Jamaica's traditional exports, particularly bauxite and alumina, led to a decline in the ratio of trade to GDP, the most common indicator of the openness of an economy. This was exacerbated by the mounting difficulties for sugar and banana exports in a liberalized international trade regime that saw the withdrawal of the preferential access to European markets for goods from the African Caribbean and Pacific (ACP) group of countries.

8.2.2 Liberalization measures

Imports

1982–1984: Prior to 1982, the trend towards more managed trade was stopped by the conditions set under two IMF loans of the late 1970s. The first positive effort to liberalize trade came in 1982 as a condition for World Bank financing.[4] The government removed a large number of items (180) from the Restricted Imports List, and eventually abolished import licensing and quota requirements on all but a small number of items. Except for CARICOM imports, a new system of tariffs was imposed. The process of liberalization was projected to begin with the substitution of the equivalent tariffs for quantitative restrictions. King and Handa (2000) have argued that this stage of the process frustrated the intent of trade liberalization. The full process was succinctly articulated by Rajapatirana (1995): 'Trade liberalization involves the replacement of quantitative restrictions with tariffs, reduction of those tariffs to lower protection, reduction of the variance in protection across activities and increasing the transparency of trade policy making.'

1987–1991: Prior to 1987, import substitution was supported by 'high tariff rates, stamp duties imposed on top of the tariffs, a wide array of non-tariff restrictions, complex customs procedures, and a large number of exceptions to the general rules' (World Bank, 1994). The tariff reform programme of 1987–1991 sought to:

- Reduce the bureaucratic obstacles by simplifying the duty system and its administration, increase transparency, reduce the scope for discretionary actions
- Reduce the overall level of tariffs and rationalize the structure of protection by reducing the widely dispersed rates. (World Bank, 1994).

In *1991*, the import monopoly of the Jamaica Commodity Trading Company (JCTC).[5] was abolished. The JCTC had been established in 1981 with a monopoly on a wide range of basic goods, including food, cars, pharmaceuticals and energy. Profits from these items were used to subsidize agricultural imports. The World Bank had identified a number of inefficiencies associated with its operation, not the least of which was that the majority of the subsidies intended for the poor were benefiting the non-poor.

Also in 1991, the government began to aggressively implement the CET of CARICOM, reducing, thereby, the average level of import duties. Phase I of the reform of the CET reduced the tariffs from a range of 1–45 per cent to a range of 5–30 per cent between 1990 and 1993. The revision of the CET was an element in the CARICOM strategy of reducing production costs, stimulating efficiency, protecting sensitive industries and encouraging new types of production activities (ECLAC, 1999). Phase II was implemented in early 1995 (Phase III was skipped) and Phase IV in 1999.

King and Handa (2000) summarize the trade liberalization measures of the 1990s as follows:

> In 1990, the average tariff rate was 25 per cent (Table 8.1). The first tariff reduction exercise occurred in 1991 and reduced the average tariff to 22.1 per cent. More importantly, the exercise started a process of simplifying the tariff code to reduce the tariff dispersion. The estimated standard deviation of tariffs fell from 20.7 to 16.8 per cent at this time. The second round of liberalization in 1993 saw average tariffs reduced to 15.9 per cent, and with further simplification of the tariff code the standard deviation fell to 13.4 per cent. In 1995, another implementation dropped average tariffs to 14.0 per cent. Finally, by the last round, which was effected in 1999, the average was brought

Table 8.1: Average import tariffs, 1989–2002

Year	Average[a] import tariff (%)	Standard deviation of tariffs	Average[b] import tariff (%)
1989	25.0	20.7	n.a.
1990	25.0	20.7	n.a.
1991	22.1	16.8	20.3
1992	22.1	16.8	n.a.
1993	15.9	13.4	n.a.
1994	15.9	13.4	n.a.
1995	14.0	13.4	14.0
1996	14.0	13.4	20.8
1997	14.0	13.4	10.9
1998	11.8	14.7	9.7
1999	n.a.	n.a.	8.9
2000	n.a.	n.a.	10.6
2001	n.a.	n.a.	
2002	n.a.	n.a.	8.9

Sources: [a] King and Handa, 2000: 30, table 2. [b] World Bank, 2004: 144, fig. 7.1.

> to 11.9 per cent. Even with this, a fair amount of trade interference still persists since the dispersion of tariffs remains high, with some tariffs, particularly those on raw materials for manufacturing, at zero, while on some final goods that compete with domestic industries, the tariff is near to (and in a few cases above) 100 per cent.

Apart from tariff reductions, other measures have also been taken that facilitate trade. The government is implementing a trade facilitation project, begun in 1993, that seeks to upgrade the quality of the customs service so that it facilitates, rather than hinders, international trade. In 2002, the government started using actual import prices as the basis for customs valuation instead of the traditional reference price, a move that led to a reduction in import values in addition to making valuation more transparent (World Bank, 2004).

Exports

Liberalization of international trade regimes under the aegis of the WTO has reduced Jamaica's (and other ACP producers') preferential access to the European markets, especially for sugar and bananas (Myers, 2004), and further changes are expected along similar lines. The impact of these changes has not been as important to Jamaica's export earnings as movements in the price of aluminium, which determine the earnings from bauxite and alumina exports. There are other factors as well, such as the reaction of the multinational mining companies to the levy regime imposed by the government on production in 1974 and the adjustments in subsequent years; there was also a temporary loss of smelting capacity for Jamaican bauxite when Kaiser's Gramercy plant in Louisiana was damaged in 1999. Measures to liberalize international trade would have had little impact on Jamaica's mineral exports, since the sector had never been protected; it is therefore arguable that Jamaica became a more attractive investment prospect for the mining companies as a result of liberalization of the economy, and, in particular, the financial liberalization that removed exchange controls and controls on the movement of capital.

Like the bauxite and alumina sector, it was less trade liberalization and more the overall thrust to a market-driven economy that boosted investor confidence in the tourism sector.

There was some short-lived success in non-traditional manufacturing exports, primarily apparel, produced in the free zones. The World Bank (2004) noted: 'Favourable location, low labour costs, and strong government incentives initially allowed Jamaica to take advantage of opportunities under the US Caribbean Basin Economic Recovery (CBI) Act, attracting investors from Far-Eastern exporters.' However:

> the North American Free Trade Agreement (NAFTA), the emergence of new, low-wage competitors in Central America, and rising labour costs in Jamaica, together with negative developments in the market, combined to erode Jamaica's competitive position, resulting in a decline of the industry in the latter 1990s. Some 47 companies closed and/or relocated operations between 1996 and 2000, though during 1999, six plants became operational, including an expansion, with a total capital investment of US$2.5 million. Plant closures have reduced employment in the Apparel industry by 10,000 over the past 5 years, and by 2000, export of garments had declined to US$360.5 million, and US$289 million by 2001. (World Bank, 2004)

8.2.3 Absence of major reversals of the trade liberalization process

The trend of declining protection was interrupted by the imposition of 'additional stamp duties' on 'agricultural products, beverages, tobacco, and aluminium products' (World Bank, 2004).[6] Beyond the inefficiencies in implementing change, and attempts to slow down the process, especially with regard to agricultural products, there have been no deliberate attempts to reverse the liberalization process.

8.2.4 Financial liberalization

In 1990, as a complement to the trade liberalization, Jamaica began liberalization of the financial markets by licensing commercial banks to trade in foreign exchange and to hold foreign-currency-denominated deposits. The following year, exchange controls were eliminated. In return for promised balance-of-payments support from the IDB, the government also discontinued its policy of subsidizing interest rates for certain sectors of the economy, particularly agriculture, and eliminated other controls on the capital market. Financial liberalization made Jamaica more attractive to foreign investors and it also stimulated rapid growth of the financial sector in a speculative boom that inevitably imploded.

8.2.5 Implementation

In summary, trade liberalization was one of several policy changes that were implemented over two decades (1980 to 2000) in the context of the IMF stabilization programme and World Bank and IDB structural adjustment programmes, along with USAID balance-of-payments support funding to the government of Jamaica. Even with the change in policy orientation of the new government in 1980, there was initial resistance to rapid liberalization of the economy, and measures were implemented slowly and often not in the spirit of the commitments given in the various international agreements. It is arguable that other elements of the policy reform, particularly the stabilization programmes involving tight demand management and tight monetary policy, tended to counter the expected impact of trade liberalization on the balance of payments and on economic growth.

8.3 Economic impact of trade liberalization

8.3.1 Impact of trade liberalization on economic growth

The fastest growth of the last two decades was in the period 1986–1990, when the growth rate of GDP rose to a robust annual average of 5 per cent – very high growth by Jamaica's recent standards. This period was preceded by the first major trade liberalization programme (1982–1986), and occurred despite the severe damage wreaked by Hurricane Gilbert in 1988.[7] As mentioned earlier, Jamaica had entered into three IMF standby agreements and received two World Bank sectoral adjustment loans during the period, 1986–1990. Two of the principal factors accounting for the high growth rates were the growth of tourism and the sharp decline in oil prices. It is arguable that with a liberal import regime, the tourism sector was able to access imported supplies much more easily. Since it had always had priority access to imports, even during the period of tightest restrictions, the impact of trade liberalization measures per se on the tourism sector was probably not that great.

Throughout the 1990s the economy grew much more slowly. The decade began with the liberalization of the financial markets and, in particular, the foreign exchange market. Following a four-year speculative boom, the rapidly growing financial sector experienced a major crisis. The government opted to bail it out, and succeeded in doing so in record time, but at major costs, which reversed the gains made in the Government's finances in the previous years. 'The crisis, one of the largest in the world (in terms of GDP), was resolved relatively quickly and has led to significant improvement in regulation and supervision of the financial system but also to a huge increase in an already large public sector debt' (World Bank, 2004). On balance, the marginal movements of the GDP in the second half of the 1990s meant that the economy was virtually stagnant, but there was an indication that the declining growth trend was being reversed.

There are several reasons for the weak growth performance:

1. The rate of growth of GDP underestimates the actual growth of the economy because of the significant size of the informal economy. (The IDB, 2002, estimated the informal economy, excluding illegal activities such as the trade in illegal drugs, to be upwards of 40 per cent of GDP in 2001).
2. The stagnation in the 1990s was in part a consequence of the financial crisis of the mid-1990s 'and the consequent monetary tightening that left a massive, costly debt overhang' (World Bank, 2004). The crisis itself resulted from introducing financial liberalization without the appropriate regulatory mechanisms being put in place. In hindsight, the liberalization of the capital account appears to have been done in a hurry, without proper preparation. High interest rates attracted investment funds into government securities.
3. Negative international economic conditions affected in particular the bauxite/alumina and tourism sectors, on which the performance of the Jamaican economy critically depended.
4. As a result of capital inflows, attracted by the high interest rates, the real exchange rate was appreciating even as the nominal rate was depreciating for most of the period 1983–2000.
5. The rise in real wages after 1996 was yet another disincentive to export activities. There is ample evidence that many garment producers operating in the free zone in from the late 1990s onwards relocated to other countries in Latin America and the Caribbean because of rising costs in Jamaica. The three most commonly cited costs were the costs of security, utilities and labour (i.e. the cost of labour in relation to its productivity). There is evidence that labour productivity declined further in the latter half of the 1990s.
6. High crime rates required high expenditures on security by firms, resulting in higher operating costs.
7. According to a Ministry of Foreign Affairs and Foreign Trade, *News Release* (17 February 2003): 'Foreign Direct Investment (FDI) moved from US$129.7 million in 1994, to US$722 million in 2001, making Jamaica the second largest earner in the Caribbean'. However, this high rate of investment did not have the anticipated growth impact on the economy because much of the capital created – physical infrastructure – was underutilized. Enterprises were restricted to single rather than multiple shifts because of the risks of crime. Moreover, much of the FDI funded a change in titles of existing enterprises (e.g. change in ownership of the electricity monopoly) rather than creating new productive capacity.

8. The World Bank (2004) also noted the views of some Jamaican entrepreneurs that the high rates of interest on government bonds made investment in production, with the risks and costs this entailed, far less attractive to investors.

In summary, these factors, individually and collectively, counteracted whatever growth impetus trade liberalization was expected to have.

8.3.2 Industrial development

In the 1990s, in the wake of the trade and financial liberalization processes, the sectoral composition of the GDP shifted sharply in favour of services, and against the goods producing sectors and the 'producers of government services'. Transport, storage and communications grew the fastest because of imports of motor vehicles and telecommunications equipment. Prior to trade liberalization, motor vehicle imports had been highly restricted. In the 1990s, or owing to the easing of import restrictions, imports of used Japanese vehicles grew rapidly in Jamaica as in the rest of the Caribbean. The boom in telecommunications services in Jamaica was driven by the international growth of the industry, which in turn was spurred by the information technology and telecommunications revolution. But in part, it was also facilitated by the deliberate liberalization of the telecommunications sector, which eventually eliminated the monopoly that had been guaranteed to Cable and Wireless (a United Kingdom multinational), when the State-owned Jamaica Telephone Company was divested in 1988 (Davies, 2003).

Other fast growing sectors were finance, electricity and water sector, and tourism. All of these services are import-intensive, and therefore must have benefited from the trade liberalization measures.

Only mining and agriculture, as goods producing sectors, showed marginal increases in the 1990s. Manufacturing and construction, the two sectors that drove the industrial development of the domestic economy in the high growth years of the 1950s and 1960s, both contracted over the course of the 1990s.

The decline of manufacturing began in the 1980s, even in the apparel subsector, the most successful in the post-1980 period. In 1992, the PIOJ in its annual *Economic and Social Survey of Jamaica* (ESSJ) summarized the problems facing the manufacturing sector. It singled out complaints by the sector's leaders of the high interest rates (that were associated with stabilization of the economy) and the unfair competition that had been triggered by trade liberalization. The ESSJ (1992) noted that, while the manufacturers opposed tariff reduction on the grounds that it exposed them to competition from extra-regional producers, they welcomed the reduction of duties on raw materials and capital goods.

The evidence indicates that trade liberalization led to a decline in manufacturing for the domestic market, an increase in apparel exports from the free zones, but an overall decline in the contribution of the manufacturing sector to GDP. A principal characteristic of the evolution of the manufacturing sector in Jamaica was its dependence on imported inputs instead of on local agricultural and mineral production. Free zone manufacturing for export had even fewer linkages with the domestic economy than the traditional manufacturing sector had maintained.

A study by ECLAC (1999) on the impact of trade liberalization on government finances in Jamaica concluded that liberalization of the economy did not have a negative impact on government revenue because as the tariff rates fell, imports increased and more duty was collected. Furthermore, the General Consumption Tax (GCT)[8] introduced in 1991 (and charged on imports after duty) more than compensated for any losses in revenue. In the same year as the GCT was introduced, the government began to implement the CET of CARICOM, as a result of which the average level of import duties was reduced. As mentioned earlier, in Phase I of the reform of the CET, tariffs were reduced from a range of 1–45 per cent between 1990 and 1993 to 5–30 per cent. The revision of the CET was an element in the CARICOM strategy for reducing production costs, stimulating greater efficiency, protecting sensitive industries and encouraging new types of production activities (ECLAC, 1999).

While import duties were replacing quotas, and then themselves being reduced, tariffs were supplemented or replaced by the GCT (levied on imports) and the Special Consumption Tax (SCT). The net effect was continuous absolute growth in international trade taxes. These taxes recently accounted for almost 30 per cent of total revenue.

8.4 Development impact of trade liberalization

8.4.1 Adjustment costs of trade liberalization, unemployment, duration of unemployment

The total unemployment rate declined from 26.6 per cent on average between 1980 and 1984 to 21.3 per cent between 1985 and 1989. This was due to a slower rate of growth of the labour force and the rapid increase in female employment in the second half of the decade, in the expanding apparel export sector in the free zones. In the 1990s, the unemployment rate levelled off, averaging 15.5 per cent between 1990 and 2002. Part of the reason for the fairly constant unemployment rate, despite the small number of jobs created, was the high rate of emigration, averaging more than 20,000 per year, which, in effect, siphoned off the natural increase in the labour force.

Major changes in the level, rate and sectoral composition of employment are undoubtedly, at least partially, the result of the policy changes that sought to transform the economy into a liberal, market-driven economy. However, it is impossible to identify the impact of the trade liberalization component from the other policy changes that were introduced. We surmise that the shift in manufacturing output from consumer goods for the domestic market to apparel for export was in part the result of the competition from imported consumer goods made possible by trade liberalization. Without protected markets, many erstwhile manufacturers found it more profitable to switch to the distribution of imported brand name consumer goods. The rapid growth of employment in the distributive trades in the 1980s supports this conjecture.

Witter and Anderson (1991) showed that the structural adjustment polices reduced the real value of wages throughout the 1980s. And King and Handa have argued that the adjustment at the beginning of the 1990s sharply reduced the real value of wages, and that it was not until 1996 before wages caught up with where they had been in 1989. By 1998, they were '29.3 per cent higher – during a time when the economy stagnated'. They go on to argue that 'While average wages in the tradable sector was 85 per cent of those in the non-tradable activities in 1989, by 1998 they were only 69 per cent. Further, the relative fall in wages in tradables occurred across skill levels' (King and Handa, 2000).

8.4.2 Social safety net programmes

One of the contributing factors to the fiscal crisis in the mid-1970s was the rapid escalation of expenditure on social programmes, particularly free health care and education. With each of its agreements with the IMF and the other international financial institutions, the government was forced to cut expenditure. Unable to reduce its international financial obligations, the burden of adjustment fell on the social programmes. By 1991, especially with the sudden liberalization of the foreign exchange market, the poverty level rose to 38.9 per cent. This prompted the World Bank to initiate a poverty alleviation programme.

In 2002, the government of Jamaica reorganized its social safety net programmes around the Programme of Advancement through Health and Education (PATH). This is a conditional cash transfer programme administered by the Ministry of Labour and Social Security (MLSS) that pays benefits every two months. It is the centrepiece of the social safety net that brings together three traditional programmes: the Food Stamp, Poor Assistance and Poor Relief programmes, with the objectives of providing assistance to vulnerable groups, improving the efficiency of delivery of benefits, and increasing transparency in the selection of the beneficiaries. In the pursuit of these objectives, PATH benefits are intended to assist in raising the level of human capital through improvements in education and health. The target number of beneficiaries for PATH was 200,000, or about 8 per cent of the total population, by the end of 2004. It is anticipated that PATH will have 236,000 beneficiaries when it is operating at its maximum.

8.4.3 Impact of trade liberalization on poverty levels and other development indicators

Between 1991 and 1994, the poverty rate was halved, rose sharply in the mid-1990s, and then fell again in 1997 and 1998, years when the inflation rate receded into single digits, and the inflow of remittances rose rapidly. Both of these had a positive impact on per capita real consumption, and are the most likely explanations for the decline in poverty rates in a period when the growth rate of the economy was marginal.

8.5 Policy lessons and implications

8.5.1 Conclusions and policy lessons

Jamaica's experience clearly indicates the necessity of proper sequencing of policy reforms. It is especially important to ensure stability before initiating trade and financial liberalization. In the transition from a protected to an open economy, new enterprises have to be established, and existing ones retooled, reorganized and re-engineered to become competitive. In both cases, new investments are required. However, there is the possibility, as the Jamaican experience demonstrates, of a perverse outcome of reforms, when speculative behaviour promises high returns at low risk. In particular, gambling that the Jamaican currency will be depreciated is almost risk-free, and purchasing government securities at high interest rates is even less risky. In these circumstances, it is not attractive to invest in productive activities that have to overcome many bureaucratic obstacles, and which have to cope with social inefficiencies, such as industrial uncertainties, unreliable utilities and social instability due to crime.

In the urgency of the initial decision-making to cope with the foreign exchange crisis of the late 1970s and early 1980s measures to liberalize imports were adopted and implemented before appropriate and relevant regulatory processes and mechanisms had been put in place. The following were some reactions to the inevitable problems of liberalization without regulation: poor quality goods and services, arbitrary pricing, misleading advertising, and, generally, business practices that took advantage of the weakness of the consumer. Apart from the social and economic costs that such practices triggered, it contributed to the general state of uncertainty that has made the transition to a liberalized economy all the more difficult.

Adapting to a more market-oriented economy requires a change in the mind set of the business community. In this regard, the government could have done more to educate the business classes in the requirements for survival in the changing international circumstances and in a liberalized economy. There is also a need for institutions that provide the relevant education and training on a continuous and affordable basis. In Jamaica's case, it is clear that the formal educational system has reacted slowly to the changed demands. A measurable indicator is the provision of information technology training that remained specialized for far too long when the demand for it as a generalized offering had been long since identified.

In Jamaica, the view that protection should be removed quickly has contended with the view that there needs to be a period of transition long enough for enterprises to become competitive. The first view holds that as long as there is protection, there is no incentive to be come competitive; while the second view holds that without sufficient time, it is impossible to become competitive, and national industry will be sacrificed to foreign competition. A compromise position is to identify the list of national priorities that should be allowed a well defined but extended period of adjustment, with appropriate steps to develop competitiveness that can be monitored. For Jamaica, it is possible to make a case for industries that support food security and employment and foster the agro-industrial potential in which Jamaica enjoys a competitive advantage, although this view is not wholly accepted.

Many producers will need assistance to become competitive. Ultimately, this assistance will require funding and new knowledge. There is therefore scope for capacity building of the productive sector that will benefit from international assistance that should be accessible with the help of the State. One of the most frequently cited reasons for the recent export success of the Trinidadian manufacturing sector has been the support of the government in facilitating the funding of re-tooling. The indebtedness of the Jamaican State means that no budgetary resources are left after servicing the debt to assist the productive sector's drive for competitiveness. Indeed, the government requires international financing to fund public investment for modernizing physical infrastructure, such as the ports and roads, and the public sector to reduce bureaucratic delays that are costly to business, as well as for improving the education system.

8.5.2 Major country issues in the Doha Development Round

In an 'Update' provided by the Foreign Trade Department, Ministry of Foreign Affairs and Foreign Trade (16 December 2004), the government of Jamaica notes that cutting higher tariffs more deeply could force reductions in applied tariffs on a number of products that are sensitive or yield significant duties. The challenges facing Jamaica in NAMA are greater than those of agricultural access because there are no exemptions, like the Special Products category for agriculture. 'Furthermore, the stated goal of reducing high tariffs and achieving overall reduction or elimination of certain tariffs threatens not only the policy space which is afforded though our bindings, but also their maintenance for revenue purposes.' Jamaica will have to be careful to ensure that the scope and timing of the reductions 'do no harm to our vital interests with respect to trade and economic policies'.

The context for these concerns is the new trade policy articulated by the government in 2001 that seeks to:

- Create new, diversified exports by facilitating the growth of domestic capital as the basis for diversifying exports and facilitating market penetration;
- Displace imports (i.e. steadily reduce the share of imports relative to output); and
- Increase the flow of net positive returns from overseas assets, which have been generating significant remittances and other capital flows for Jamaica.

Jamaican policy-makers are keen to ensure that any formula adopted, particularly the non-linear formula, does not disadvantage Jamaica too much, given the country's record of concessions in trade liberalization negotiations over the past two decades of adjustment. Jamaica's experience with liberalization offers many lessons, and perhaps explains the search for a programmed approach, that is properly scoped, phased and timed, to further the objective of tariff reductions in the NAMA process.

Notes

1 This strategy was articulated by W. Arthur Lewis, who had been impressed with the success of Puerto Rico's Operation Bootstrap in the late 1940s.
2 For an authoritative account of this process, see Girvan, 1971.
3 It was to be informed by the ideology of democratic socialism, a variant of the kind of Western European social democracy practiced in some Scandinavian countries in the 1970s.
4 The World Bank made three structural adjustment loans to Jamaica between 1982 and 1985 for a total of US$190 million. It discontinued its lending in 1985 because it was dissatisfied with the pace of policy changes.
5 The JCTC was actually the successor to Jamaica Nutrition Holdings that had been established in 1975 to engage in bulk imports of basic foods and became a vehicle for bilateral food aid. It was therefore an important element of the government's response to the rising import bill of the 1970s.
6 The World Bank provides examples of how increased rates of additional stamp duties (raised from 32 per cent to 80 per cent) on agricultural products, such as beef (with a tariff at the bound rate of 100 per cent), more than tripled the duty, from about 85 per cent to 260 per cent, so as to provide substantial protection for domestic producers. However, it should be noted that the level of protection could have been lower if imports, particularly from the United States, had not been subsidized.
7 ECLAC (2004) estimated the damage at US$595 million.
8 The GCT is a sales tax. When it was introduced, its rate was 10 per cent on a limited range of goods and services. Since then the rate has been increased in two stages to 15 per cent, and the range of goods and services exempted from the tax has been reduced.

References

Bloom, D. E. et al. (2004) Jamaica: globalization, liberalization and sustainable human development: progress and challenges in Jamaica. Geneva in M. Agosin et al. (eds), *Making Global Integration Work for People: Analytical Issues and Country Assessment Studies*, Geneva: UNCTAD, Occasional Paper, UNCTAD/EDM/Misc.176.

Davies, C. (2003) Refocusing the Jamaican State: Privatization and regulation of key utilities. Speech for the joint workshop on Risk, Regulation, Accountability and Development organized by Centre for the Analysis of Rich and Regulation (CARR), Centre on Regulation and Competition (CRC) and Aston Business School, University of Manchester, 26 June.

ECLAC (1999) The impact of trade liberalization on government finances in Jamaica, LC/CAR/G.574. Santiago, 1 November. Available at: http://www.eclac.cl/publicaciones/PortOfSpain/4/LCCARG574/carg0574.pdf

ECLAC, UNDP and PIOJ (2004) Assessment of the socio-economic and environmental impact of Hurricane Ivan on Jamaica, Santiago: ECLAC.

Girvan, N. (1971) Foreign capital and economic underdevelopment in Jamaica, Institute for Social and Economic Research (ISER), Mona, Jamaica: University of the West Indies.

King, D. and Handa, S. (2000) Balance of payments liberalization, poverty and distribution in Jamaica (mimeo), May Kingston, University of the West Indies, Department of Economics.

Myers, G. (2004) *Banana Wars: The Price of Free Trade*. London: Zed.

Rajapatirana, S. (1995) Post-trade liberalization policy and institutional challenges in Latin America and the Caribbean, Policy Research Working Paper 1465. Washington, DC: The World Bank, Latin America and the Caribbean Technical Department, Advisory Group, May.

Witter, M. and Anderson, P. (1991) The distribution of the social cost of Jamaica's structural adjustment, 1977–1989. Paper prepared for the research project on The Impact of Structural Adjustment on the Social Debt in Jamaica, sponsored by the International Labour Office, Geneva, and the Planning Institute of Jamaica, May.

World Bank (1994) Jamaica: a strategy for growth and poverty reduction: country economic memorandum. Report No. 12702-JM, Washington, DC, 12 April.

World Bank (2004) The road to sustained growth in Jamaica. Washington, DC: May, 222 pages.

WTO (2004) Trade policy review – Jamaica. Report by the Secretariat, Geneva: World Trade Organization, October.

9
Malawi

Kennedy Mbekeani

9.1 Introduction

9.1.1 Economic and trade environment

Main features of the economy

Malawi is a small landlocked country, bordering Mozambique, the United Republic of Tanzania and Zambia. The country's population is estimated at 11 million. With a per capita GDP of $163, it is one of the world's poorest countries.

Malawi's growth performance has generally been weak. Between 1981 and 1990, GDP (in constant 1995 $) grew at an average annual rate of 2.2 per cent. During the period 1990–2002, the GDP grew at an average annual rate of 3.2 per cent, but growth slowed to 1.7 per cent in 2001, before shrinking by 1.5 percent in 2002. The slow growth of GDP was mainly due to economic mismanagement and the poor performance of the agriculture sector. Severe droughts in 1992 and 1994 led to decline in real GDP (at factor cost) of 7.9 per cent and 11.6 per cent, respectively, while favourable harvests in 1995 and 1996 were largely responsible for real GDP growth averaging 9.25 per cent in those years.

The country has a predominantly agrarian economy and is dependent on subsistence farming, with 75 per cent of the population living in the rural areas. However, the share of agriculture in GDP has been falling from a peak of 49 per cent in 1993 to 37.6 per cent in 2003. Likewise, the share of industry has been declining, from a high of 31.5 per cent in 1992 to 14.6 per cent in 2003. The services sector is now the main contributor to GDP, with a share of 47.8 per cent in 2003.

Inflation, as measured by the consumer price index, remained very high over the period 1990–2002, with an average 12-month inflation rate of 29 per cent, peaking at 40 per cent a year between 1994 and 1999.

While it has moderated in recent years, it still remains high: in 2002 inflation was 14.7 per cent.

Malawi's savings and investment rates are very low. Gross investment was 8.1 per cent of GDP in 2003, which was 4.4 percentage points lower than the previous year. Gross national savings were −7 per cent of GDP in 2003.

Malawi's exports are highly concentrated. Primary commodities constitute the bulk of merchandise exports, of which nearly 90 percent are agricultural commodities. Tobacco accounts for about 53 per cent of total exports followed by tea and sugar, which account for about 8 per cent each. Malawi has a niche place in the international tobacco market. It is the second largest producer and exporter of burley tobacco, behind the United States, but it does not compete directly with the United States as it produces a different variety. Similarly, Malawi does not compete with varieties produced by large producers such as Brazil and India. Manufacturing exports account for about 10 per cent of total exports. These include mainly textiles and clothing and, to a lesser extent, furniture and processed food products.

Exports of services grew at an average annual rate of 6.9 per cent between 1990 and 2002 and have grown further in recent years: 27.3 per cent in 2001 and 13.2 per cent in 2002. Growth in imports of services has been slower than exports: between 1990 and 2002, imports grew by 2.4 per cent, which was almost half the growth experienced during the period 1980–1996.

There has been some re-orientation of trade from traditional markets such as the United Kingdom and Germany, and Malawi's main export markets today are South Africa, which took 23.3 per cent of exports in 2003, followed by the United States – 13.5 per cent, Germany – 11.2 per cent and Japan 4.6 per cent.

Malawi has performed poorly in international trade: between 1990 and 2002, imports of goods increased by an average of 10.7 per cent per annum while exports increased by only 5.3 per cent, with the highest growth (21.4 per cent) recorded in 2002. In 2001, exports increased by 6.1 per cent, but declined by 1.3 per cent the following year. This gap between growth in exports and imports led to a widening of the trade deficit, from $15 million in 1992 to $150.8 million in 2002, although in 1998 it registered a surplus.

In early 1995, Malawi embarked on an adjustment programme designed to restore financial stability and set the basis for sustainable economic growth. A fiscal adjustment over the period 1994–1997 resulted in the reduction of the overall deficit (excluding grants) by 20 percentage points. This was a consequence of significant measures undertaken to curtail expenditure and to improve the administration and collection of taxes. The fiscal adjustment permitted the adoption of a tight monetary policy that helped reduce the inflation rate from its peak of 98 per cent in July 1995 to less than 7 per cent in 1996.

In the context of re-establishing the basis for sustained growth, the authorities embarked on an ambitious programme of structural reform. In the agricultural sector, reforms were aimed at providing smallholder farmers access to cash crops and to liberalizing the marketing of agricultural output, including terminating the monopsony position of the marketing parastatals as the sole purchaser of smallholder crops. Additionally, the marketing of inputs was liberalized, encouraging the participation of private traders in this activity and increasing the supply of inputs to farmers. However, this achieved the opposite effect, as small-scale, rural subsistence farmers were faced with the burden of travelling long distances to sell their produce. Also, subsistence farmers could not afford the high price of fertilizer, and this resulted in lower yields.

Structural reforms designed to liberalize the economy and facilitate the growth of private enterprise were also implemented in several other areas. In the external sector, the exchange and trade systems were reformed with the introduction of a market-based exchange rate system in February 1994 and a formal, foreign exchange inter-bank market in September 1996. All restrictions on external current account transactions were removed, and in December 1995, Malawi accepted the obligations under Article VIII of the IMF's Articles of Agreement. The external trading environment was significantly liberalized with a phased reduction of the temporary export levy and import duties, and a decrease of the weighted average tariff rate from 18 per cent in 1994 to about 15 per cent in 1996.

9.2 Trade liberalization and its impact

9.2.1 Trade liberalization

Overview of the reforms

Throughout most of the 1980s, Malawi maintained a restrictive and complex trade and exchange rate regime that was based on the discretionary allocation of foreign exchange for imports, pervasive non-tariff barriers, a large number and wide dispersion of tariff bands, high tariff protection against imports, restrictive licensing requirements on imports and exports, and surrender requirements on export proceeds.

Beginning in 1988, and continuing through most of the 1990s, the government implemented a series of measures aimed at liberalizing the trade regime (Box 9.1). Much of this was done under the World Bank/IMF

Box 9.1: Malawi's key trade reforms (1988–1998)

Eliminating non-tariff barriers (1988–1997)

- February 1988 – Exchange controls on about 25 per cent of imports of non-petroleum raw materials and spare parts were eliminated. However, petroleum imports remained unrestricted.
- August 1988 – Liberalization of foreign exchange controls was extended to an additional 50 per cent of non-petroleum imports, including raw materials, industrial spare parts, and intermediate goods (including most goods related to commercial transport and some consumer goods).
- January 1991 – Introduction of a narrow and temporary negative list that freed all other items from the requirement for prior foreign exchange approval. The negative list covered, among others, alcoholic beverages, precious metals, motor vehicles and electrical goods.
- February 1994 – The negative list for imported commodities was abolished. However, following a shortage of petroleum imports, the government reinstated a State import monopoly through the Petroleum Control Commission.
- June 1997 – All licensing requirements on imports and exports were abolished, except for items related to health, security and the environment.

Consolidating the tariff structure (1988–1996)

- 1988 – Customs duties and import levies were combined into one tariff schedule, followed by a broadening of the tax base.
- 1992–1993 – The differential in the surtax levied on imports and domestic goods was eliminated in combination with an upward adjustment of import duty rates.
- 1996 – The number of tariff bands was reduced.

Reducing tariff protection (1988–1997)

- 1988 – Maximum tariffs on non-government imports were reduced from 70 per cent to 45 per cent of the c.i.f. value, with

(*continued*)

Box 9.1: (continued)

a weighted average of about 21 per cent. Some tax rates were later abolished. Government imports were exempt from customs tariffs.

- April 1996 – The maximum tariff rate was reduced from 45 per cent to 40 per cent, resulting in a weighted average import tariff rate of about 15 per cent. Nonetheless, the tariff structure contained 10 bands (including for zero-rated items) ranging from 0 to 40 per cent. The import bands were 0, 5, 7.5, 10, 15, 20, 25, 30, 35, and 40 percent. However, only a few items were levied at the 5, 7.5, 15, 20, and 25 per cent rates.
- April 1997 – The import duty rate on raw materials used in manufacturing was eliminated and the maximum rate (on finished products) was further reduced from 40 per cent to 35 per cent. The temporary export levy on tobacco, tea and sugar, which was introduced in April 1995, was lowered from 10 per cent to 4 per cent in April 1997. However, the export levy was extended to coffee under the 1997/98 budget.
- June 1997 – All licensing requirements on imports and exports were eliminated, except for items related to health, security and the environment, completing the removal of non-tariff barriers.
- 1999 – Maximum tariff rate was reduced to 25 per cent.

Liberalizing the export regime

- February 1994 – The export surrender requirement was abolished, except for tea, sugar and tobacco; at present 40 per cent of proceeds are still subject to surrender requirements.
- April 1995 – A 10 per cent temporary export levy on tobacco and sugar was reduced to 8 per cent.
- 1997 – Temporary export levy on tobacco and sugar was further reduced 4 per cent and concurrently extended to include coffee.
- 1997 – The corporate tax on firms in export processing zones was eliminated.
- 1998 – The export levy was eliminated.

structural adjustment programmes. The trade reform programme, which started in the latter half of the 1980s and was deepened in the mid-1990s, consisted of two distinct approaches: (i) reducing the restrictiveness and complexity of the trade regime in the context of the World

Bank and IMF structural adjustment programmes; and (ii) improving market access through bilateral and regional agreements.[1]

The reforms introduced since the late 1980s have substantially liberalized trade, by eliminating licences and their bureaucratic requirements, simplifying the import regime by amalgamating tariffs, reducing dispersion by cutting the number of tariff bands, reducing protection by progressively cutting tariff rates and equalizing domestic taxes between imports and domestic goods, and increasing transparency by reducing the use of discretion. As a result of the reforms, Malawi now has one of the most liberal and transparent trade regimes in Africa.

The export regime was also liberalized by reducing export surrender requirements and export levies, even though the process proceeded more slowly than that of the import regime.

Measures affecting imports

Prior to the reforms, imports had been subjected to cumbersome, lengthy, and costly procedures including the obtaining of an import licence (subject to a fee of 5 per cent of value) and foreign exchange approval from the Reserve Bank of Malawi through a commercial bank. The application process alone normally took about a month, with further administrative delays on arrival of the goods. Allocation of foreign exchange was subject to substantial discretion. Guidelines used by the Reserve Bank of Malawi reflected perceived national priorities within the limitations of the foreign exchange budget. The import tariff system was prohibitive and complex. Imports attracted a maximum tax rate of 75 per cent, an import levy of 10 per cent and surtax rates of 0–35 per cent for non luxury items and 55–100 percent for luxury goods. Government imports were exempt from customs tariffs.

Imports may still be subject to four types of duties: the customs tariff, excise duties (on some products), surtaxes, and anti-dumping duties. The domestic surtax and excise duties are applied to imports and domestically produced goods in a non-discriminatory manner.

Malawi's applied tariffs have been reduced from an average of 30.7 per cent in 1994 to 13.1 per cent in 2001 (Table 9.1). The manufacturing sector is the most protected followed by agriculture. The applied average MFN tariff rates on manufactured goods and agricultural products are 13.7 per cent and 12.2 per cent respectively.

Malawi's tariff structure continues to be characterized by the phenomenon of tariff escalation. The lowest tariff rate (5 per cent) is applied to 'necessities', consisting predominantly of capital goods and other inputs; the middle rate (15 per cent) is applied to intermediate goods;

Table 9.1: Malawi's average applied tariff levels

Product category	1994	1998	2001
Tobacco products	44.3	10.0	25.0
Wearing apparel; dressing and dyeing of fur	44.8	39.9	25.0
Tanning and dressing of leather; manufacture of luggage, handbags, saddles, harnesses and footwear	43.7	36.4	24.8
Furniture; manufacturing n.e.c.	44.1	38.3	23.5
Wood and of products of wood and cork, except furniture; manufacture of articles of straw and plaiting materials	31.9	25.2	19.7
Textiles	47.1	28.5	19.3
Office, accounting and computing equipment machinery	42.8	35.9	18.2
Motor vehicles, trailers and semi-trailers	32.9	24.8	18.0
Radio, television, and communications equipment and apparatus	37.6	39.8	17.6
Food products and beverages	34.5	24.1	17.6
Rubber and plastic products	34.6	21.0	15.3
Other non-metallic mineral products	28.5	19.1	14.3
Fabricated metal products, except machinery and equipment	31.0	19.7	14.1
Medical, precision and optical instruments, watches and clocks	31.2	23.3	13.8
Total average	**30.7**	**20**	**13.1**

Source: UNCTAD/World Bank, WITS/TRAINS Database.

and the highest rate (25 per cent) is applied to 'non-essential' goods, consisting mainly of consumer goods.

Malawi applies the highest tariffs on tobacco products, wearing apparel and dressing and dyeing of fur, tanning and dressing of leather, luggage, hand bags, saddles, harnesses and footwear (Table 9.1). High tariffs are also applied on wood and wood products, textiles, food products and beverages and, rubber and plastic products. Higher tariffs are also applied on four other products that Malawi need not protect: manufacture of office, accounting and computing machinery; motor vehicles, trailers and semi-trailers; manufacture of radio, television, and communications equipment and apparatus; and, manufacture of medical, precision and optical instruments, watches and clocks. Higher tariffs are applied to these products because of the need to protect a few smaller local producers who are able to lobby government for protection.

It should be noted that, because of bilateral agreements and preferences given on a reciprocal basis to other members of the Common

Market for Eastern and Southern Africa (COMESA)[2] and the Southern Africa Development Community (SADC),[3] a large proportion of trade is subject to lower effective tariffs. COMESA has focused on the acceleration of regional integration through trade facilitation and the elimination of non-tariff barriers and intraregional tariffs. A timetable was set for the progressive reduction of tariffs, with the target of free intraregional trade by 31 October 2000. However, only nine countries (Malawi, Djibouti, Egypt, Kenya, Madagascar, Mauritius, Sudan, Zambia and Zimbabwe) met the 31 October 2000 target. COMESA also planned to adopt a common external tariff by 2004 with three tariff bands of 5, 15 and 30 per cent. Malawi already surpasses this liberalization objective.

SADC began implementation of a free trade area in September 2000. It will take about 12 years for the agreement to become fully effective. As a least developed member, Malawi will start reducing tariffs against South African goods only in 2005. Currently about 40 per cent of Malawi's imports come from South Africa.

Measures affecting exports

During the 1980s, exports were restricted to ensure an adequate supply of goods for the domestic market. A large number of goods, including maize, beans, groundnuts, and petroleum, could not be exported at all. Many other exports were subject to licensing. Specific duties were levied on exports of hides and skins, and tobacco, and foreign exchange earnings were required to be surrendered to the Reserve Bank of Malawi.

The export regime has been liberalized substantially since 1988. There are no general licensing requirements for exports and no export tariffs. Only four commodities require an export licence (implements of war other than arms and ammunitions; petroleum products; wild animals, trophies, and products of such animals; and maize and maize meal). Nevertheless, exports of tobacco, tea and sugar remain subject to a surrender requirement of 40 per cent of foreign exchange receipts. Tobacco production has been liberalized, but exports are permitted only through a single auction house.

Malawi's external trade arrangements have changed with the provision of preferential market access to the United States through the African Growth and Opportunity Act (AGOA) and to the EU through the Everything-but-Arms (EBA) initiative. An important question is whether these initiatives provide meaningful additional market access for Malawi, and, therefore whether they can contribute to stimulating exports and growth and reducing poverty. The preferential market access provided by AGOA had a small positive impact on apparel exports. For agricultural commodities of interest to Malawi, AGOA does not provide additional market access. Tariffs remain high (35 per cent) on tobacco imported for cigarettes, such as Malawi's burley tobacco, and relatively low on tobacco imported for other than cigarettes (5.6 per cent). For many of the other agricultural commodities, such as sugar, raw cotton, coffee, black tea and certain kinds of peanuts, they are either governed by a tariff-rate quota or are not eligible under the general United States agricultural policy.

Since Malawi already receives highly preferential access to the EU market under the Cotonou Agreement, the impact of the EU's EBA on enhancing market access will be negligible except for sugar. Under the EBA, all duties on sugar will be eliminated by 2009. In the interim, the EU will continue to offer a tariff-free quota that is to increase by nearly 15 per cent per annum. Given the substantial price advantage that the quota provides to sugar producers in beneficiary countries, there is considerable potential for an expansion of sugar exports to the EU.

After the expiry of the Cotonou preferences in 2007, Malawi is likely to continue enjoying preferential access to the EU market under the EBA, but it will face increased competition from other LDCs that previously did not have preferential market access to the EU.

The main obstacles to Malawi's exports are transport costs and supply-side constraints. The country's production output has been declining since the mid-1990s. The ability to export is constrained by high transportation costs, which make Malawi's products uncompetitive in export markets. Commodity exports entail high volumes and therefore high shipping costs, while they fetch low prices in the export market compared to manufactured products, such as wristwatches, that require lower transportation costs and fetch very high prices.

9.2.2 Economic impact of trade liberalization

Malawi's economic performance following liberalization has been mixed. Between 1990 and 2002, its GDP grew at an annual average rate of 3.2 per cent. However, in 2001 growth was below 2 per cent, and in 2002 the economy shrank. Key to the dismal performance in 2001 and 2002 was the deteriorating manufacturing sector. Between 1993 and 2003, the sector declined on average by 2 per cent per annum. In 2002 the sector declined by 11.4 per cent, thereby reducing its share in GDP to 9.9 per cent.

Exports

Tobacco remains Malawi's single most important export commodity, accounting for over 60 per cent of total exports. This is followed by tea and sugar with 8 per cent and 6.5 per cent respectively. Non-traditional exports, which are predominantly within agriculture, registered strong growth in the 1990s, albeit from a small base, increasing their share in the total export basket from 6.7 per cent in 1990 to 12.7 per cent in 1997–2003. In particular, exports of cotton products increased rapidly, together with exports of flowers and special vegetables to Europe, reflecting production by the EPZs.

Malawi's total exports increased significantly, from $278.8 million in 1988 to $436.9 million in 2001. Exports of tobacco, which increased from $178.4 million in 1988 to $259.6 million 2001, were largely responsible for the overall increase. However, exports of manufactured goods fell sharply from $8 million in 1988 to $4 million in 2001. This is a reflection of the negative impact of liberalization on local manufacturers, who failed to compete with imports in the domestic market and did not have enough capacity to produce for exports. Consequently, most of them were forced to close down.

The pursuit of liberal trade policies has reduced the anti-export bias in the trade regime and improved the domestic environment for export expansion. Despite these improvements, however, production and export performance have not been strong. In the 1990s Malawi's exports grew by approximately 1.8 per cent per annum, which is less than the average export growth of sub-Saharan Africa of 3.4 per cent per annum.

Imports

In the aftermath of the 1992 drought, Malawi's import capacity was severely constrained by a lack of foreign exchange. Non-maize imports declined by 10 per cent between 1993 and 1994, and by 4.3 per cent in 1995. Changes in imports reflected the changes in disbursements of balance-of-payments assistance, and commodity and project inflows.

Production

Total manufacturing production shrank from an annual average of $535.8 million during the period 1989–1991 to $293.9 million in 1998. Food production was the hardest hit. The value of production increased at the start of liberalization, from $67.2 million in 1998 to a high of $218.4 million in 1992. However, since then food production consistently declined and reached a low of $26.1 million in 1998. Production of textiles dropped to their lowest levels in 1998. The levels of production had been declining since 1994 from a high of $93 million in 1993 to $13.5 million in 1998. This resulted in the eventual closing down of the David Whitehead and Sons textile mill in 2002.

The production of beverages fared better, reaching $78 million in 1998 from $13.8 million in 1988. The other products in which production increased after liberalization were industrial chemicals, other chemicals, plastic products and fabricated metal products. However, their production levels have since been declining.

Apart from the impact of the trade liberalization, the disappointing performance stems from a variety of factors, including macroeconomic instability that was due to economic mismanagement and weak infrastructure. During the mid-1990s, fiscal mismanagement triggered inflation. This had a negative impact on the manufacturing sector. Borrowing to expand production became expensive and a number of small businesses were forced to close down. Even imports of machinery, which had picked in 1997 to $207 million from $156 million in 1989, fell to $161.9 million in 2001.

9.2.3 Development impact of trade liberalization

Malawi suffers from poor statistics on key development indicators such as employment. However, the available statistics show that life expectancy has declined significantly. This is mainly due to HIV/AIDS and not to trade liberalization. Of course, trade liberalization has not assisted in creating the wealth that will enable people to have a balanced diet and afford to buy essential medicines. The illiteracy rate has declined due to the introduction of free primary education. However, this has been followed by a drop in the quality of education due to a higher student–teacher ratio and to the hiring of untrained schoolteachers.

On the whole, trade liberalization has not had a significant impact on Malawi's economic development. The country remains one of the poorest in the world and the poorest in Southern Africa.

9.3 Policy lessons and implications

Malawi's record of economic reforms has been mixed, although some significant headway has been made since year 2000. The slow rate of progress in reducing existing economic distortions may explain the country's weak growth record. The poor quality of the infrastructure of services and utilities adversely affects exports. High transportation costs will continue to limit Malawi's exposure to international competition.

Malawi's trade liberalization programme has produced an open and transparent regime. The emphasis placed on eliminating non-tariff barriers has exposed domestic industries to international competition, but has failed to improve the capacity of domestic firms to compete. Concurrent measures to find alternative sources of tax revenue have enabled the reforms to proceed without major policy reversals, thus increasing their credibility. However, new taxes have prevented consumers from benefiting from lower tariffs.

Overall, Malawi has not been able adequately to exploit the opportunities provided by lower tariff and non-tariff barriers, or the bilateral and multilateral agreements for market access, because of weaknesses in its productive capacity. This has meant that it has not been able to fully exploit the non-reciprocal market access provided by South Africa. The contraction of output in industries that were previously protected has not been offset by a corresponding development and growth of export industries; exports have continued to be concentrated in a few agricultural commodities. There is need for comprehensive reforms to tackle supply-side constraints and other bottlenecks, including high transportation costs and poor infrastructure.

Malawi's trade continues to be restricted by some remaining structural weaknesses. These have in the past included relatively high transport costs, associated with its landlocked situation, compounded by poor security conditions in neighbouring countries and oligopolistic practices. Greater competition in transportation should reduce these problems. However, haulers' charges are still high, reflecting inefficiencies in Malawi's industry and restrictions in the region on third-party carriers as well as low volumes.

As a least developing country, Malawi has preferential access to most markets. While it will be exempt from making tariff cuts in the WTO negotiations, Malawi's effective tariffs will be affected by its membership of SADC and it is also negotiating an Economic Partnership Agreement with the European Union together with other developing countries.

Trade preferences have played a crucial role in Malawi's trade. They have made a positive impact on Malawi. For example, AGOA and non-reciprocal trade agreements with the EU and with South Africa have boosted clothing and textile exports from Malawi by attracting investment, creating employment and promoting diversification through the establishment of clothing and textile industries. This preferential initiative has also triggered upstream processing activities, with an enormous impact on poverty alleviation efforts. Additionally, Malawi has benefited from preferential exports to the EU market of such products as sugar, paper and leather goods, textiles and clothing. The phasing out of import quotas for clothing and textiles is a concern for Malawi. Its exports will face intensified competition, particularly from China, resulting from the termination of the Agreement on Textiles and Clothing as of 1 January 2005.

However, in the WTO negotiations, reductions of MFN rates will reduce the preferential margin, with negative effects on Malawi's trade flows. Since the country relies on non-reciprocal preferences as a development tool, any reduction of such preferences implies increased competition in its traditional export markets. Consequently, the resulting adjustment costs will disrupt the sequencing necessary for its further growth and industrialization. Therefore, Malawi's loss of preferential tariff margins, will need to be compensated by additional support to meet its trade and development needs.

The biggest challenge for Malawi lies in the formulation of strategies to help firms adjust to global competition. Government policies will play an important role in the adjustment process.[4] A key responsibility of the government is to ensure that firms are given the 'right' incentives to induce investment in activities in which Malawi has a comparative advantage, and to assist in facilitating adjustment to technological changes and policy shocks. The strategy should aim to overcome market failures and other distortions that may increase the cost of adjustment.

Notes

1 Even though Malawi acceded to the WTO in 1994 its membership did not provide new market access opportunities because it already benefits from the Cotonou Agreement and the Everything-but-Arms (EBA) initiative of the EU and the Africa Growth and Opportunity Act (AGOA) of the United States.
2 COMESA currently has 19 members: Angola, Burundi, Comoros, Djibouti, Egypt, Eritrea, Ethiopia, Kenya, Madagascar, Mauritius, Rwanda, Seychelles, Sudan, Swaziland, Uganda, the Democratic Republic of the Congo, Zambia and Zimbabwe.
3 SADC has 13 members: Angola, Botswana, the Democratic Republic of the Congo, South Africa, Swaziland, the United Republic of Tanzania, Zambia and Zimbabwe. Madagascar has applied to join.
4 See Hoekman and Smarzynska Javorcik (2004) on policies for facilitating firm adjustment.

References

Hoekman, Bernard and Smarzynska Javorcik, Beata (2004) Policies facilitating firm adjustment to globalization, World Bank Policy Research, Paper 3441, Washington DC: World Bank.

10
The Philippines

Ramon Clarete

10.1 Introduction

This paper examines the Philippines' experience with trade liberalization policies in the 1980s and 1990s, and their impact on the economy. Ex-ante assessments of the impact of freer trade on the Philippine economy using computable general equilibrium models report net positive gains (e.g. Habito and Cororaton, 2000; Cororaton, 1998; Clarete 1991). However, an ex-post assessment of the effects of trade liberalization produces less favourable results. Per capita income in the country has changed very little over the past 25 years. The economy appears unable to provide an adequate number of jobs for its labour force, and nearly one million Filipinos are working outside the country. Moreover, while trade has expanded, the increasing concentration of exports in semi-conductors and electronic components is cause for concern.

This divergence is due to transaction costs: when import restrictions are lowered, the owners of activity-specific existing capital assets and currently employed workers in import-substituting industries face adjustment costs. In the absence of transaction costs, these import-substituting firms are likely to move out of their current business activities and invest resources in export-oriented production. But if transaction costs in the export sector of the economy are substantial, it becomes difficult for the firms and workers adversely affected by the more liberal import policies to adjust to the new trading opportunities. Those jobs in the import-substituting industries that are lost due to freer trade are unlikely to be fully replaced with new ones in export-oriented activities because of the transaction costs involved. Thus such costs have the potential of distorting, if not preventing, the expected reallocation of productive resources.

10.2 The Philippines economy: overview and recent trends

The Philippine economy had experienced slow growth during the period 1980–2001. The average annual growth rate of GDP has been only 2.4 per cent, which barely keeps up with that of its population of nearly 80 million. One of the fastest growing in Asia, the Philippine population expanded at an annual rate of 3 per cent in the early 1970s, followed by 2.4 per cent in the mid-1980s and 2.3 per cent in 2000.

The country's relatively rapid population growth is hampering efforts to solve its unemployment and underemployment problem (Orbeta and Pernia, 1999). In 2001, the unemployment rate was estimated at 10.1 per cent of a labour force of 32.6 million. The underemployment rate was even higher: an estimated 18 per cent of the labour force. If about one million Filipinos did not have jobs abroad, the unemployment problem would have been even more serious. Their annual remittances, which amounted to $8.5 billion in 2004 according to the Bangko Sentral ng Pilipinas, substantially bolster disposable incomes in the Philippines, alleviating significantly the level of poverty in the country.

Nearly half of the employed are in the services sector, which provided only about one-third of all jobs in 1980. The agriculture sector, which was the source of half of all available jobs a quarter of a century ago, now accounts for only 37.5 per cent of employment. The industrial sector has failed to create any significant number of new jobs for the labour force.

The employment distribution of the different sectors reflects their respective contributions to GDP. The shares of agriculture and industry have steadily fallen since 1980, while the value added of the services sector in proportion to GDP increased. In 1980, the value added from the agriculture sector was 25.1 per cent of GDP in 1980, but this declined progressively to reach 20.1 per cent in 2002. Likewise, the value added share of industry, about one-third of which is manufacturing, declined progressively, from 38.79 per cent in 1980 to 33.8 per cent in 2002. It was only the services sector's share which showed an increase, from 36.1 per cent in 1980 to 46.2 per cent in 2002.

The Philippines has increasingly depended on cash remittances from overseas Filipino workers to support its balance of payments. Over the past two decades, net income inflows have become an important asset item in the country's balance of payments. By 2002, net income inflows more than exceeded the country's current-account deficit. This is particularly important, given that, since 2000, net private FDI has been declining to reach a little over $1 billion in 2002 from nearly $1.5 billion in 2000. The importance to the country of the cash remittances from overseas Filipino workers is thus clear: were it not for these receipts, the country would have experienced serious balance-of-payments difficulties in 2002.

Over the last 20 years, the country's trade has increasingly become concentrated in a few exportable items – mainly machinery and transport equipment – while losing competitiveness in its traditional export items. For example, coconut exports constituted nearly 10 per cent of total merchandise exports in 1980, but after two decades their share was only slightly over 1 per cent. Processed food exports were nearly a quarter of total exports in 1980, but their share dropped to nearly 4 per cent in 2002. The mining industry shows a similar pattern: in 1980, its exports represented about 25 per cent of total exports, but by 2002, their share had fallen to less than 1 per cent.

10.3 Trade reforms and recent trends

In 1982, the Philippine government introduced an unilateral, comprehensive trade reform programme aimed at increasing the competitiveness of the Philippine economy. It was implemented in three phases during the 1980s and 1990s. The Tariff Reform Program (TRP), implemented from 1981 to 1985, narrowed down the tariff structure from a range of 100–0 per cent to 50–10 per cent. This was accompanied by the Import Liberalization Programme (ILP), which sought to eliminate non-tariff import measures, but it was interrupted by the economic and political crises in the country in the mid-1980s. It was not until the change of government in 1986 that this programme was resumed. The number of regulated items was reduced from 1,802 in 1985 to 609 in 1988, and export taxes on all products except logs were removed.

The government launched the second phase of its trade liberalization programme in 1991 with Executive Order (EO) 470, which aimed at lowering tariff rates over a five-year period. The realignment involved the narrowing of the range of the tariff structure through a series of rate reductions for commodity lines with high tariffs and increases in commodity lines with low tariffs. Specifically, the programme aimed at clustering the commodities within a tariff range of 10–30 per cent.

In 1992, EO 8 introduced tariff protection measures to replace quantitative restrictions (QRs) on imports of 153 commodities. The tariffication raised the tariff rates applicable to affected commodities by 100 per cent of their pre-EO 8 levels. In effect, the tariff rates imposed were higher than the tariff equivalent rates, which are the tariff protection rates indicated by the respective proportionate difference between local and world prices of commodities in a number of cases, especially during the initial years of the conversion. However, EO 8 had a built-in programme for a five-year phase-down of the tariffed rates, and it realigned tariff rates for 48 items.

The unilateral tariff reform programme entered its third phase in 1994 with four Executive Orders, two of which are listed for 1994: EO 189 issued on 1 January 1994 reduced tariff rates on capital equipment and machinery; and EO 204 issued on 30 September 1994 lowered tariff rates on imported textiles, garments, and chemical inputs. But by far the largest overhaul of the country's tariff code was EO 264, introduced on 22 July 1995, which reduced tariffs on 4,142 lines of the Harmonized System (HS) in the manufacturing sector. This was followed by EO 288, introduced on 1 January 1996, which reduced tariffs on 'non-sensitive' agricultural products. The TRP Phase III provided for a four-tier structure of tariff rates: 3 per cent for raw materials and capital equipment that are not available locally; 10 per cent for raw materials and capital equipment that are available from local sources; 20 per cent for intermediate goods; and 30 per cent for finished goods. The objective was to eventually achieve a 'low, nearly uniform' tariff rate in the Philippines by 2002. The Philippine government made this offer in its Individual Action Plan presented at the summit meeting of leaders of the Asia Pacific Economic Cooperation (APEC) forum in Subic in 1996. It was also considered a necessary step in the implementation of the impending ASEAN Free Trade Agreement.

In the Uruguay Round, the Philippines, along with all other WTO Members, committed to eliminating all its quantitative import restrictions on agricultural products, except rice, and to converting the underlying trade protecting its protective ordinary customs duties. The Philippine Congress passed Republic Act (RA) 8178 on 29 March 1996 to implement this international treaty obligation. Accordingly, EO 313 was issued which specified the tariff equivalent rates for each agricultural QR. Rice was exempted because the Philippine government asked for special treatment in accordance with Annex 5 of the WTO Agreement on Agriculture, which expires in 2005.

Table 10.1 shows the trade-weighted average tariff rates on imports from 1988 to 2003. The progressive reductions in tariff rates by sector were larger for manufacturing than for agriculture. However between 1994 and 1998, agricultural protection increased as a result of the 'tariffication' of non-tariff import restrictions in that sector, as provided for by the WTO Agreement on Agriculture. David (1997) observed that quantitative restrictions were replaced by applied tariffs, most of which were equal to the high binding tariffs; these had the effect of increasing protection for agriculture. Even the tariffs on imports that are close substitutes

Table 10.1: Trade-weighted average tariff rates applied on Philippine imports: 1988 to 2003(%)

	1988	1990	1994	1998	2000	2001	2002	2003
Agriculture, forestry and fishing								
Agriculture, hunting and related service activities	18.18	16.86	15.67	20.35	9.27	7.77	6.77	6.30
Forestry, logging and related service activities	10.65	10.11	5.61	0.67	0.77	0.88	0.70	0.70
Fisheries and aquaculture	31.45	23.46	25.34	8.29	5.82	5.45	5.80	4.42
Mining								
Mining of coal and lignite; extraction of peat	19.98	10.00	14.05	9.62	6.55	6.54	4.14	3.57
Extraction of natural gas and industry-specific services	10.00	10.00	10.00	3.00	3.00	3.00	3.00	3.00
Mining of metal ores	10.00	10.00	10.00	3.00	3.00	3.00	2.99	2.99
Other mining and quarrying	11.91	11.43	4.22	3.23	3.24	3.01	2.18	2.18
Manufacturing								
Food products and beverages	32.16	20.93	30.57	25.49	12.93	11.73	12.73	11.97
Tobacco products	49.54	29.89	49.66	20.00	9.98	9.96	6.98	6.98
Textiles	38.73	27.63	28.36	13.90	9.37	8.97	6.58	4.96
Wearing apparel; dressing and dyeing of fur	49.92	30.00	49.40	24.88	19.22	19.48	14.53	9.73
Tanning and dressing of leather; luggage, handbags, footwear	36.21	23.80	30.97	13.25	8.49	8.37	6.71	5.45
Wood and of products of wood and cork, except furniture;	32.36	21.35	21.80	13.68	9.82	9.56	7.82	5.64
Paper and paper products	34.50	19.89	20.87	10.04	6.82	6.68	4.58	3.60

(*continued*)

Table 10.1: (*continued*)

	1988	1990	1994	1998	2000	2001	2002	2003
Publishing, printing and reproduction of recorded media	25.05	18.66	18.60	10.62	6.43	6.17	4.43	3.98
Coke, refined petroleum products and nuclear fuel	19.71	11.49	10.31	3.00	3.00	3.00	2.64	2.64
Chemicals and chemical products	19.36	12.66	11.94	5.55	4.79	4.29	3.76	3.63
Rubber and plastics products	31.13	24.88	23.87	10.87	8.25	10.43	9.77	9.16
Other non-metallic mineral products	36.70	14.78	20.63	12.73	7.62	7.52	5.70	4.54
Basic metals	15.18	12.82	12.68	6.39	5.35	3.95	2.88	2.79
Fabricated metal products, except machinery and equipment	30.17	26.51	26.54	13.44	9.28	9.17	6.51	5.05
Machinery and equipment n.e.c.	22.36	12.24	12.29	4.70	3.33	3.27	1.90	1.71
Office, accounting and computing machinery	19.36	10.44	10.03	3.01	0.04	0.02	0.02	0.02
Electrical machinery and apparatus	26.45	17.76	18.42	7.81	5.24	4.64	3.25	2.68
Radio, television, and communication equipment	21.83	11.43	11.62	3.21	0.47	0.29	0.12	0.09
Medical, precision and optical instruments, watches	17.63	13.92	13.66	4.80	2.72	2.61	2.30	2.29
Motor vehicles, trailers and semi-trailers	31.70	25.06	21.49	15.05	13.07	11.36	11.14	11.14
Other transport equipment	14.23	11.84	11.67	7.20	9.78	9.72	8.80	8.79
Furniture; manufacturing n.e.c.	41.96	27.07	31.36	16.33	10.00	9.32	6.74	5.40
Electricity, gas, steam and hot water supply	10.00	10.00	10.00	3.00	3.00	3.00	3.00	3.00
Total average	**22.43**	**14.79**	**15.22**	**7.16**	**4.13**	**3.86**	**2.82**	**2.60**

Source: WTIS/Trains UNCTAD Computations.

for the tariffed imported commodities, such as feed wheat and barley substitutes for corn, were likewise raised to ensure protection for the corn farmers. The dramatic drop in tariff protection for agriculture between 1998 and 2000 reflects the changing basket of agricultural imports. Between 1996 and 1997, the agricultural products that were imported were those subject to tariff quotas, for which a relatively high out-of-quota tariff rate was imposed. This increased the trade-weighted average. Thereafter, imports of other agricultural items affected the average tariff rate on agricultural imports.

Manasan and Pineda (2000) have estimated that the overall average effective protection rate in 2000 was lower than its level in 1990 by 48 per cent, reflecting the tariff reforms of the 1990s. As with nominal tariffs, the cuts in effective protection were larger for manufacturing than for agriculture. The EPR for manufacturing was reduced by at least one-third compared to that for agriculture, which was reduced by only 31 per cent over the same period. Food processing has been the most protected in the manufacturing sector, while agriculture enjoys the highest effective protection among the primary and mining sectors. Both these sectors experienced an increase in their effective protection in 1996. The dispersion of sectoral EPRs for industry was lower in 2000 compared to what it had been in 1990.

The government's key purposes in liberalizing trade policies have been to achieve greater efficiency in resource allocation and to make consumers better off. Trade protection distorts allocation of resources, as they tend to move towards economic sectors that are protected by import restrictions rather than to those in which the country has a comparative advantage. With trade liberalization, this distortion is removed. As a result, the economy gains from the ensuing reallocation of resources towards industries with the greatest export potential – arising from technology or resource endowment advantages – as well as to those industries whose products are the most valued by consumers.

Critics have expressed reservations about trade liberalization and the serious threats that globalization poses to the country's economy. In their view, Philippine producers are ill-prepared for increased market competition, and are therefore likely to close down, resulting in the loss of job opportunities for Filipinos. While they acknowledge that winners may emerge, their number would be smaller than those forced out of business. Workers displaced by freer trade face adjustment costs in searching for new job opportunities and developing the appropriate skills for new jobs.

Reduced prices are expected to harm producers, particularly the primary producers or those at the top of the supply chain. In agriculture for example, the growing competition provided by competitive imported fruits and vegetables are generally expected to push down prices of tropical fruits and vegetables in the domestic market. With logistical costs relatively higher for local farmers, increased trade would reduce farm incomes and increase poverty in rural areas.

Commenting on the trade-related problems of Philippine agriculture, Clarete (1999) ascribes the lack of competitiveness in Philippine agriculture to two types of failures. The first pertains to the government's failure to provide the required public support services necessary to increase productivity. The second is due to the failure of producers to keep their production costs down to the minimum. The policy in 1996 to provide maximum trade protection to the country's farmers may have had adverse consequences on their ability to become competitive in that high tariff protection is a disincentive to achieve higher levels of productive efficiency. And since the producers' incomes are artificially propped by trade protection, the government is not politically compelled to act on the lack of infrastructure and common service facilities.

10.4 Assessing the effects of freer trade policies

10.4.1 Effects using simulation models

Habito and Cororaton (2000) simulated the effects of trade liberalization using a 50-sector computable general equilibrium of the Philippine economy. Its benchmark year is 1994, which makes the model particularly appropriate for simulating the actual trade policy reforms that took place after the ratification of the Philippines' accession treaty at the end of that year. The analysis involves simulating the effects of tariff rate changes from 1995 to 2000. These changes reflected both unilateral and multilateral tariff reforms, the latter representing the country's concessions to its trading partners covering applied tariffs on agriculture imports. The tariffication of non-tariff measures in agriculture ended up increasing agriculture tariff protection in 1996. With respect to non-agriculture tariffs, the changes depicted in the analysis are unilateral. The authors performed sets of calculations covering nominal tariff reforms, implicit tariff reforms, and transaction valuation reform.

The ex-ante assessment of tariff reforms from 1995 to 2000 by Habito and Cororaton (2000) yielded a cumulative impact on real GDP of 2.3 per cent. The results indicated a relatively smaller drop in the number of jobs in both the agriculture and services sectors. However, this was more than compensated for by new jobs created in the manufacturing sector. Thus, overall, not only did real GDP increase, but also the inequality of its distribution declined, the poorest quintile income group receiving the largest share of the GDP growth.

10.4.2 Merchandise trade

In the early stages of the reform, aggregate imports exceeded exports for most of the years since 1985, contributing to the build-up of a trade deficit. However, Habito and Cororaton (2000) observed that merchandise exports performed well in the 1990s. Except in 1993, export growth from 1991 to 1998 was significant. This led them to conclude that the export sector generally benefited from market opening in other countries and from the removal of trade barriers unilaterally or as offshoots of the WTO agreements. Even the slowdown of the economy in 1997–1998 did not prevent the export sector from posting consistently high rates of growth.

However, merchandise export growth was not as robust as it could have been because 'the reductions in tariff and import restrictions have not been accompanied by a consistent exchange rate policy that favours (or is neutral to) exports' (Austria, 1997). The real effective exchange rate depreciated by 31.1 per cent during the period 1982–1988, but appreciated from 1989 to 1996 because of the increase in foreign direct investment, from about $0.5 billion in the 1980s to $1.5 billion in the 1990s. Intal (1997) noted that the Philippines lost its competitiveness relative to its East Asian competitors in the 1990s. As a result, export expansion decelerated, from an average annual growth rate of 11.3 per cent in the second half of the 1980s to only 9.7 per cent in the first half of the 1990s. The depreciation of the peso following the Asian crisis probably helped boost export performance during the crisis, but it failed to arrest the slowing down of export growth. In the second half of the 1990s, exports expanded by only 3.6 per cent.

However, a different finding may be reached by breaking down overall export performance by sector. In fact, exports of machinery and transportation equipment virtually explain aggregate export performance in the 1990s. Although exports of coconut oil (which is an important component of animal and vegetable oils and fats) recovered in the first half of the 1990s, and boosted overall export performance, their contribution was less than $1 billion. Miscellaneous manufacturing also accounted for higher export earnings, which rose significantly through the 1990s, peaking at nearly $5 billion in 2000, but falling thereafter. The other export sectors showed either a decline or hardly any improvement. Food and live animals, beverages and tobacco, and manufactured goods did not register any discernible pattern of export expansion.

Merchandise imports expanded much faster than exports in the 1990s until the Asian crisis halted that trend. Since 2000, only a few sectors have recovered, but only moderately, including beverages and tobacco and food and live animals.

To what extent can the changes in merchandise trade be attributed to reductions in applied tariffs on Philippine imports and those faced by Philippine exporters? If the changes in applied import tariffs are correlated with the increases in import values since 1990, the response of imported intermediate goods, such as chemicals and chemical products, or machinery and transport equipment, was positive. However, imported machinery and transport equipment, used in the production of exports of electronic products and semi-conductors, slowed down in response to the Asian crisis about three years earlier than the sector's exports.

Overall, a post-hoc assessment of the liberalization differs from the ex-ante analysis using an equilibrium model of the Philippine economy. For most of the period covered by the analysis, imports exceeded exports, which meant that the country experienced a trade deficit as a result of trade liberalization. Second, rather than revealing a fairly diverse basket of exports from a large number of industries, as the simulation-based analysis indicated, the ex-post assessment indicates a concentration of exports in only a few industries.

10.4.3 Production and employment

Freer trade policies are expected to move resources towards industries in which the country has a comparative advantage. Table 10.2 shows the shares of 27 manufacturing industries in total manufacturing between 1980 and 1997. Food products and refined petroleum have been the top two industries in terms of production since 1980. These two industries contributed, on average, over 21 per cent and over 15 per cent respectively to total manufacturing output. Other important sectors are other chemicals, transport equipment, textiles, wearing apparel, beverages, iron and steel, and professional and scientific equipment.

Total employment growth fluctuated around its average of 2.7 per cent over the last two decades, but with two fairly large downturns. These coincided with problems in the agriculture sector. One occurred in the mid-1980s and the other in 1997, both caused by droughts brought on by El Niño. Agriculture not only failed to provide new jobs to new entrants into the work force, but also led to job losses, thereby pulling down total employment growth. Overall economic performance was also affected by the Asian financial crisis. By the early 2000s agriculture recovered, resulting in a resumption of employment.

Those who oppose trade liberalization and Philippine membership of the WTO use the loss of jobs in agriculture to prove their point that

Table 10.2: Manufacturing production: 1980–1997

	1980	1985	1988	1990	1992	1994	1996	1997
Total manufacturing (USD million)	17'368	12'081	18'252	24'322	28'805	32'273	46'003	45'935
Share to total (%)								
Food products	21.72	21.87	21.65	24.69	20.16	19.84	20.28	20.28
Beverages	2.70	6.26	6.54	5.64	5.79	5.59	5.93	5.93
Tobacco	5.77	5.86	4.21	3.10	3.01	3.16	2.92	–
Textiles	7.27	4.59	5.08	4.68	3.98	3.12	3.21	–
Wearing apparel	2.68	2.15	3.95	4.34	4.43	4.29	4.17	–
Leather products	0.15	0.08	0.14	0.19	0.20	0.14	0.15	–
Footwear	0.22	0.24	0.17	0.19	0.36	0.42	0.40	–
Wood products	3.91	2.42	2.84	1.84	1.36	1.08	1.08	–
Furniture	0.96	0.52	1.00	0.88	0.68	0.66	0.64	–
Paper and products	2.93	2.41	2.66	2.12	2.58	2.03	2.04	–
Printing and publishing	1.51	1.08	1.08	1.24	1.27	1.29	1.48	1.48
Industrial chemicals	4.53	3.26	3.75	3.12	3.28	2.67	2.73	2.73
Other chemicals	8.22	6.77	7.94	7.08	7.79	7.42	7.28	7.28
Petroleum refineries	15.33	21.46	11.55	11.31	11.81	13.10	12.29	12.29
Misc. petroleum and coal products	0.04	0.10	0.13	0.09	0.13	0.10	0.13	0.13
Rubber products	1.56	1.26	2.19	1.50	1.89	1.16	1.20	1.20
Plastic products	1.40	1.17	1.74	1.59	1.91	1.83	1.83	1.83
Pottery	0.36	0.17	0.20	0.20	0.32	0.29	0.27	0.27
Glass and products	0.65	0.82	0.78	0.65	0.65	0.67	0.64	0.64
Other non-metallic mineral products	0.94	1.81	1.97	2.36	2.55	2.60	2.51	2.51
Iron and steel	3.00	4.24	5.13	4.98	4.62	4.15	4.63	4.63
Non-ferrous metals	0.67	2.43	3.10	2.27	1.60	2.06	2.16	2.16
Machinery and equipment n.e.c.	2.40	1.70	1.58	1.87	1.72	1.93	1.87	1.87
Office, accounting and computing machinery	1.29	0.75	0.86	0.82	0.93	1.35	1.60	1.60
Transport equipment	4.04	4.81	6.66	8.22	10.95	11.99	11.58	11.58
Professional & scientific equipment	5.01	1.13	2.31	4.13	5.15	5.99	5.89	5.89
Other manufactured products	0.05	0.14	0.16	0.07	0.11	0.20	0.23	0.23

Source: UNSTAT 2003 ISIC Revision2.

more trade is bad for Philippine agriculture. They link the contraction of agriculture during the El Niño-induced drought to the Philippine government's implementation of provisions of the WTO's Agriculture Agreement, particularly those related to market access. This was quite simply a case of spurious correlation (Clarete, 1999). However, agricultural employment recovered starting in 2000, even though the Philippines continued to implement the multilateral trade reforms in agriculture. Thus the agriculture sector continues to be an important generator of jobs in the Philippines. However, like industry, its performance in terms of providing jobs in the rural areas falls short of requirements.

Industrial employment growth has been better than expected. The sector's employment growth averaged 2.9 per cent over the period 1980–2000, which was higher than the growth rate of the economically active population. The economic contraction in 1985 appeared to have a moderate impact on employment in this sector, and, indeed, a much lower impact than that of the Asian crisis in 1997–1998; it reduced employment by about 4.7 per cent, or about two percentage points higher than the negative 6.9 per cent of agricultural employment. This shows that agricultural production is affected much more by weather conditions, such as the El Niño-induced drought, than by changes in economic policies.

The services sector provides the best job opportunities for Filipinos. It has been generating jobs at the rate of about 4.5 per cent per annum. Since 1998, this sector has overtaken agriculture in providing jobs to Filipinos. In 1980, agriculture provided nearly 9 million jobs as against the services sector which provided 5.6 million. By 1998, the latter provided 12.6 million jobs or over 1 million jobs more than agriculture.

Contrary to the results obtained from simulating the effects of trade reforms using models of the Philippine economy, industry rather than making up for the observed reduction of jobs in agriculture and services in the ex-ante analysis, has turned out in this ex-post assessment of the effects of these reforms to be part of the problem. According to the results from the simulations, trade liberalization should have resulted in resources of industries rendered uncompetitive moving into those that were given a boost by lower import restrictions. However, the shares of the various manufacturing sectors to total manufacturing production barely changed, indicating that resources hardly moved.

10.4.4 Development indicators

Is the Philippines better off as a result of progressive trade liberalization over the past 25 years?

In terms of per capita income, the country is not better off, as this has remained more or less unchanged, even falling slightly from $1,173 (at 1995 prices) in 1980 to $1,165 in 2001. There were years when the average Filipino was worse off than in 1980, but relative to that year, when trade reforms began, the average Filipino's standard of living has remained roughly the same. However, this is no indication that freer trade has made the country either better or worse off. Per capita income could have declined if trade had not been liberalized or if the Philippines had not joined the WTO. On the other hand, per capita incomes might have increased had trade protection not been reduced or, worse still, increased.

Looking at a few other development indicators, at least for the years for which data is available, there are positive trends of progress. Life expectancy at birth has risen by slightly more than eight years. The literacy rate has improved: the proportion of illiterate adult females fell from 13.2 per cent in 1985 to just short of 5 per cent in 2001, and the illiteracy rate of adult males fell from 11.22 per cent to 4.7 per cent (World Bank, 2003).

The data also indicate that more Filipinos have access to infrastructure services and technologies. While the number of computer users is low, it has been rising, from nearly 3,500 per thousand persons in 1990 to nearly 21,700 in 2001. The use of mobile phones in the Philippines is among the highest in the world, with 15 per cent of Filipinos using them in 2001.

The incidence of poverty appears to be on the decline (Habito et al., 2000), although it worsened in the early 1990s. In 1985, the incidence of rural poverty was far worse than that of urban poverty, at 50.7 per cent compared to 33.6 per cent in the urban areas. There was an impressive decline in the incidence of urban poverty, which fell by 15.1 percentage points over the period 1985–1997. However, the number of rural poor fell by only 6.3 percentage points over the same period. Overall, the incidence of poverty declined from 44.2 per cent in 1985 to 32.1 per cent in 1997.

10.5 Transaction costs

The preceding discussion reveals important differences between the results emerging from an ex-ante analysis of the effects of trade liberalization using a general equilibrium model and the ex-post assessment of secondary data. The former reflect the underlying assumptions of the model, while the latter are the realization of a host of factors and economic shocks. This analysis does not proceed from the perspective that the two ought to be identical. Rather, it considers whether the movements of key development indicators over more than 25 years of progressive trade liberalization in the Philippines are consistent with a priori expectations. The analysis shows that they differ from the anticipated results.

The role of transaction costs in decision-making with respect to resource allocation cannot be emphasized enough. If trade protection is reduced, the expected reallocation of resources to export-oriented industries may not happen as quickly, or even at all, because of transaction costs. In conventional models of international trade, transaction costs are zero. That is, they assume that producers, consumers and the government have perfect information about everything that is relevant for their respective decisions, agreements are easy to make and property rights are well defined and easily enforced. When the effects of lower import restrictions on resource allocation are analysed with those models, resources are expected to move towards export-oriented industries, and consumers purchase more imported products.

However, in reality, transaction costs have the potential of dampening these effects, and, worse, preventing them from occurring at all. It is not surprising then that critics claim that globalization has led to less import substitution without the corresponding gain in export revenues, resulting in the loss of jobs and a worsening of the poverty situation. The examination of the economic data on production, employment and merchandise trade in the Philippines would seem to validate this claim. Reducing tariff protection goes as far as it can in generating jobs, lowering prices and improving productivity. However, if the country has a serious problem with transaction costs, the benefits that can be derived from trade reforms will not be maximized. This is consistent with Rodriguez and Rodrik (2000), who cautioned against oversimplifying the case that trade policies are a substitute for other macroeconomic reforms fundamental to economic development.

There are two interpretations of transaction costs in the literature (Allen, 1991). The type of transaction cost faced in the example above covers the costs associated with the transfer of assets. The neo-classical definition of transaction costs covers all market-related infrastructure, including highways, feeder roads, sea and air ports, communications, banking facilities, and other common services, which, taken together, define the capability of a group of producers to take advantage of known market opportunities. These costs cannot be passed on to the market because the producers concerned are price-takers. The burden of these costs falls on them and serves as a disincentive to participation in any market exchange. If the volumes are so large that the combined supply of producers in a given area constitutes a significant share of the market, then these necessary logistic costs may be passed on to the market. However, if other suppliers of the same homogeneous product or a close substitute can demonstrate that they have lower logistic costs, then the former group of producers have a comparative disadvantage and will set benchmark costs for the industry. Non-marginal suppliers with higher than the benchmark costs can supply them, but they will have to bear these transaction costs.

The relatively poor Philippine export performance may therefore be explained substantively by this problem of transaction costs rather than market access difficulties. As discussed earlier, most export sectors in the Philippines experienced a decline in their share of total export receipts, with the notable exception of electronic products. Because lack of market access involves MFN tariffs, other trading partners face the same set of import duties in importing countries. For example, when Philippine coconut oil exporters lost market share to their competitors producing coconut oil substitutes, including palm oil or other lauric oils, that problem reflected the growing perception of importers that the Philippines cannot be relied upon to meet the lauric oil requirement of the various industries in the importing countries. That perception stems from the inability of the Philippines to improve its efficiency in moving products from point of production to the market – a logistical rather than a market access issue. The problem is probably due to logistic cost disadvantages and the lack of responsiveness of Philippine exporters to the changing demands of the importers of the country's goods. Hence, those importing firms that had once bought coconut oil shifted to substitutes that assured a more reliable and adequate supply.

Exports require investments, which in turn depend upon the investment climate of the country. A good environment for investments requires a regime that keeps transaction costs of defining and enforcing property rights low (Coase, 1937).[1] High Coasean transaction costs dampen investments. These cover the costs incurred in acquiring information, negotiating the terms of transactions, monitoring the performance of the parties to an agreement, enforcing the terms of the agreement, adapting the agreement to the changing environment, and settling disputes. Absence of information per se is not a transaction cost, but it is an important component of the latter if considered in the context of making an economic transaction.

10.6 Concluding remarks

This ex-post assessment has sought to examine the impacts of trade liberalization in the Philippines since the 1980s on production, trade, income, income inequality and poverty. It compares these impacts with ex-ante simulations of the effects of trade reforms.

The Philippine experience reveals a case of only partial positive adjustment to a freer trade regime due to transaction costs. When trade-related costs or costs of enforcement of property rights are high, the investment needed to seize the opportunities created by freer trade fail to materialize. Consequently, the structure of the industrial sector, particularly manufacturing, barely changed. It is important for the Philippines to address this issue of transaction costs in its pursuit of greater integration into the global trading system. Improved economic performance, made possible by freer trade, involves a growing number of economic agents engaged in a cooperative, competitive, and mutually gainful exchange of assets to create additional wealth. Lower transaction costs are necessary for this to happen.

Contracting parties in trade negotiations request market access for products in which their economies have a comparative advantage. An understanding of what makes up that advantage is important and transaction costs offer important insights towards this. An economy may have a comparative advantage in producing a product because it may have the better technology or factor endowments. However with poor logistics systems it may lose the production advantage to those more efficient in moving their products to markets. This is particularly important in today's world when supply chains that span several countries and involve more than one product are increasingly being organized to cut down logistic costs as well as to take advantage of specialization and economies of scale. Furthermore, the investment climate of an economy is critical in multinational companies' decisions to include that economy in their production and logistical networks. This requires effective enforcement of property rights and adequate infrastructure capacity in host economies.

Note

1 While Coase (1937) first used the term 'transaction costs', Williamson (1979) developed the concept to refer to costs associated with determining and enforcing property rights.

References

Allen, D. W. (1991) What are transaction costs? *Research in Law and Economics*, 14: 1–18.

Austria, M. (1997) The emerging Philippine trade environment. Paper prepared for the Department of Foreign Affairs and Trade of Australia under the project entitled, The Philippines: Beyond the Crisis.

Clarete, R. (1991) General equilibrium effects of the EO 413 tariff reforms in the Philippines. Paper prepared for the Philippine Center for Economic Development.

Diliman, Quezon City, Philippines, University of the Philippines School of Economics.

Clarete, R. (1995) How valuable is MFN treatment to the Philippines? *Philippine Review of Economics and Business*, XXXII (2), December.

Clarete, R. (1999) Trade-related problems and policy issues in Philippine agriculture. *Philippine Review of Economics and Business*, XXXVI (1), June.

Coase, R. (1937) The nature of the firm. *Economica*, 4: 386–405.

Cororaton, C. (1998) The Philippine tariff structure: an analysis of changes, effects and impacts. Micro Impacts of Macroeconomic Adjustment Policies Project (MIMAP), Philippines, Research Paper. Paper presented during the third MIMAP Annual Meeting on 2–6 November 1998 in Kathmandu, Nepal.

David, C. (1997) Agricultural policy and the WTO Agreement: The Philippine Case. PIDS Discussion Paper No. 2001–09. Makati City, Philippine Institute for Development Studies. Discussion Paper No. 97–13.

Habito, C. and Cororaton, C. (2000) WTO and the Philippine economy: An empirical and analytical assessment of post-WTO trade reforms in the Philippines. Study report for the USAID/Philippines AGILE Programme. Manila, Philippines.

Habito, C. et al. (2000) Farms, food and foreign trade: the World Trade Organization and Philippine agriculture, Study report for the USAID/Philippines AGILE Programme. Manila, Philippines.

Intal, P. (1997) Sustaining the Philippine economic resurgence. Paper presented at the symposium in honour of Dr Gerardo Sicat and Dr Jose Encarnacion, Jr. Makati City, Philippine Institute for Development Studies, 23–25 September.

Manasan, R. and Pineda, V. (2000) Assessment of Philippine tariff reform: 1998 update. Study Report for the USAID/Philippines AGILE Programme.

Orbeta, A. and Pernia, E. M. (1999) Population, growth, and economic development in the Philippines: What has been the experience and what must be done? PIDS Discussion Paper No. 99–22. Makati City, Philippine Institute for Development Studies.

Rodriguez, F. and Rodrik, D. (2000) Trade policy and economic growth: A skeptic's guide to the cross-national evidence. Harvard University Kennedy School of Government, Cambridge, MA. http://ksghome.harvard.edu/~.drodrik.academic.ksg/skepti1299.pdf

Williamson, O. (1979) Transaction cost economics: the governance of contractual relations. *Journal of Law and Economics*, 22: 223–61.

World Bank (2003) World Development Indicators 2003, Washington DC.

World Bank (2004) Sustaining trade liberalization. WB 2004 Philippines DB10. World Bank Resident Mission, Manila, Philippines.

11
Zambia

Manenga Ndulo and Dale Mudenda

11.1 Introduction

Zambia (population 10.5 million) is among the poorest of the least developed countries (LDCs) in the WTO. Real per capita income was estimated at $421 in 2003, which is 28 per cent lower than it was in 1980, at $584. It is estimated that 84.6 per cent of the population lived below the poverty line in 1998, compared with 49 per cent in 1980 (Seshamani, 1999). The rate of growth of real output is low; real GDP was estimated at $4.9 billion in 2003 compared with $3.4 billion in 1980 – an increase of only 47 per cent in 23 years. This is despite an abundance of unutilized agricultural resources.

The Zambian economy is heavily dependent on the production of a single commodity: copper. In 2002, copper accounted for nearly 68 per cent of total exports, contributed about 8 per cent to GDP and represented an important source of government revenues. Zambia is also rich in agricultural resources, but much of that potential remains underutilized. The country was able to sustain a high rate of real growth from independence in 1964 until about 1974, when it suffered a major external shock in the form of a drastic, 40-per-cent fall in the price of copper. Thereafter, copper prices remained weak and unstable. Coupled with high prices of imported fuel that raised import costs, it highlighted the weaknesses of the economy: its dependence on one commodity, a weak manufacturing base, an underdeveloped agriculture sector and a rapid opening up of the economy. It meant that the effects of the shock were transmitted to all sectors of the economy. Consequently, real GDP per capita collapsed. Since these adverse shocks, the economy has undergone two major episodes of adjustment. The first adjustment period (1985–1987) was brief because the domestic economy could not support the adjustment costs. The second adjustment has been under way since 1991. However, since 1996 the intensity of the adjustment effort has been moderated, though not reversed.

Prior to the first adjustment period, Zambia had a controlled economy, with a protected import-substituting industrial sector and an underutilized agriculture sector. The country produced a narrow range of exports comprising mainly copper and a few agricultural and manufactured goods. There was an extensive system of domestic price controls, trade restrictions and government allocation of foreign exchange. This created severe internal and external disequilibria within the country; it also resulted in the emergence of an underground economy in international trade and a parallel market in goods and assets in domestic trade. The country also had a huge external debt, which worsened after the external shock, mainly because the government responded by borrowing in order to resolve the crisis. All these elements affected the nature of trade policy reform.

11.2 Trade policy and reform

Zambia has undertaken major trade policy reforms since 1985. Between independence in 1964 and the mid-1970s, the country's trade regime was relatively unrestricted compared with what followed. Tariffs were high, varying between zero and 150 per cent, there were exemptions and outright bans on certain imports, and a system of import licensing. There were also export taxes on mineral exports.

In 1975, following the collapse of the copper price in 1974 and the consequent shortage of foreign exchange, the government imposed greater restrictions on trade. It introduced quantitative restrictions on imports, in addition to the existing high tariffs, and used import licences, import bans and foreign exchange controls to regulate the use of scarce foreign exchange and to protect domestic industry. By the early 1980s, quantitative restrictions on imports had become so extensive that the structure of protection could not be determined by the tariff schedule alone (World Bank, 1984).

The first major attempt at tariff reform began in 1985. However, this reform process ended in 1987 when the adjustment costs became unbearable and led to social protests and unrest, and was reversed in 1987–89.

The second period of trade reforms has been implemented since 1991 and has involved a second wave of tariff reform. This began in 1989 with the New Economic Recovery Programme supported by the IMF and World Bank. The objectives of Zambia's trade policy are set out in policy framework papers and in the national policy document (GRZ, 1994). The country has moved away from an inward-focused strategy of import

Table 11.1: Main trade-related reform measures, 1991–2003

Year	Policies
1991	Nominal tariff levels reduced to a range of 0–50 per cent.
1993	Nominal tariff levels reduced to a range of 0–40 per cent.
1994	All controls on current and capital accounts abolished.
1995	Import sales tax changed to import VAT.
1996	Nominal tariff levels reduced to a range of 0–25 per cent. SADC Trade Protocol signed.
2000	COMESA FTA signed, with zero duty for traded among the nine members.
	SADC tariff reduction phase begins, with objective to establish a SADC FTA by 2012.
	AGOA Agreement signed.
2001	EU's EBA established, offering duty-free access to LDCs' exports, except for armaments and three sensitive products.
2003	Zambia Export Processing Zone Authority established.

substitution, dependent on high levels of tariff protection, to an outward-oriented, export-led strategy based on open markets and international competition. The objective is to create opportunities for the country to develop. In this regard, it has opted for a liberal import and export regime aimed at directing resources to the most productive areas necessary for export production. This will help it achieve the immediate objective of promoting non-traditional exports. Tariffs are to be used as a strategic instrument of tariff policy. The government aims to arrive at a simplified and broad-based tariff structure that promotes development and takes account of the revenue implications and adjustment costs to industry.

Under the reforms, the maximum nominal tariff rate was reduced to 50 per cent in 1991. In the 1993 budget, nominal tariff rates were reduced further and rationalized to 0, 20, 30 and 40 per cent. However, the major tariff reform effort was in 1996, when the nominal tariff rates were reduced to their current levels of 0, 5, 15 and 25 per cent. Table 11.1 shows some of the major trade-related measures carried out during the second period of reforms. Table 11.2 shows the broad sectoral breakdown of applied MFN tariffs as well as rates by stage of processing. There is a simplified four-band structure with a dispersion of 0–25 per cent; it gives a simple import tariff average of 13.6 per cent with a standard deviation of 9.3 per cent.

The trade regime has been fully liberalized, involving a reduction of the level of nominal tariffs, their rationalization and the removal of all impediments to trade. On imports, nominal tariffs have been lowered

Table 11.2: Dispersion of Zambian applied MFN tariffs in 1997

	Average tariff (%)	Tariff range	Standard deviation	Variation coefficient
All tariff lines	13.6	0–25	9.3	68.6
By sector:				
Agriculture	18.2	0–25	8.5	46.7
Mining	7.5	0–25	5.9	79.1
Industry	13.5	0–25	9.3	69.3
By degree of processing:				
Primary products	14.4	0–25	9.2	63.8
Semi-processed products	9.5	0–25	8.8	92.4
Finished products	16.5	0–25	8.6	52.3

Source: Independent Management Consultancy Services, 1999.

and import licensing has been dismantled except for sanitary and phytosanitary (SPS) purposes and for conformity with the United Nations Convention on International Trade in Endangered Species of Wild Fauna and Flora (CITES). Import controls are maintained only for environmental, moral, health and security reasons. All quantitative restrictions on imports have been abolished and many exemptions eliminated. Import customs valuation has been changed from a free-on-board (f.o.b.) basis to a cost, insurance and freight (c.i.f.) basis. In order to further rationalize the tariff system, the tariff bands were reduced to four bands, and their current levels are 0, 5, 15 and 25; any tariff changes are done within these bands. Many specific rates have been changed to ad valorem duties. Domestic and import sales tax rates were unified, and, subsequently, a value added tax replaced the sales tax. The current value added tax is 17.5 per cent for both domestic and imported goods. On exports, all export restrictions have been removed. Export documentation is maintained only for statistical purposes. This reform has been supported by the creation of institutions to promote exports, such as the Export Board of Zambia and the Zambia Export Processing Zones Authority.

Among the measures directly affecting imports, a distinction can be made between those relating to imports that serve as inputs in export-oriented production, and those applied to other imports not used in export production. To try to reduce the anti-export bias and expand non-traditional exports, the government has introduced a duty-drawback system and manufacturing under bond, neither of which seems to work very well. Concerning imports intended for local consumption or as inputs into local production that is not exported, in principle, the overall import policy is liberal, with no quantitative restrictions on imports. Import licences were abolished in 1992, and have since been given automatically. There is a general consensus in the government and the private sector for the need to move from a regime of quantitative restrictions to tariffs. The most important factor determining imports are tariffs. In this policy stance, the government has been generally consistent despite enormous pressure from the private sector to impose controls on certain imports.

Internal constraints on Zambia's export performance have to do with the unstable and weak macroeconomic performance of the economy and the lack of a supply-side response. The range of exports, especially industrial exports, is too small, both in terms of product mix and export markets. Other problems include inadequate exploitation of natural resources, poor infrastructure services, lack of export finance, low productivity, underutilization of productive capacity, high production costs and high transport costs (Commonwealth Secretariat, 1993; World Bank, 2003).

The major external constraint to increased exports is the range of tariffs and non-tariff barriers facing the country's exports to the world market (Commonwealth Secretariat, 1993; World Bank, 2003). Zambia faces relatively high tariffs on export products in which it has a comparative advantage, such as food products and beverages, tobacco, textiles, wearing apparel, tanning and leather. For example, the tariff on tobacco in 2003 was as high as 65 per cent. There are generally tariff peaks on Zambian exports.

Zambia's exports are mainly to the United States, the EU, Japan SADC and COMESA. The relevant rates for COMESA and SADC are regional preferential rates. Most of Zambia's trade with the rest of the world is at preferential rates. For example, the trade with the EU and the United States is either on GSP terms or at preferential rates under the Cotonou Agreement or AGOA.

As for non-tariff barriers, there are several such barriers faced by exporters to the EU market, which, as pointed out earlier, is one of Zambia's major export markets. These non-tariff barriers take such forms as sanitary and phytosanitary standards, pest risk assessments and minimum residual levels in food products. The exporters also face a complex tariff structure and import requirements, as well as restrictive rules of origin (IMCS, 2003). In addition, all Zambian exports to the EU are subject to strict inspection at port of entry, which adds costs and delays. The EU has also set marketing standards such as size and packaging of goods. Tariff profiles in agriculture rates on agriculture goods are very complex, restrictive and far from transparent.

11.3 Effects of the reforms

11.3.1 Overview

Economic reform in Zambia has been bold, broad-based and far-reaching. Significant progress has been made in many areas. But there have also been major problems in sustaining the pace of implementation of the reform programmes. A problem is that the programmes placed too much emphasis on short-term adjustment of the balance of payments and fiscal deficit through the reduction of aggregate demand. This was difficult to sustain because aggregate demand had already been severely cut earlier. There was a need for policies that would expand domestic supply.

It has also been argued that the speed and sequencing of the reform programmes was too fast so as to prevent entrenched interests from reversing them. But because adjustment had been delayed for too long, the social costs of going too fast were considered excessive. Domestic industry and workers had no time to adjust, which made the programmes unpopular.

11.3.2 Macroeconomic impact

There is no doubt that the reform effort in Zambia has stabilized the macroeconomic situation: the fiscal and balance-of-payments deficits have been reduced, as have the inflation rate and interest rates. However, a major weakness has been its inability to produce real growth. Real GDP growth was stagnant at 0.8 per cent during the 1991–2000 period, increasing to 3.3 per cent in 2001–2003 and to an estimated 4 per cent in 2003. This real growth rate is insufficient to regenerate the economy and arrest the continuing decline in per capita incomes.

High levels of investment in the early 1970s were financed from domestic savings. Since the State was heavily involved in the economy, and budgetary revenues from copper where high in the 1970s and early 1980s, there was considerable public investment in the 1970s and early 1980s. However, the gap between savings and investment has since widened. Gross domestic savings, which stood at 19.3 per cent of GDP in 1980, dropped to an average of 6 per cent in the 1990s, and to 5 per cent in 2003. Likewise, domestic investment sharply declined from 23.3 per cent of GDP in 1980 to an average of 14.4 per cent in the 1990s. It now stands at 16 per cent of GDP.

The fall in domestic savings and the permanent trade deficit meant that the country had to rely on external resources to finance investment. It had to borrow from commercial lenders and multilateral institutions, thereby exacerbating the debt problem. The lack of investment in the economy has adversely affected performance and prospects for real growth as well as its ability to resolve supply-side constraints affecting export production. Export-oriented producers are faced with considerable structural rigidity, such as high energy costs, poor roads, poor marketing institutions and poor telecommunications, which results in unreliable and uncompetitive production of goods for export (World Bank, 2003).

11.3.3 Effects on exports

One of the major objectives of the reforms has been to diversify the sources of export earnings from copper to non-traditional exports. This has succeeded: the value of non-traditional exports increased from $90 million in 1990 to $360 million in 2002 (GRZ, 2004: 16), which represents an increase in export earnings from 8 per cent in 1990 to 39 per cent in 2002. However, recent rates have stagnated and do not meet the government's target growth rate of 15 per cent. The diversification has been slow because of difficulties in accessing export markets, which are highly protected. In addition, there are supply-side constraints to increased output. Diversification efforts have focused on both agriculture and industry. The agriculture sector has tended to concentrate on high-value export crops such as floriculture, cotton and tobacco.

A closer examination of the export structure of the manufacturing sector reveals that there has been a dramatic change in the composition of manufactures for export. Whereas, exports of building materials were more or less constant throughout the period, at about 5 per cent, those of engineering products almost halved, falling from 47 per cent in 1993 to 21 per cent in 1998. On the other hand, exports of textiles, processed and refined goods, and petroleum oils increased. The share of textiles rose sharply, from 16.7 per cent in 1993 to 30.5 per cent in 1995, before a slight fall to 28.2 per cent in 1998. Likewise, the contribution of processed and refined foods increased from 22 per cent in 1993 to 33 per cent in 1998.

11.3.4 Effects on industrial output

After 1994, there was a restructuring of manufacturing output. This took place despite the fact that the competitiveness of the sector had been adversely affected by unstable macroeconomic factors such as a high inflation rate, high interest rates and a volatile exchange rate. Output in the sector continues to be constrained by inadequate infrastructure services such as electricity, transport, development finance and technology (GRZ, 2003). Most manufacturing activity is concentrated in food, beverages and tobacco, and textiles and leather, reflecting their competitiveness. The chemicals sector is still relatively important because of the few capital-intensive oil refineries and fertilizer plants. The basic metals and metal products sector has lost its prominence. Labour-intensive sectors, where Zambia has a comparative advantage, have good export potential.

The effects of the reforms on the textile and clothing sector are discussed in Box 11.1.

Box 11.1: The effects of trade liberalization on the textiles and clothing sector in Zambia

During the 1970s and 1980s, Zambia set up import-substituting industries for which the raw materials were usually imported. These industries thrived on a domestic market that was protected with high tariffs and quantitative restrictions. Consequently, the industries neglected to enhance their competitiveness and efficiency, which prevented them from entering export markets. Thus with trade reforms in the 1990s, these industries were threatened. A case in point is the textiles and clothing sector.

This sector had over 140 companies in the 1980s, employing 25,000 workers. During the first episode of adjustment in the 1990s, these companies, which had previously been protected from competition, found themselves facing stiff competition from imports overnight. They had little time to readjust. As a result, the sector experienced mass closures of its garment factories and a scaling down of operations. Employment levels fell to below 2,500 workers.

The major input into the textiles industry is cotton, which has poverty ameliorating effects because cotton production in Zambia is based on out-grower schemes. The major activity in the textiles sector is spinning and weaving, knitting and garment making. Two textile mills, Kafue Textiles and Mulungushi Textiles, dominated spinning, although there were also a small number of spinning plants.

The two largest mills were orientated to production for the domestic market of local chitenge fabric. They met about 80 per cent of domestic market requirements. After liberalization, imports flooded the country, particularly second-hand clothing. Fabric and second-hand clothing imports reached such levels that by the mid-1990s only about 50 apparel out of 140 manufactures in the 1980s remained in business. Today no more than 10 clothing manufacturing companies exist and capacity has shrunk to the point where they are

(*continued*)

Box 11.1: (continued)

unlikely to be able to compete regionally or internationally. The surviving textile firms are engaged in the spinning of yarn from locally grown cotton for export. Others are producing woven and knitted fabrics, toweling and industrial wear (primarily for the domestic market), such as school uniforms, protective wear for the mines and professional uniforms, for which they are able to compete in terms of service and delivery. However, they are operating at low levels of capacity utilization. With the collapse of the clothing manufacturing companies, the demand for fabric dropped drastically, resulting in weavers and knitters operating at only 40 per cent of capacity utilization.

Zambia is a major cotton producer in Southern Africa, with privileged access to four major markets: SACU, COMESA FTA, the EU and the United States. Zambia's textile and garment exports to SACU countries are exempt from the double transformation rule for textiles and garments. Zambian producers of textiles and clothing are granted duty-free access on quotas under the SADC Trade Protocol. Members of the COMESA FTA are entitled to duty- and quota-free access for fibres, textiles and clothing originating within the FTA. Under the Cotonou Agreement, Zambian textiles and clothing have duty- and quota-free access to the EU market, while under AGOA, Zambia's exports of garments to the United States market are exempt from both quotas and tariffs.

Despite the difficulties experienced by the textiles and clothing sector, it continues to play a significant role in the Zambian economy. It is one of the most import earners of foreign exchange in the non-traditional sector, due mainly to the spinning sector. Between 1991 and 1997, the sector recorded a growth rate of 438 per cent, from $9.4 million in 1991 to $50 million in 1997. The main market for Zambian textile exports, mainly yarn, was the EU. However, recently, because of AGOA, some of this market share has been lost to South Africa and Mauritius. Exports within the COMESA FTA and SADC are negligible.

The level of imports of second-hand clothing has been extremely high, causing the collapse of the garments industry in the 1990s. Also, many structural constraints are affecting the sector, such as the high cost of borrowing, low capacity utilization, a limited domestic market, poor infrastructure, high energy costs, high transport costs, high cost of telecommunications and inappropriate labour policies.

11.3.5 Effects on revenues

One of the most important effects of trade reform is its impact on the share of trade taxes in government revenue. A major argument for retaining high tariffs and delaying trade reform during adjustment is that trade liberalization would deprive a government of trade tax revenues. However, trade reforms have not adversely affected the levels of tax revenue: trade taxes increased from an average of $150 million between 1986 and 1990 to an average of $195 million between 1991 and 2002.[1] As a percentage of total government revenue, trade taxes accounted for an average of 26 per cent and 30 per cent, respectively, during the two periods.

The country has, therefore, been able to sustain its revenue levels despite liberalization. This can be attributed to the structural change in the composition of Zambia's imports and exports. According to Musonda and Adam (1999) the pre-adjustment period was characterized by government allocations of foreign exchange to low-tariff consumer goods. Liberalization of trade led to a rise in the proportion of the high-tariff goods such as vehicles, capital equipment and construction materials, thereby increasing the average tariff yield on imports. Thus the fiscal impact of the trade reforms between 1991 and 2002 has been more or less favourable.

11.3.6 Effects on the labour market

The liberalization programme led to sharp structural changes in the economy as whole, the greatest impact being on the labour markets. As already stated, in the pre-liberalization period most of the firms were State-owned and in the import-substitution sectors. They were protected by high tariffs, as they were considered infant industries, and depended mainly on State financing.

Trade liberalization exposed these domestic firms to external competition, which, owing to their weak economic base, most could not withstand. As a result, they were forced to either close down or relocate to neighbouring countries (mainly Zimbabwe and South Africa) where production costs were perceived to be low. These changes had a negative impact on Zambia's labour markets. In the period 1981–1990, formal employment as a percentage of the labour force averaged 23 per cent, but it fell to an average of 12 per cent in 1991–2000, when the liberalization programme was in full swing, and by 2003 it had fallen further to 8.1 per cent. In their survey of firms Musonda and Adam (1999: 494) found that in almost all the firms they sampled employment had fallen by over 50 per cent during liberalization. The public service reform programme exacerbated this situation with large job cuts in an effort to make the civil service more efficient. The massive job losses between 1991 and 2000 deprived people of their livelihoods, thereby increasing the poverty level.

Since independence in 1964, mines have been the largest employer in Zambia. However, employment in the mines declined from an average of 13.6 per cent in 1981–1990 to an average of 9.7 per cent between 1991 and 2003. That of the manufacturing sector also fell from 12.5 in 1980 to an average of 11.4 per cent between 1991 and 2003. Meanwhile, formal employment in the services sector grew, from 62.4 per cent of total formal employment in 1980 to an average of 65.3 per cent in 1991–2003 and to 66.3 per cent between 2001 and 2003. That of the agriculture sector grew more sluggishly, from 8.6 per cent in 1980 to 15.4 per cent in 2003. Overall, employment in the formal sector was 23.3 per cent of the total labour force in 1980 and 8.1 per cent in 2003.

Consequently, the unemployment rate in Zambia is quite high and most of the people are self-employed in the informal sector. According to the 2000 census, the agriculture sector has the highest rate of self-employment, followed by manufacturing and services. According to the census, close to 60 per cent of the population engaged in agriculture consisted of unpaid family members, and a large proportion of the population is involved in cross-border trade and informal trade.

In brief, the recent liberalization of trade and the associated adjustment measures have resulted in a fall in employment levels in Zambia by over 50 per cent. In turn, this has led to an increase in the informalization of the labour market in Zambia.

11.3.7 Adjustment costs

Critics have alleged that the 1991 reforms were undertaken without fully studying and understanding their implications and costs. There was no effort to introduce safety nets and mitigating measures to support the reform effort. The main reforms, besides trade liberalization, included privatization of the State-owned firms, liberalization of the agricultural input markets and marketing, public sector reform, financial sector liberalization and removal of exchange rate controls. These reforms were bound to cause dislocations in the economy unless properly managed and planned, which was not the case. For example, with regard to privatization of State-owned firms, by 1997 as many as 224 firms were privatized, while others were liquidated or relocated to neighbouring countries, as they were unable to withstand new competition. As a result, many workers were laid off. There were no institutions set up to deal with this problem. In the case of the public sector, in 1996 the government halted the public service reform programme arguing that the social cost of retrenching the civil servants was too high.[2] The failure to set up institutions to mitigate the social consequences of the adjustment process can be attributed to the limited consultation with stakeholders regarding the adjustment packages and the government's reliance on the multilateral institutions and bilateral donors to design and fund such institutions.

11.3.8 Poverty

The impact of trade liberalization on poverty can be traced through the labour market. If trade liberalization stimulates the production of labour-intensive products then the rewards to labour must increase. If the poor form part of the labour market and incomes rise, then trade liberalization will be poverty reducing. However, the experience of the second adjustment episode is that formal employment fell, real GDP growth was inadequate, and, consequently, real incomes declined. This is reflected in the continuous deterioration of the socioeconomic indicators. The Living Conditions Monitoring Surveys of 1996, 1998 and 2002 show that the prevalence of poverty in Zambia rose in the decade between 1990 and 2000 and still affects over two-thirds of the population, with rural poverty being as high as 74 per cent.

Due to economic deterioration and rising poverty levels, the health and education indicators worsened between 1990 and 2000, compared with what they had been in the 1980s. In 1980, life expectancy was 52.5 years, but dropped to 48.5 years in 1995 and increased marginally to 49 years in 2002. This was mainly because of a deterioration of the health standards and higher infant mortality rates caused by the HIV/AIDS pandemic. The HIV/AIDS infection rate was 20 per cent of the population in 1998 and 16 per cent in 2002: it has affected all aspects of the social and economic fabric of the society, reducing productivity and increasing health care expenditure. The infant mortality rate rose from 99 per 1,000 live births in 1980 to 123 in 1990, and fell to 95 in 2000. However, the under-five mortality rate continued to worsen, from 121 per 1,000 in 1980 to 151 in 1990 and 162 in 2000.

In terms of education, gross primary school enrolment rates declined during liberalization. The gain from 89.9 per cent in 1980 to 98.7 per cent in 1990 was lost in 2000 when the enrolment rate fell to 78.2 per cent. According to the World Bank (2003), the low enrolment rate of school-going children is largely due to the inability of their parents and guardians to meet the cost of schooling. Overall, the literacy rate is 68 per cent, but is characterized by a wide gap between men and women and between urban and rural dwellers.

According to an assessment of Zambia's social and economic performance by the World Bank (2003), the country saw significant progress in the area of structural reforms during the 1990s, but full macroeconomic stability and sustainable growth remain elusive. All the social and education indicators deteriorated: infant mortality, adult illiteracy, malnutrition and poverty remained very high.

11.4 Conclusions and policy lessons

The failure of the reform process to produce real growth presents challenges to policy-makers, but it does not negate the necessity of reform. It points to the need for a well-designed adjustment programme involving all stakeholders, and well sequenced, taking account of adjustment costs. It should be based on a package of measures concerning trade, the exchange rate and macroeconomic reforms, along with institutional changes to address supply-side constraints. Liberalization in Zambia was too rapid, unsequenced, and often without the support of the stakeholders.

The second period of reform has brought about considerable structural changes in the Zambian economy and trade reform has increased competition and efficiency. This can be seen in the transformation of both the agriculture and manufacturing sectors. The manufacturing sector was heavily protected before the reforms. Consequently, it was inefficient, with high costs, and unable to compete on the international market. Its production structure has since been transformed and is dominated by industries in which the country has a comparative advantage. Consequently, manufactured exports have increased, particularly in non-traditional industries. To accelerate this process, supply-side issues need to be addressed, especially those that adversely affect the competitiveness of Zambian products.

It is important for the reform process to produce growth to compensate losers from the adjustment process. Simultaneously, there is need for support from the multilateral institutions, and for a net inflow of external resources, which have been inadequate.

The liberalization measures have led to a change in relative prices, and created incentives for investment in potentially expanding sectors such as industry and agriculture. However, the major problem in Zambia is that despite extensive adjustment to relative prices and liberalization, there has not been a sufficient investment response (Adam and Bevan, 1995), necessary to support the reform process.

An assessment of the structure of industrial production in Zambia and its export performance shows it has a comparative advantage in food, beverages and tobacco, textiles and leather, and wood and wood products. These are products of export interest to Zambia, but they face tariff peaks and tariff escalation in the markets of developed countries. The post-Doha work programme of the WTO should address this in the trade negotiations, especially in respect of LDCs. Only then will the multilateral trading system be seen to create opportunities for LDCs to grow so that they can resolve their problems of poverty and development. The negotiations should therefore concentrate on two main issues in respect of the LDCs, including Zambia. The first is that developed countries should provide bound duty-free and quota-free market access for products originating from LDCs, which are of export interest to them. This can be looked at in terms of special and differential treatment provided only to LDCs. This is the only way that Zambia can benefit from the post-Doha work programme because it already has market access opportunities to the markets of the developed countries through preferential schemes. It could be done at once or under a phased programme so that technical assistance can help the LDCs work on their supply-side constraints and prepare to take advantage of the opportunities created by greater market access. The second is that developed countries should strive to eliminate completely their tariff peaks and tariff escalation that are concentrated in products of export interest to LDCs, which would create market access opportunities for the LDCs.

Notes

1 Ministry of Finance and National Planning, Macroeconomic Indicators, 1986–2002.

2 Those retrenched were to be paid from donor funds, which were not forthcoming. The labour markets remained inelastic and most of those retrenched remained unpaid for several years.

References

Adam, C. and Bevan, D. (1995) Investment, uncertainty, and the option to wait: implications for government and donor policies in Zambia, Unpublished Manuscript. Oxford: Centre for the Study of African Economies, University of Oxford.

Anderson, P. and Ndulo, M. C. (1992) Structural adjustment, inflation and political commitment in Zambia: a short analysis of the New Economic Programme of 1989, *Macroeconomic Studies*, 28/92, SIDA, Stockholm.

Commonwealth Secretariat (1993) Export development policies and strategies for Zambia. London: Commonwealth Secretariat.

Government of the Republic of Zambia (GRZ) (1994) Industrial, commercial and trade policy, Lusaka: Ministry of Commerce, Trade and Industry.

Government of the Republic of Zambia (GRZ) (2003) *Economic Report*, 2002, Ministry of Finance and National Planning, Lusaka.

Independent Management Consulting Services (1999) COMESA tariff reduction impact study for Zambia, Lusaka: COMESA.

Independent Management Consulting Services (2003) Regional case studies on access to the European Union market for goods and services: Zambia country report, Lusaka: COMESA.

Musonda, F. and Adam, C. (1999) Zambia, in Oyejide T. A., Ndulu, B. and Gunning, J. W. (eds), *Regional Integration and Liberalization in Sub-Saharan Africa: Country Case Studies*, New York: St. Martins Press – now Palgrave Macmillan.

Seshamani, V. (1999) Some observations on the challenge of poverty in Zambia, Unpublished Manuscript, Lusaka: Department of Economics, University of Zambia.

World Bank (1984) *Zambia: Industrial Policy and Performance*, Washington, DC.

World Bank (2003) *Zambia: The Challenge of Competitiveness and Diversification*, Washington, DC.

12
Comment: the Process of Trade Liberalization in the Eight Countries

Diana Tussie and Carlos E. Aggio

12.1 Introduction

The evidence presented in the eight country case studies shows that over the past 20 years, but particularly during the 1990s, these countries implemented gradual liberalization of their trade regimes. This was pursued at multilateral, regional and bilateral levels. Their trade policy changes stemmed from the commitments negotiated multilaterally through the Uruguay Round of trade negotiations. But there were also major elements of broader economic policy strategies such as structural adjustment programmes (SAPs). The annex provides a summary table mapping out the trajectories pursued by these countries (Table 12.A.1).

After decades of highly interventionist trade regimes, all eight countries initiated tariff reforms, which resulted in gradual but considerable reductions of the MFN average tariff rate and its dispersion. A number of quantitative restrictions (QRs) on imports were eliminated or converted into their corresponding tariff equivalents. Trade liberalization was also manifested in the removal of items from restricted imports lists and the simplification of export-import activity through, for example, the elimination of export-import licences. In other words, the trade reforms made international trade more accessible and simpler in all countries.

Alongside trade liberalization, all countries have signed some type of trade agreements with neighbours and/or other trade partners (Table 12.1). They are all signatories to at least one free trade agreement (FTA) through which they grant and receive preferential market access. The two African countries in the group, Malawi and Zambia, have preferential access to major developed countries: with the EU through the EBA initiative and the Cotonou Agreement, and with the United States through AGOA. Bulgaria has an FTA with the EU and Bangladesh also has preferential

Table 12.1: Bilateral and regional trade arrangements

Country	Bilateral or regional trade agreements
Bangladesh	South Asia Free Trade Agreement (SAFTA) BIMST-EC (Bangladesh, India, Myanmar, Sri Lanka and Thailand) Economic Cooperation MFA quota-free access to the EU market
Brazil	Customs union of MERCOSUR (Argentina, Brazil Paraguay and Uruguay), 1995 MERCOSUR FTA with Bolivia and Chile MERCOSUR FTA with Andean Community Agreement with EU members for preferential access (1993) EFTA (1999)
Bulgaria	CEFTA (1999)
	Various FTAs entered into bilaterally with countries in the region: with Bosnia Herzegovina, and Serbia and Montenegro in 2001; with Estonia, Israel Lithuania, Latvia, TFYR of Macedonia and Turkey in 2002; and with Albania in 2003
India	SAFTA BIMST-EC IOR-ARC
Jamaica	CARICOM COMESA
Malawi	SADC EBA, Cotonou
Philippines	AGOA APEC AFTA COMESA
Zambia	SADC EBA, Cotonou AGOA

Source: Country case studies.

access to the EU for its garment exports. For the remaining countries, the main trade arrangements have been established with countries in the same region. While trade liberalization provided incentives to tradables, bilateral and regional trade agreements made trade more attractive with certain partners. As will be shown in the next section, these arrangements have had a considerable impact on recent trade flows, changing both the basket of goods traded and the trade partners.

The other common feature of all the countries is that trade reform has not been a stand-alone policy, but part of much broader policy strategies. In Bangladesh, Jamaica, Malawi, the Philippines and Zambia, trade liberalization was part of a SAP promoted and funded by the IMF and the World Bank. In Bulgaria, trade liberalization was part of the reforms undertaken in the process of transition to a market economy from a previously centrally planned system. In Brazil, trade reform was part of a stabilization plan, and, finally, in India it was a component of a set of policies aimed at changing the regime from a highly interventionist one to a more liberalized economic framework. All told there have been important changes in all eight of the country case studies.

12.2 Impact on economic and social development

The fact that trade reform has been part of far-reaching economic policies reduces the possibility to disentangle trade liberalization effects on economic growth and social development. However, in this section an effort is made to present the main recent trends in economic and social indicators. They are analysed in association with the policy changes described, but without attributing any causal relationship. The eight countries have been grouped into four sets of two.

12.2.1 Malawi and Zambia (small, highly indebted poor countries of sub-Saharan Africa)

These two countries started trade and economic reforms in the mid-1980s, but these were pursued more vigorously during the 1990s. Having meticulously followed the SAP agenda promoted by the international institutions they currently stand out, comparatively speaking, as two of the most liberalized economies in the region. In addition, they benefit from preferential access to the two major world markets: the EU and the United States.

Recent economic performance has been unsatisfactory due to their low capacity to generate real economic growth. Supply-side constraints have been a major problem, preventing them from taking full advantage of various preferential schemes. In the case of Zambia, part of the explanation for its poor economic performance lies in the collapse of the international copper price, since the country strongly depends on the production and export of this single commodity: in 2002, copper accounted for nearly 68 per cent of its total exports, contributed about 8 per cent to its GDP, and represented an important source of budgetary revenue. The value of Zambian non-traditional exports increased from $90 million in 1990 to $360 million in 2002, representing an increase in their share of export earnings from 8 per cent in 1990 to 39 percent in 2002. However, the contraction in output of previously protected industries has not been offset by a sufficiently vigorous development of its export industries.

The reforms have also had a negative impact on social indicators. The World Bank (2003: 8) summarizes the performance of Zambia's social and economic indicators as follows: 'The country saw significant progress in the area of structural reforms during the 1990s but full macroeconomic stability and sustainable growth proved elusive. All the social and education indicators deteriorated. Infant mortality rates, adult illiteracy, malnutrition and poverty remained very high.'

Poverty reduction remains a major challenge for these countries, all of which are heavily dependent on exports for economic growth. There is a need for comprehensive reforms to tackle supply-side constraints and other bottlenecks, including poor transportation and infrastructure. Their non-agriculture activities are almost non-existent, and therefore the challenge is to create and develop an industrial sector that could compete internationally. Further liberalization under NAMA is likely to pose further challenges if it erodes the preferential access of these countries to important world markets.

12.2.2 Bulgaria and Bangladesh (characterized by export dynamism based on exploitation of preferential access to developed-country markets, and undergoing major institutional reforms)

Bangladesh and Bulgaria have undergone extensive institutional transformation. Bangladesh became independent in 1971 and, in the 1990s Bulgaria started the process of transition to a market economy from a previous centrally planned system.

The socioeconomic performance of these countries has been fairly positive. Bulgaria experienced moderate economic growth, and, during the period 1991–2002, Bangladesh grew at an average annual rate of 5 per cent. In both cases, international trade has played an important role in their economic success. Reform and liberalization measures made their economies increasingly open to external flows. In the case of Bulgaria, this is reflected in the high share (over 80 per cent) of imports and exports of goods and services in GDP. Total external trade increased by 40.1 per cent in the period 1996–2002.

There are some common features in their export performance. First, export growth has been concentrated in a few industrial sectors. Textiles and clothing constitute the main exports, as neither of these countries has been subject to quota restrictions under the WTO Agreement on Textiles and Clothing (ATC). The sector accounts for over 80 per cent of Bangladesh's total merchandise exports. Secondly, export markets are also highly concentrated by virtue of preferential treatment. Nearly 75 per cent of Bangladesh's exports in 2002 went to developed-country markets (43 per cent to the EU, and 29 per cent to the North American Free Trade Area (NAFTA)). In 2003, the EU accounted for over half of Bulgaria's total trade. More than 70 per cent of Bulgaria's trade is now conducted through preferential arrangements, including with the EU, the European Free Trade Association (EFTA) and the Central European Free Trade Agreement (CEFTA). Thirdly, FDI has played a major role in the export dynamism of both countries. In particular, multinational firms in the clothing sector have invested in these countries to take advantage of their quota-free privileges.

However, the development impact of their transformation has been different. In Bulgaria, the transition process and the more open economy has resulted in a high and persistent level of unemployment and a high share of long-term unemployment. In addition, the low level of real incomes is a major social problem resulting in a large number of people in need of social protection and assistance; there are high relative and absolute poverty levels and a large proportion of the population lives close to the poverty line. Available estimates for Bangladesh, on the other hand, indicate that during the 1990s it succeeded in reducing poverty on average by 1 per cent per annum.

Given the pre-eminence of textiles and clothing in the export structure, any significant change in the external market conditions affecting this sector, particularly in the context of the expiry of the ATC at the end of 2004, could have serious implications for the trading prospects of Bangladesh, and, to a lesser extent, Bulgaria.

12.2.3 Jamaica and the Philippines (weak economic results, but with apparent social improvements)

Recent trends show that the economic performance of these countries has been modest. The Philippine economy has not been able to raise the standard of living of its population above its level of the 1980s. At 1995 prices, a Filipino in 1980 had $1,173 compared to $1,165 in 2001. Jamaica registered a slightly better situation. Its period of fastest growth in the last two decades was 1986–1990 (at an average annual rate of 5 per cent), but throughout the 1990s the economy grew at a much slower rate.

Trade reform did produce an impact on trade flows. In both cases, import dynamism exceeded export dynamism. In the Philippines, aggregate imports exceeded exports for most of the years since 1985. Export growth in the 1980s was flat, but, starting in 1990, aggregate exports expanded dramatically and peaked in 2000, despite the Asian financial crisis. However, aggregate exports expanded at a slower rate than that of imports. At the same time, there was a marginal decline in the openness of the Jamaican economy, measured by the ratio of the sum of exports and imports of goods and services to GDP, over the two decades. Imports of goods and services as a proportion of GDP rose marginally, but not sufficiently to offset the decline in the ratio of exports of goods and services to GDP.

Despite these economic outcomes, the social development indicators of both countries have registered a positive trend. In the Philippines, life expectancy at birth rose slightly over eight years and literacy improved during the period 1980–2001. The data also indicate that over the past 25 years an increasing number of Filipinos have gained access to infrastructure and technologies. The poverty problem appeared to have been alleviated, but it worsened in the early 1990s. There has been an impressive decline in the proportion of poor families in urban areas. In the case of Jamaica, unemployment fell in the 1980s and remained fairly constant in the 1990s, while poverty also declined.

12.2.4 Brazil and India (populous countries, among the largest economies in the world, with vast natural resources, but having amongst the widest income inequalities in the world)

Both countries, given their size, have offered numerous incentives for inward-oriented growth over a long period. However, their trade regimes, which started to show signs of obsolescence and slow growth, were liberalized along with moves towards more open economies. But in both cases trade liberalization was more timid than that of the other sets of countries examined here.

In the case of Brazil, GDP growth rates in the 1960s and 1970s were superior to average world GDP growth rates, but in the 1980s and 1990s performance began to slow down, and failed to offer enough employment opportunities to absorb the economically active population. Trade liberalization went hand in hand with regional trade agreements and with a new economic policy environment committed to stable macroeconomic conditions. These led to a period of overvaluation of the currency. The impact of trade liberalization, along with overvaluation, is best indicated by the import penetration coefficient, which increased from 3.2 per cent in 1990 to 11.8 per cent in 1999. This occurred in all the sectors, leading to a higher percentage of domestic consumption of imported goods. The share of exports fell from 9 per cent to 6.5 per cent, but when the currency was devalued in 1999, it increased to 15 per cent by 2003. Brazil's main export markets are its regional partners, especially for manufactures. Overall returns for the period have been disappointing. Clearly, adverse conditions internationally have influenced these results, but problems also abound in domestic policies relating to the exchange rate, public debt and high interest rates, and there have been difficulties in implementing all the economic reforms.

In contrast, Indian economic growth since 1991 has been impressive. There does not seem to be any consensus on whether the trade reforms implemented in the 1990s have been successful, and to what extent, but they cannot be discounted. As to their distributional impact, regional inequality in India has increased since the reforms were introduced. Also, even though the manufacturing sector has perked up, overall it continues to account for only 17 per cent of India's GDP. Employment trends in the manufacturing sector have not been positive. There was an increase in the national unemployment rate from 6 per cent in 1993/94 to 7.3 per cent in 1999/00. Between 1993 and 2000, the organized manufacturing sector created only 350,000 jobs, which can be attributed to rigid labour markets.

Given the high incidence of poverty in both countries, it is clear that trade alone cannot address this problem; improvements in income distribution will also be necessary to achieve a faster pace of poverty reduction.

12.3 Conclusions: what next?

So what are the lessons that can be learnt from these studies? The contribution of these studies is that they focus on issues of the utmost importance. Reforms in all countries were so deep and all-encompassing that it is difficult to separate the effects of the trade reforms from the other reforms and arrive at any definite conclusions about their impacts. Trade liberalization never happens as projected, and it rarely happens in isolation from other reforms, both economic and political.

All told, it is difficult to gauge the overall legacy of the reforms; no doubt the policy reforms, especially those concerning trade policy, moved in the right direction. But, except for India and Brazil, there was significant (and painful) overshooting. It would have been wiser and less costly to move gradually, rather than in the rough and tough manner witnessed in some of the other countries. Except for Brazil and India, the other six countries selected for the study had a shallow industrial base at the beginning of the exercise. The supply response has been extremely poor in Malawi and Zambia in particular, while neglect of the social implications in the planning of the adjustment process has had serious human welfare consequences. Government efforts to deal with economic dislocation and job losses have been at best reactive and marginal. Threatened workers and communities have had virtually no policy options other than to plea for protection after they are already in serious trouble – a legacy that subsequent governments are left to resolve with reduced degrees of liberty in foreign economic policy. Even in countries that opted for a gradual pace of liberalization, such as Jamaica, Malawi and Zambia, reforms have been so deep and extensive that it is no longer possible to envisage a reversal. Unemployment can no longer be addressed through a return to old-style protectionism, even if in many cases the economy has not yet adjusted to its full potential because of inflexible markets.

In Bangladesh, Jamaica and the Philippines, emigration first provided labour markets with safety valves, and, subsequently, remittances provided financial flows for offsetting trade deficits and balance-of-payments disequilibria. New behind-the-border policies, be they related to competition or the labour markets, must now come into play.

The termination of the WTO Agreement on Textiles and Clothing at the end of 2004 has significant implications for overall trade in this sector, but it will affect a selected number of successful garment exporters less than might be expected. Some countries have started to explore possible 'coping strategies'. Bangladesh's Board of Investment, for example, has suggested a strategic alliance between Dhaka and New Delhi. This association would combine Bangladesh's strengths in the garment sector with India's raw material production following the phasing out of quotas. Joint ventures may in fact be profitable. As a least developed country, Bangladesh will continue to benefit from the Generalized System of Preferences (GSP), giving it an approximately 12-per-cent duty advantage. Moreover, in order to promote investment, all six Bangladeshi special economic zones benefit from the power sector's 15-year tax holiday. Similarly under AGOA, the United States has granted some African countries 'third country fabric' exemption, which would allow them a favourable rules-of-origin regime in order to use inputs from third countries for export of their final products to the United States market.

Most trade reforms (India being the outlier) have been locked in by regional agreements North–South and, as in the case of Brazil, South–South, where liberalization was tied to the MERCOSUR agreement. This has important implications for overall trade negotiations. On the one hand, preference holders, be they firms or countries, may feel threatened by further MFN tariff liberalization, the NAMA negotiations in particular. This may explain the current lack of interest in these negotiations. On the other hand, since tariffs are highest in the trade corridor linking developing countries, the 'tricks' of mutually liberalizing is being implemented through the growing web of South–South preferential agreements, regardless of progress at the WTO.

Not being capable, or even wanting, to turn the clock back, some lessons can still be drawn for the process of continuous reforms. Given the diversity of reforms, one may doubt blanket claims of the unambiguously positive impacts of trade liberalization. Many analysts, give the false impression that a better economic future is possible simple by inhibiting global competition. Others, however, refuse to consider various conditions and pre-emptive measures with due regard for political and economic variables; yet these cannot be ignored.

It is known that even without abandoning modern orthodox methodology and findings, under certain assumptions and circumstances, trade and growth can be shown to be immiserizing for a country. True, a major message for these models is that while government actions are necessary to correct distortions, and thus laissez-faire is not advisable, it is highly unlikely that the best policies would involve trade restrictions. Thus free or freer trade is still desirable. But if best policies are not feasible, a great deal of intervention may be needed, and can be justified, depending on a country's judgement of its particular constraints and its willingness to accept non-economic considerations. Judgements will differ depending on whether the civil servants in charge of these matters have the requisite skills.

What would a pre-emptive strategy look like? While a government may not care for industrial policies or be in the business of picking winners, it cannot ignore the losers. The problem of specific losses has to be addressed with concrete and practical initiatives that take account of potential destabilizing effects. It can generally be anticipated, with a high degree of certainty, when an industry or a set of workers is threatened by global competition. A reverse industrial policy to support vulnerable communities and industries should be able to offer displaced communities a viable alternative early in the game – and well before having to choose between trade and devastation.

References

Banister, G. and Thugge, K. (2001) International trade and poverty alleviation, IMF Working Paper WP/01/54, Policy Development and Review and African Department, Washington, DC: International Monetary Fund.

Matusz, S. and Tarr, D. (1999) Adjusting to trade policy reform, World Bank Policy Research Working Paper No. 2142, Washington, DC: World Bank.

McCulloch, N. A., Winters, L. A. and Cirera, X. (2001) *Trade Liberalization and Poverty: A Handbook*, London: Centre for Economic and Policy Research.

Rodriguez, F. and Rodrik, D. (1999) Trade policy and economic growth: a skeptic's guide to the cross national evidence, available at: http://ksghome.harvard.edu/~drodrik/skepti1299.pdf.

World Bank (2003) *Zambia: The Challenge of Competitiveness and Diversification*, Washington, DC.

Annex

Table 12.A1: Summary of trade liberalization process

	Bangladesh	Brazil	Bulgaria
Summary	Over the past three decades the country has come a long way in the evolution of its economic policy orientation, from a highly interventionist regime to a substantially liberalized economic regime.	During the 1990s, after decades of a protectionist trade regime, Brazil implemented a series of major reforms, including trade liberalization and stabilization plans.	Bulgaria has been undergoing almost 15 years of profound reforms in the process of transition to a market economy from a previously centrally planned system. Trade liberalization and integration into the multilateral trading system have been among the top priorities and major elements of the reform strategy.
Bilateral and regional trade arrangements (RTAs)	SAFTA South Asia Free Trade Area BIMSTEC (Bangladesh, India, Myanmar, Sri Lanka and Thailand) MFA quota-free access to the EU.	Customs union of MERCOSUR (Argentina, Paraguay and Uruguay and Brazil) MERCOSUR FTA with Bolivia and Chile FTA with Andean Community	FTA agreement with EU members for preferential access (1993) EFTA (1999) – CEFTA (1999) Various FTAs arranged bilaterally with countries in the region. With Bosnia Herzegovina and Serbia and Montenegro (2001), with Estonia, Israel, Latvia, Lithuania, TFYR Macedonia and Turkey (2002), and with Albania (2003).

Main trade policy changes	During the latter half of the 1980s, a series trade reforms were implemented under an SAP. The SAP emphasized rationalization of the import regime, simplification and reduction of effective protection, elimination of negative and restricted lists of industrial imports and facilitation of imported raw materials and intermediate and capital goods, including required imports for direct and indirect exporters. Throughout the 1990s, Bangladesh consistently reduced import duties. The average unweighted rate of customs duty fell from 47% in 1993 to 196% in 2003. The weighted average fell from 23% to 12% in the same period. The maximum import duty was reduced from 350% to 30%. Between 1991 and 1993, the first serious slashing of QRs occurred, which reduced the number of items in the import control list from 325 to 193. Between 1993 and 1997 the number of restricted items was reduced to a range of 111–120 items.	The first broad tariff reform included a programme of unilateral tariff reductions in four stages, and the elimination of quantitative controls of 1,200 products (1990). The Treaty of Asuncion established the Southern Common Market, MERCOSUR (1991). Customs union of MERCOSUR (Argentina, Paraguay, Uruguay and Brazil) entered into force, encompassing around 85% of tariff lines with a maximum CET of 20% (1995). Tariff increase demands caused by trade deficit following the Plan Real (1995). FTA with Bolivia and Chile which is almost completed (through MERCOSUR) (1996). FTA between MERCOSUR and the Andean Community to be completed in 2020.	During the transition process, Bulgaria's overall trade policy objective was geared to the gradual liberalization of its trade regime. This was pursued at multilateral, regional and bilateral levels. However, its main trade liberalization efforts have been implemented through a series of regional and bilateral FTAs. Bulgaria acceded to the WTO on 1 December 1996, whereupon it bound all its MFN tariffs under the GATT, 1994. Since then, trade liberalization has been much faster: applied MFN tariff rates were reduced to a simple average of less than 12% in 2003 (17.2% in 1996); the applied simple average MFN rate was set at 21.7% for agricultural products and 8.6% for industrial products.

(*continued*)

Table 12.A1: (*continued*)

	India	Jamaica	Malawi
Summary	Reforms in the 1990s were manifold, encompassing macroeconomic and external trade aspects. The macroeconomic (stabilization) programme placed emphasis on addressing the fiscal and current-account imbalances. The unilateral liberalization coincided with multilateral trade negotiations undertaken as part of the Uruguay Round trade negotiations.	The process of trade liberalization began with stabilization programmes (in the late 1970s), and accelerated with structural adjustment programmes (1980s). In the 1990s, the trade liberalization process was continued with reform of the common external tariff of the CARICOM, pressure to comply with the WTO's international trade regime, and the restructuring of trade relations with the EU (embodied in the Cotonou Agreement) and commitments taken in the context of the process to establish a Free Trade Area of the Americas (FTAA).	Throughout most of the 1980s, Malawi maintained a restrictive and complex trade regime that was based on pervasive NTBs, a large number and a wide dispersion of tariff bands, high tariff protection against imports, restrictive licensing requirements, and surrender requirements on exports proceeds. The reforms introduced since the late 1980s have substantially liberalized trade.
Bilateral and regional trade arrangements (RTAs)	SAFTA BIMST-EC IOR-ARC	CARICOM	COMESA SADC EBA, Cotonou Agreement AGOA
Main trade policy changes	The export-import policy (in effect from 1992–1997 (Foreign Trade Regulation Act 1992) significantly	Trade liberalization measures included: removal of 180 items from the restricted	Exchange controls were removed on 50% of imports of non-petroleum raw materials and spare

reduced trade restrictions. Import tariffs were reduced gradually by compressing the top tariff rates, while rationalizing the tariff structure by reducing the number of tariff bands. The highest tariff stood at 355%, simple average 113% weighted average 87%. This was further reduced to 71% in 1993/94 and to 41% in 1995/96. The different import license systems continued to function, but were reformed to make them less restrictive (OGL, VABALdrop). Special Economic Zones (SEZs) were introduced through the Export/Import Policy of 2000 to provide an internationally competitive and 'hassle free' environment for export-oriented firms.	imports lists and eventual abolition of import licensing and quota requirements for all but a small number of items. Except for CARICOM imports a new system of tariffs was imposed (1982). Simplification of The duty system and its administration was simplified, the overall level of tariffs was reduced, along with a rationalization of the structure of protection by reducing widely dispersed rates (1987–1991). The import monopoly of the Jamaican Commodity Trading Company was abolished (1991). The average tariff was reduced to 22.1% (1991) 15.9% (1993), 14.0% (1995) 11.9% (1999). The standard deviation fell from 20.7% to 16.8% (1991) 13.4% (1993).	parts and intermediate goods. Maximum tariffs were reduced on non-government imports, from 70% to 45% (averaging 21%) (1988). The differential between surtax levied on imports and domestic goods was eliminated, in combination with an upward adjustment of import duty rates (1992). The export surrender requirement was abolished except for tea, sugar and tobacco (1994). WTO-accession export levy on tobacco and sugar was reduced to 8% (1995) and then to 4% in 1997, then extended to coffee. The maximum tariff rate was reduced from 45% to 40% (1996) to 35% (1997) 25% (1999). All licensing requirements on imports and exports were abolished, except for items concerning health, security and the environment. The maximum rate was cut to 35% (1997). The export levy was abolished (1998).

(*continued*)

Table 12.A1: (*continued*)

	Philippines	Zambia
Summary	Prior to the 1980s, the country pursued import substitution policies. The adverse effects of anti-trade and protectionism led to policy reforms, including a series of tariff reform programmes since 1981. These reforms were unilateral although those undertaken in the 1980s were done in the context of the World Bank structural adjustment programmes. In the 1990s, the government continued its trade liberalization programmes.	Zambia has undertaken major trade policy reforms since 1985. Between independence in 1964 and the mid-1970s, it had a fairly unrestricted trade regime with high tariffs varying between zero and 150%. That trade regime ended in 1985 with the first attempt at tariff reform, but was interrupted between 1987 and 1989. In 1991, the current reform programme was launched, which has fully liberalized trade, making the country comparatively one of the most liberal economies in the region.
Bilateral and regional trade arrangements (RTAs)	APEC AFTA	COMESA SADC EBA Initiative Cotonou Agreement AGOA
Recent main trade policy changes	Recent policies have included: implementation of a comprehensive trade reform programme aimed at increasing the competitiveness of the economy (1980); a tariff reform programme from 1981 to 1985 which narrowed down the tariff rate structure from a range of 100–0 to 50–10 per cent; and an import liberalization programme (ILP), which did away with non-tariff import measures.	Nominal tariff levels were reduced to a 0–50 per cent range (1991). Nominal tariff levels were reduced to a 0–40 per cent range (1993). All controls on current and capital accounts were abolished (1994). Nominal tariff levels were reduced to a 0–25 per cent range. The SADC Trade Protocol was signed (1996).

	With the change of government in 1986, the trade reform programme was resumed. It involved lowering tariff rates over a five-year period (1991); and the conversion of quantitative import restrictions (QRs) for 153 commodities into their corresponding tariff protection measures (1992). Two laws were passed in the early 1990s which provided for trade protection in agriculture: the Magna Carta for Small Farmers and the Seed Industry Development Act (1991–92). TRP III (1994).	COMESA FTA was created, with zero duty on goods originating among the 9 members (2000). SADC tariff reduction phase down began with the objective of establishing a SADC FTA by 2012. Became a beneficiary of AGOA (2000). EU EBA was established offering LDCs duty-free access for their exports except for armaments and three sensitive products (2001). Zambia Export Processing Zone Authority was established (2003).

Source: Country case studies.

13
Comment: Reflections on the Trade Reforms and Policy Implications

Patrick Messerlin

13.1 Introduction

The case studies included in this book cover a wide range of countries; they provide a rich array of information due to their coverage of a long period of time, and raise interesting issues for future research. Their perspectives concerning the last three decades generate a few common observations (beyond all the differences that one could expect between countries such as India, Malawi, Brazil and Jamaica) that are useful for drawing policy lessons. This brief note focuses on one of these common points: the 'real' liberalization process.

13.2 Challenging the current view of the liberalization process

The currently dominant view is that developing countries have undergone substantial liberalization over the past two decades (for instance, the last World Bank Development Reports). Evidence supporting this 'optimistic' view is based on the decline of the average level of tariffs and the increase in trade among developing countries over this period. Indeed, detailed information on average tariffs by country presented in Fernández de Córdoba, Laird and Vanzetti (2004) seems to support this optimistic view.

The country studies included in this book are extremely useful because they put this optimistic view in a wider perspective, which largely challenges it; they offer a better understanding of what has actually been happening during the past three decades, and what should be done in the coming ones.

In fact, the country studies have two common recurrent themes (not, however, sufficiently emphasized by some of them). First, strong pockets of protection have survived over the last three decades, particularly in the economic activities that were already well established before the beginning of the liberalization process. Second, during this period, the path to freer trade has been very hesitant – to say the least – a feature which is partly, but not completely, related to the first point.

Before examining in detail the challenge to the current optimistic view raised by these studies, it is useful to underline the fact that the picture they provide is not so surprising when one looks at the history of trade liberalization in the industrialized countries, and at their current situation. Six decades after the establishment of the GATT and the launching of trade liberalization, the OECD countries still substantially protect sectors such as steel, clothing and few others, which were their largest industrial sectors in the early 1950s. This observation would be even stronger if one were to include agriculture, which is beyond the scope of this book. The OECD countries' most liberalized sectors are those which did not exist, or were relatively small, in the 1950s. In fact, during these last six decades, most of them did not have the time to build their own protection instruments, as best illustrated by the information technology products. As a result, the outcomes outlined in the country studies in this book should not be so surprising, particularly since they deal with developing countries which are at the stage of the liberalization process that most OECD countries had already reached in the 1960s.

13.3 A better understanding of the liberalization process

But how then is it possible to reconcile the much more cautious view about the liberalization process suggested by the country studies and the data which support the current optimistic view? In particular, how can the survival of strong pockets of protection be consistent with the tariff decline and trade growth mentioned above?

A first, obvious, answer would be to list the wide range of non-tariff trade barriers which are still being used by developing countries during their liberalization process: from non-tariff barriers to export taxes (which are equivalent to import taxes, and prevalent in several countries surveyed in this book) to norms and standards. Similarly, one could mention the still large gap between 'bound' and 'applied' tariffs, particularly among the least developed countries, which imposes a particularly heavy toll on small, isolated economies. However, this answer, though certainly powerful, does not seem central enough to be convincing on its own.

It seems more interesting – including from a policy perspective lesson – to focus on what really happened to tariffs during the decades covered by the country studies. Clearly, these studies suggest that the simple average level of tariffs, on which the current optimistic view relies, is a very imperfect indicator of the level and structure of protection. More precisely, it overstates (probably grossly) the real magnitude of liberalization. Such an average is calculated over the whole tariff schedule, which comprises 6,000–10,000 tariff lines. Most economies produce in substantial quantities goods which correspond only to a small range of these tariff lines (in fact, most economies produce the whole range of goods, but many of these products are produced in negligible quantities). This concentration of production means that vested interests ready to fight for keeping protection unchanged are themselves very concentrated. Of course, other vested interests, such as domestic firms assembling imported parts (a not negligible share of production in developing countries), should also be taken into account. However, their political leverage tends to be (much) weaker than the leverage of the first group of vested interests for a host of reasons, among which, they do not look like 'real' producers and they do not produce noticeable quantities, hence they do not mobilize large numbers of workers. Relying on a simple average tariff level for assessing the liberalization process – as the current optimistic view does – tends to conceal the very slow trade liberalization in the sectors where there is initially domestic production into the more rapid trade liberalization in the larger of group of other products (most of which are unable to mobilize strong domestic vested interests).

This very simple observation suggests the need for a better assessment of the real pattern of the liberalization process. Trade liberalization in most developing countries has so far consisted mainly of reducing protection imposed on goods which are not (or only in small quantities) produced at home. Such liberalization is not insignificant, but its asymmetrical pattern has important implications for domestic growth (as examined below).

Before looking at these implications, the above simple observation deserves three remarks. First, it is important to realize that the magnitude of the statistical bias embedded in the current optimistic view is likely to be larger for small economies than for large economies, hence larger for developing countries than for the industrialized countries. The reason for this difference in bias is that small economies are likely to produce in significant quantities a smaller range of products than large economies, implying that averages are much less likely to reflect the real picture in their case than for larger economies. In some of the country studies, the core of domestic industrial production may consist of less than 100 tariff lines (maybe even less than some 10 tariff lines).

Second, another indicator often used for supporting the current optimistic view (the import-weighted average tariff) is even more biased in understating protection than the simple average. It weights low tariffs by unconstrained (large) imports and high tariffs by restricted (possibly nil) imports. The indicator which would provide the least distorted view of the liberalization process would be the average tariff, weighted by domestic production. Further research should thus attempt to estimate such an average tariff (indeed, it should not be so difficult for the least developed countries, where significant production involves so few products). This would be all the more useful if the countries under examination have a wide range of tariff rates.

Lastly, it is useful to underline that in fact, the country studies included in this book are very consistent with easily observable negotiating tactics. During the two last decades, trade negotiators have been great admirers and supporters of the concept of 'early harvest', a concept meaning that one should target first 'easy' liberalization, leaving for 'better' times the liberalization of 'more difficult' or 'sensitive' products. In other words, they have advocated leaving aside the politically powerful industries at the beginning of the liberalization process. History (and the country studies) suggests that, generally, 'better' times come after several decades, if ever.

13.4 Implications for growth and policy lessons

The country studies give a clear indication that the magnitude of trade liberalization effectively implemented by developing countries during the past two decades or so has been (probably much) more limited than the one suggested by the current optimistic view. This better appraisal of what has actually occurred has interesting implications from which useful policy lessons can be drawn.

First, such limited liberalization implies that the existing domestic resources used in the traditional sectors – particularly the factors of entrepreneurship and capital, which are relatively scarce in developing countries – are likely to move only slowly out of the traditional sectors and towards new activities. This 'reluctant' manner in which liberalization has been implemented may have handicapped domestic entrepreneurs and capital more than foreign firms, which can limit or shape their activities into a sequence of short-term profitable operations by tapping into initially unused domestic labour or resources; this increases, by the same token, the volatility of a country's growth (a feature frequently cited in the country studies). Similarly, a 'zig-zag' liberalization process may handicap domestic firms more than foreign firms (which can limit more easily their activities to a sequence of profitable short-term operations). This may be all the more true because liberalizing sectors with small domestic production and limiting the liberalization of the traditional sectors may even increase the relative margin of protection (i.e. the effective rate of protection) of the latter, and make these sectors even more attractive than before the beginning of the liberalization process.

It is therefore hard to expect such liberalization to boost economic growth and a noticeable shift towards diversification – the two most widely expected outcomes of liberalization. In this context, it is not surprising that one of the recurrent themes of the country studies is the disappointing performances of the countries following such a liberalization. The fact that most of these liberalizations have followed a 'zig-zag' course, with many hesitations and, in some cases, even reversals, has reinforced this failure to boost growth and diversification.

It would be interesting to test all these remarks by providing some counterfactual evidence based on the experiences of a few countries that have had a more decisive liberalization policy (which, unfortunately, is outside the scope of this book). The most direct criterion for defining the appropriate countries should not be the average level of (tariff or non-tariff) protection, but rather the level of reduction of protection on the products existing prior to liberalization. A proxy for such a direct criterion would be the introduction of a uniform tariff (defined as the imposition of the same tariff rate on all the goods), since such a tariff effectively reduces the level of protection on all the production existing prior to liberalization. Only a few economies (Chile, Hong Kong (China) and Singapore) adopted a uniform tariff before the 1990s (allowing a time span similar to the one adopted by the countries studied in this book). None of them is examined in this book. In fact, the only appropriate example would seem to be Chile, because the zero tariffs imposed by Singapore and to a lesser extent by Hong Kong (China) on their imports of goods are largely irrelevant for economies which, almost exclusively, produce services. Calculating a meaningful level of protection of these two economies would have to take into account the protection of their services activities, and this may well reveal that their economies are significantly protected.

The Chilean example is interesting for two reasons. It shows that the economic difficulties feared by developing countries when considering liberalization (particularly the fear of no or little diversification after opening up their domestic markets) tend to be largely solved by the markets. But it also shows that the high speed at which the uniform tariff was reduced by the Chilean government in the early years imposed severe adjustment costs on Chilean resources (particularly labour). This observation suggests that the main reason for the choice of liberalizing 'at the margin' adopted by the countries surveyed in this book may be their desire to minimize adjustment costs. This result has been achieved, but at the cost of a small (if any) and often volatile impetus to growth. The best alternative to both the Chilean case and the cases examined in this book would be to liberalize across-the-board, à la Chilean, but at a slower pace than in Chile. The speed, rather than the sectoral pattern, of liberalization becomes the crucial parameter: too rapid liberalization generates high adjustment costs, while too slow liberalization reduces the impact on growth (the impact on volatility is uncertain, but it should not be negative). In sum, acting firmly and in a time-consistent manner may be more crucial than acting swiftly. Launching a credible liberalization process does not mean rapid liberalization (though it may require a not too distant horizon for achieving a given result in order to be credible).

13.5 Special and differential treatment revisited

The fact that developing countries have different rights and obligations than developed countries through 'special and differential treatment' (SDT) has always been a difficult issue in the multilateral trade regime. The country studies included in this book offer several policy lessons.

Problems related to SDT are even more acute in the WTO negotiations because developing and developed countries alike face a situation that is largely unknown. When SDT was established 40 years ago, developing countries constituted a relatively homogeneous, well-defined group. Thus it did not really matter that being considered a developing country was a self-selection process, all the more because all of them protected their producers heavily. Although the industrialized countries were only marginally concerned by competition from developing countries, they granted SDT with little consideration for development, and did not hesitate to exclude a few key sectors for developing countries: shoes, clothing or agriculture. It is no wonder, then, that SDT did not work well in the past.

Today, developing countries in the WTO constitute a completely heterogeneous group. The country studies make this point very clear despite the choice of the countries examined, which (rightly) is not representative of one-third of the 'developing countries' in the WTO, namely those which have a GDP per capita higher than the poorest Member States of the European Union. This makes it increasingly more difficult for the industrialized countries and the poorest countries alike to still consider them as developing countries. Even in countries such as India or China, there are regions with a level of wealth and activities comparable to what exists in industrialized countries. Recent years have shown that developing countries can rapidly enter sectors, such as a broad range of services, which, only a few years ago were seen as the exclusive territory of rich economies. All the success stories – from the Republic of Korea and Singapore to China and India – have very little to do with SDT. Rather, they reflect better domestic governance and classic economic recipes for growth: a sound macroeconomic policy, a progressive but firm pace towards freer trade, and an ever wider set of improved domestic regulatory policies.

Does that mean that the days of SDT are over? No. But it definitively requires a new approach which may be emerging in many capital cities, but is far from perceptible in Geneva, where trade negotiators are still too glued on outdated fights.

A first aspect of this 'new' SDT approach is related to the poorest countries. These countries can be defined by one key feature: they lack the crucial input for growth, namely, a critical level of good governance. As a result, they still need preferential access to rich markets; indeed, rich countries can still do a lot in this respect, such as opening up their farm and clothing markets and simplifying their rules of origin. That does not mean that the poorest countries should make no concessions. As shown by the study on non-agricultural market access, as underlined by Francois, J. and Martin, W. (2003), the poorest countries will gain mostly from trade liberalization between developing countries – a situation reflecting the substantial, but still considerably incomplete move of many developing countries towards freer trade during the past decade. They should focus on cutting their high tariffs and binding them – a progressive but firm move towards a uniform and moderate tariff, as recently done by countries such as India or China.

In this context, a common theme of the country studies, the fact that tariffs are only part of the 'transaction costs' of trading goods and services (see in particular the study on the Philippines), is very interesting. Malawi also well illustrates this important point. Malawi's imports are seriously hampered by the fact that they transit through one distant harbour (enjoying a quasi-monopoly position) and through unsafe roads (the equivalent of 'private' tariffs). It would thus be interesting to estimate these 'private' transaction costs, and to compare these estimates with the 'public' (tariff-related) costs.

This observation raises an interesting question in the SDT context. Could one use, from a policy perspective, the opportunities generated by the 'substitutability' of private with public transaction costs, particularly in the context of the Doha Round? These could focus on trade facilitation (assuming that trade facilitation is defined in a broader way than at present, in order to include all the ways and means of decreasing private transaction costs). In other words, could the current Doha Round make 'operational' the link between tariff reduction and the improvement of trade facilitation? Conceptually, one could argue that, as improving trade facilitation takes time (since it requires investment in better physical equipment and governance), developing countries could reduce their tariffs in the short run (when the benefits of trade facilitation improvement have not yet materialized), and increase them once the 'returns' from trade facilitation investments are realized. Of course, this trade-off should make sure that the global (private plus public) transaction costs decline from the very start (initially through tariff reductions, then through much improved trade facilitation). Industrial countries would then be involved in two ways: as a source of compensating losses of tariff revenue in the initial period; and as a source of investment in the long-term improvement of trade facilitation.

Such a mechanism is probably too complex to be implemented in the naive way sketched above, and it requires too much trust (probably lacking) from both sides. However, it could be used as a conceptual benchmark for the Doha negotiations with regard to the poorest developing countries. For instance, these countries could agree to reduce their highest applied tariffs (and all their bound tariffs) in a progressive move towards a uniform and moderate tariff policy as a concession for a financial package (funded by the industrialized countries) for investing in trade facilitation and for compensating tariff revenue losses in the initial years. Thereafter, the industrialized countries could progressively withdraw from tariff compensation (and from trade facilitation in the long run), once the moderate uniform tariff policy implemented by the poorest countries begins to provide an adequate source of funds to the developing countries in question.

13.6 Trade liberalization and domestic reforms

The full benefits to be expected from trade liberalization are likely to require complementary domestic reforms. Several of the country studies emphasize the high costs of the absence of such domestic reforms in both the poorest and the emerging countries. In fact, they implicitly show what economic analysis insists on *ad nauseam*, that is, if the developing countries want 'policy space' for development purposes, they have plenty of instruments at their disposal (production and consumption subsidies or taxes in goods, services and factors of production) which can better help them achieve the desired objectives at a much lower cost for the country than can trade barriers. In general, WTO rules do not constrain these instruments. However, there are cases where WTO rules are ambiguous; hence there is considerable need for clarifying these rules in the Doha Round – a move that is demanding for rich countries as they tend to be the main beneficiaries of the current ambiguity.

It is true that the Uruguay Round has massively expanded the scope of the WTO: from services, to norms and standards, to trade-related aspects of intellectual property rights, to name only a few. All these new trade issues require a high degree of domestic regulatory policies, and, hence, important regulatory capacities. WTO disciplines on such matters are generally greatly exaggerated as pointed out below. But the fact remains that they open a completely new chapter in SDT for the following reason: if improving market access in goods (reducing trade barriers) improves domestic welfare *and* reduces regulatory costs, opening markets in services improves domestic welfare *but* may increase regulatory costs.

As a result, regulatory policies in the multilateral trading system magnify the key handicap of many developing countries – good domestic governance – and amplify the differences among them. Introducing an economically sound and politically acceptable SDT into this context will be no easy task. What matters most are two broad principles. There is the need for regulatory creativity: developing countries should not be asked to mimic rich countries' regulations inherited from decades of the rule of law. Second, trade negotiations should focus on a well-defined cluster of services offering the largest net benefits from consumers' gains and regulatory costs. In the Doha Round, an excellent candidate seems to be the cluster of services related to trade facilitation.

Last but not least, the country studies included in this book show how the WTO remains the best available instrument for all the developing countries. 'Preferential' agreements almost inevitably promote 'reverse' SDT, which favours the powerful trading partner – developed or emerging – as best illustrated by the many bilateral agreements with no provisions on farm liberalization, or with stronger TRIPS provisions than those found in the WTO.

References

de Córdoba, Fernández, Laird, S. and Vanzetti, D. (2004) Blended like Beckman: trying to read the ball in the World Trade Organization negotiations on industrial tariff, *Journal of World Trade*, 38(5).

Francois, Joseph and Martin, Will (2003) Formula approaches for market access negotiations, *The World Economy*, 26(1): 1–28 (January), Blackwell Publishing.

Index